They Called Me Trouble

---

by
C.R. Van Anden

Published by:

FriesenPress

Suite 300 – 852 Fort Street
Victoria, BC, Canada V8W 1H8

www.friesenpress.com

Distributed to the trade by The Ingram Book Company

This book is dedicated to my wife of 55 years. Her love, passion and support have meant more to me than anything else in the joy of living. God love her!

PREFACE

THE FRAMEWORK OF this sentimental journey is the fifteen years from 1930 to 1945. It was a period of the conquest of despair followed by unheard of cruelty to the vanquishing of tragic militarism. All ushered in a new America and world. It was a great time in which to spend a boy's formative years.

Looking back I wouldn't trade my life for anyone's. The exposure to two distinct ways of living taught and prepared me for the future. Perhaps it was really three ways of life, if my five years in Private School can be separated from the Scarsdale/Westchester segment. All three were very happy times, even if there were many ups and downs.

The Hudson River experiences provided the greatest contentment, security and perhaps a fuller knowledge of what being an American was all about. The town had an economy based on farming, the river, the railroad and hard physical labor in surrounding factories. Most families walked, only about 20% owned an automobile. Their lives revolved around their church, the community, the firehouse and the river. Not many had an education more than High School. The local school was small. The teachers taught with enthusiasm, dedication and warmth. Discipline was strict and nearly always fair. The school building was solidly built and Spartan. The fancy frills of today were unnecessary, learning the basics were essential.

Social activities were held at the firehouse, Yacht Club or church. The highlight of the year was the New Year's Eve dance. The ladies dressed in their Sunday best, the men squeezed in to their suits or sport coats and many wore ties. It was nearly always held at the firehouse. Occasionally, a band was hired but more often than not, records of the Big Bands were played. The dancing would have terrorized Miss Covington's Dance school in Scarsdale. Most days, dress attire for men was work clothes. The women wore their house dresses. Ladies never wore pants. The clothes lines, strung behind their homes, flapped in the wind with men's trousers, overalls, children's underwear, ladies other house dresses and unmentionables. Everyone was scrubbed clean and sloppiness was frowned upon.

The townspeople subsisted on low to medium incomes. Some, were struggling to make ends meet. But as hard as the struggle, they refused to think themselves poor. They believed in the American dream. The people voted regularly and patriotism was second nature. They loved the "Good Old U.S.A.".

In New Hamburgh, nearly every house had a front porch. Most evenings, weather permitting, the adults would move to the front porch to sit, cool off, relax and say "hello" to their neighbors or passing citizens. Many an evening, when walking through town with friends, we'd talk to those on their porches and they in turn would keep an eye on who was with whom and what romance might be springing up. Everyone knew everyone and gloried in the changing patterns of relationships.

There were few modern conveniences. Less than a third of the people had a telephone, some still used oil lamps, refrigerators could be found in only a handful of homes, more houses had outhouses than bathrooms, coal stoves were the norm and most had a compost heap in their backyard. Many young people started working between the ages of ten to twelve. on the farms or helping others in town.

Recreation was abundant. In the winter, skating, ice boating, sledding, ice fishing and tobogganing. In the spring, shad fishing, rifle shooting, laddie cake jumping (jumping from large ice slabs, broken by the thaw, to other ice slabs), boating and baseball. Summertime brought a plethora of popular activities and Fall more of the same. It was a paradise for a young boy.

Travel was largely limited to railway journeys to Poughkeepsie or Beacon. Day Liner trips to towns along the river were also made. Not many had been to New York City, a few to Albany but only one or two to foreign countries, with the exception of men who had served in the military during the Great War. Some of the wealthiest had been to the Adirondack's, Atlantic City or Maine. Of course, none of this applies to those who lived on the surrounding large estates but that was a lifestyle fast fading.

An interesting fact underlines the security felt by the great majority of the residents: hardly anyone locked their doors.

How different Scarsdale and other Westchester County towns were! They were fairly large communities populated by middle management and executive class people. Most had recently moved in to these suburbs. A large percentage had college degrees, commuted to work in New York City while their wives remained home to raise their children. Competition to show off success developed demand for live-in maids, automobiles, country clubs, more and more elaborate schools and fashionable clothes. "Society" became essential. Women, freed from housework by their maids, sought other avenues to fill their time. Joining the woman's club became almost mandatory as did membership in garden clubs or if really upper material, the Junior League.

To say the least, children were indulged. Once turning a teenager weekly allowances were the norm. (I was an exception). Dancing school was the surest entry in to "proper society". The cotillion was the summit. However, if you really had it, you were allowed your own car. The schools had auditoriums, well equipped gymnasiums, art studios, wood working shops, dramatic clubs, large playgrounds, orchestras, bands and something new- a student counselor! How did students ever survive before? Now there was barely time for education.

Politics was also undergoing a change. So many suburbanites saw the need to correct society's wrongs, not by correcting their own problems, but by feeling for, not actually helping, those less fortunate. Politicians soon caught on and legislated programs designed to help. Taxes were raised to support these altruistic programs but cleverly placed deductions were incorporated. It was all so wonderful, they cared. The suburbanites grasped at these loopholes and actually reduced their taxes. The Democratic Party was the first to grasp the wonders of this system. Handing out Alf Landon's sunflower in 1936, I was greeted with smiles but when the vote was in, the Democrats won in a landslide.

Meanwhile, a major portion of the privileged men spent hours at the "Club" playing golf with their buddies. Bragging became an art. Each was trying to outdo the others in the prestige of ownership and the wonders of their kids with whom they seldom spent time. After hitting the nineteenth hole, they'd ride home just in time for cocktails on the porch. There were no front porches, only back or side porches. They didn't want to be seen or overheard by their neighbors. When the maid announced that dinner was ready, it was swallowed without thought and the kids were off to the movies or some other place of sedentary enjoyment.

Church was a must. Not because couples wished to thank the Lord but because Harry and Gertrude would surely see they hadn't come. After all, church had become an extension of their social life. Sunday afternoon was spent resting up or attempting to look busy in the garden. By dinner time, the kids were home, Dad was tired and Mom was wondering how to get out of the charitable work she had somehow been roped into. After dinner, the radio was put on, the kids disappeared to the play room to listen to their latest records and the maid cleared and washed the dishes. In this fashion the week ended and the rat race started all over in the morning.

The proper clothes were always expensive but a necessity to maintain status. One thing for sure, the women always looked gorgeous, with the exception of those with poor taste. Women were women and men were men. (The closet doors were still kept closed.) Most women had charge accounts at the major stores. These always kept the husbands in a state of anxiety over the budget. It always amazed me how quickly the daughters caught on to the game of fashion.

If you didn't travel, you must be having difficulty making ends meet. Bermuda was a must in Spring. Skiing in Vermont in Winter couldn't be missed and in the Fall one had to go back to his or her Alma Mata for the big game. Sometimes the kids could come, particularly in Fall and Winter but never in Spring. Those of more fortunate means went to Europe. It was so very, very steeped in culture. If you hadn't been, you were lacking. The family unit was changing. Everyone had their own "musts." Seldom did these come together. Doing things as a family became the exception not the rule. But their elevated cultural attainments, social involvements and superior position in the fabric of the country gave them the right to advise and look down on the bulk of the population. It was the beginning of the "elite society". Frankly, I decided at an early age, I didn't want my life to be like that. Oh, by the way, everyone in Scarsdale kept their doors locked.

When I turned thirteen, I was sent off to Private school. No parent or other family member was there to give me advice or solace. Alone in a strange environment, responsible for my own actions and faced with boys of varying backgrounds, desires and ambitions, I couldn't run home later to seek answers as to what to do. The routine of life had changed dramatically. Strange adults were confronting me with questions and regulations on how to act and demanding almost an immediate response. Within this framework it was necessary to carve out a path to live day by day and to achieve.

Nearly all the students came from families far wealthier than mine, never had worked in their lives and lived in societies similar, if not from, Westchester. None could even imagine a small community like New Hamburgh. In this regard, it was easy for me to relate to how they behaved and thought but when I talked of my riverside town and life their eyes would gloss over and if any comment was made it was usually demeaning.

Yes Prep School life was a change but in most aspects it was an extension of Scarsdale's society.

One thing all segments taught me was: friends and foes are all part of living. All underline the diversity of this world, all make you stronger and all show the truth of:

"Forgive us our trespasses as we forgive those who trespass against us".

What follows is the result of reviewing my memory. I apologize if names are misspelled, dates are slightly inaccurate and I've left anyone out that had an impact on my young life. In certain cases I have changed the name of individuals to afford them privacy. I loved all these years and those that shared them with me.

CHAPTER 1

As LONG AS I can remember the Hudson has been "my river". This majestic water highway stretches from the heights of the Adirondacks to the narrows of New York City. It is wide from Albany to the big city. It flows between magnificent hills and palisades and has tides more than eighty miles inland. Its' history encompasses that of Indian Nations, Dutch settlers, English armies, Revolutionary war battles, famous artists, large sloops plying their trade, the first steamboats, our first Military Academy and an ever changing culture. It is truly one of America's treasures.

Navigating north approximately sixty miles from the magnificent New York Harbor you come to Newburgh Bay. The city of Beacon sits on the east bank and Newburgh to the west. Once through the bay the small town of Chelsea comes into view and almost immediately on your left is Danskammer Point with its' small light house pointing the way to Langreach, an eight mile straight stretch of river nearly a mile wide. The famous Diamond Reef, one of the best fishing spots on the river, divides the shipping channel. The western route hugs the shore of Cedar Cliff and the eastern skirts the busy little town of New Hamburgh. Here my family has lived since 1714.

As the town comes into view, you see the buildings of the Millard Lumber Company perched on its' sturdy docks. The town dock comes next with its' large freight house. Here the Hudson River steamers stop to pick up produce being shipped to New York and beyond. It is also a stopping place for many of the Day Liners — the Mary Powell, Robert Fulton, Dewitt Clinton, Alexander Hamilton, Claremont and others — who shuttled passengers up and down the river. Tucked in alongside the dock is a small foundry that supplies parts to manufacturing plants located in the back country. A little bay comes next and ends where the Yacht Club sits upon a rocky protrusion. (The men who raced iceboats on the frozen river started the club and dominated that sport from the early 1880's to the late 1930's. Then the government decided to send ice-breaking ships up the river in winter to keep the channels open. This effectively ended the sport). Even though membership was limited anyone from town could use the beaches adjacent to the clubhouse.

Just past the club is the old Lime-Dock followed by a rocky shore leading to a favorite swimming area called "Sandy Bottom". On its' far side is a continuation of the rocky shore abruptly ending at the New York Central Railway tracks. Behind this expanse of shorefront is the town proper. Three grocery stores are scattered through the village. Jake & Reeds is on Point Street opposite the town dock. Johnny Myers' Grocery is on Main Street next to the meat market and Railway Freight Office. The Post Office is next just before the abandoned Presbyterian Church. Going further east you cross the railroad tracks to find the Hudson Hotel and Petropole's small grocery store. Our beautiful old Railway station (with one of the best potbellied stoves ever built) sits behind the hotel adjacent to the tracks that enter the tunnel going north. The Eagle Hotel is on the north western side of Main Street. Such is the hub of our town. We do have a small school on top of a hill behind the Railway station. Two active churches — the Episcopal Chapel next to the Firehouse on Point Street and the Methodist at the corner of Point and River — satisfy the religious needs of a majority of the population. Fast overtaking these Protestant bastions are the Catholics who trek approximately four miles to Wappingers Falls to attend their church. In all 400 or so people call this riverside town home.

In 1932, at the age of five, this was the center of my universe. My memory goes easily back to that year. Previous years are just snatches of vague scenes and people. I lived with my Aunt Nell. Our home sat squarely in the center of town on Main Street facing the Meat Market and Johnny Myers' grocery. Stone Street was on the east side of our house and behind was a new road from a new bridge that passed over the new railroad tracks that replaced those that had run through the tunnel. In 1929 the New York Central had cut through the rock to make an open passageway for the trains. This made our property an island surrounded by pavement. Our yard was about one half acre. It was full of flowers. Between the old plum tree and an older apple tree were remnants of a path long used to reach the barn and the outhouse, both having been torn down to accommodate the new road. Each summer hollyhocks continued to bloom along the remains of that path. The only good received from the new road was the indoor plumbing that had to be installed.

So my remembrances begin.

It was the first week in June. The temperature reached the high nineties and the humidity seemed worse. All morning I kept begging Aunt Nell to take me to the river near the Yacht Club where there was a small rocky beach. Kids from town my age were allowed to play there. The water remained shallow for at least 75 feet out. A large stone poked its' nose above the surface near the half-way mark. It was perfect for pretend diving or jumping into the water.

"I want to go swimming!"

"No. Not now perhaps later when my ironing is done."

All I could think was that my friends were probably already there. Ted Jennings and Frederica Lawson lived next to the Club and always arrived first. I tried to coax my Aunt but the harder I pushed the more she tended her ironing. Lunchtime came. Hot Soup! Sitting at the kitchen table I knew swimming had been put off due to my unrelenting insistence.

The dishes were washed and put away. Aunt Nell picked up her knitting and moved to the front porch. Out there it was even hotter and no breeze at all. I decided to lie low. I went in the living room and started to play tidly -winks. While playing my eyes became heavy, I stretched out and promptly fell asleep.

"Charles! Wake up. We can go swimming now."

I awoke, looked at the tidly winks, stood and ran to our bathroom upstairs. When I came down my Aunt handed me my bathing suit, told me to put them on and dress. We were off to the beach but not before I'd been made to pick up the tidly -winks.

When we got there, Ted, Frederica, Billy Gallagher, Violet Townsend and more were already splashing and jumping in the water. I stripped down to my bathing suit and ran into the river. I loved it! As I ran in all the girls kept singing loudly:

"Charlie is my darling, Charlie is my darling but how he does cry!"

I heard it so often I paid no attention. Soon Ted and I went exploring along the shoreline quickly turning over rocks seeking small eels before they could squiggle back to the water. We

3

caught some and ran after the girls attempting to stuff the eels down their bathing suits. Such squealing! It only egged us on.

While playing, it suddenly turned dark and windy. Aunt Nell and all the mothers started calling us to get out of the water. It became very dark. The wind picked up and then dropped deathly still. Clouds climbed the sky, lightning flashed and thunder rumbled deeply. The air pressed in. My arm was grabbed and my Aunt pushed me to the road. Pants, shirt and sandals were forgotten. She started running, dragging me along. Lightning flashed and its' sharp crack made us bend over while we ran. The wind returned with a vengeance and blew so hard our running steps hardly made progress. It started to hail. Large ice pellets hit our heads, face, body and legs. I started to cry. The howling wind tore branches from trees and then Aunt Nell fell to her knees.

"My glasses, the hail broke them and they have fallen. Help me find them."

I got on my knees and looked all over the road. The hail stopped and then sheets of rain came, wave after wave. We were wet through, soaked. The glasses were forgotten and we pressed on. A voice shouted in front of Audrey Miller's house. We saw her as she screamed for us to come inside. My Aunt refused, saying we had to get home to close the windows. Down Point Street we struggled. When reaching the corner of Main, a mad dash was made for our house. Water was streaming down the new road. We sloshed through the mud and deep water. As we rushed up the steps of our front porch the wind whistled, slammed at the awning over the front stoop and tore it loose. We watched it hurtle along the road until it fetched up against the World War Memorial overlooking the river.

Once inside, my Aunt kept sobbing. She needed her glasses. I ran upstairs and got an old pair from her room. She then calmed down, hugged me and stopped crying. The lights were out and it was so dark, yet only late afternoon. My Aunt rummaged in the hall closet and found our oil lamps and lit them. All at once it seemed much safer. The rain kept on. The wind started to slow and then the lightning stopped but we could still hear thunder in the distance.

Aunt Nell went to the kitchen and put the kettle on the coal stove. She made tea for herself and hot chocolate for me. The fig newtons were brought out and we settled down for a welcome treat. The torrential rain continued. As we sat there I became conscious of the sound of running water. My Aunt also heard it.

She went to the cellar door, opened it and screamed. I ran to the door and peeked around her skirt. Water was half way up the stairs and still rising. She told me to stay while she ran across the street to the store to phone the fire department. In a few minutes she returned very upset and soaked. The phone was out. Mr. Myers told her he'd call the Fire Dept. as soon as the phone was working. We waited — me frightened the house would float away and my Aunt frustrated over the lack of action.

At seven I was put to bed. After prayers I was kissed good-night and left. My imagination went in to high gear. The water would reach upstairs, seep into my room and I would drown in my sleep. I had no supper! Out of fear I slipped out of bed and went downstairs. Aunt Nell was sitting by the west window looking toward the river watching the pounding rain. As I entered the room we heard the fire engine. It stopped on Stone Street and some men ran to our back door. They asked what the problem was. My Aunt took them to the cellar stairs. They flashed a light down and said something not meant for my ears. The men ran back to the truck, pulled out a long length of hose and shoved it through the coal shoot into the basement. Their driver pulled a switch and the engine started to pump. A few minutes later the Chief came in and said:

"As fast as we pump the water keeps coming faster."

He talked to my Aunt for a good fifteen minutes and then left saying:

"We'll check you out in a couple of hours to see how things are."

I was told to go back to bed and assured things would be all right. Sleep came slowly. At six in the morning I awoke to the sound of more pumping. I got up and went downstairs to the kitchen. Aunt Nell was feeding five firemen ham and eggs, toast, jam, coffee and apple pie! They all laughed when they saw me. I was given oatmeal with milk and honey. They were all talking but I couldn't make heads or tails out of what they were saying. They stayed for another hour running the pump and then left. For five days the pumps were kept running intermittently until water stopped seeping in.

We were in a fix. The water had destroyed the coal furnace, water logged the pump to the cisterns, our coal had become satu-rated and the place stank. Uncle Le was contacted but he said he was too busy repairing the damage done to the estate where he worked. When the phone was back in order, Aunt Nell called my father in Scarsdale. He agreed to come up the following weekend. In the meantime we cleaned up all we could — my aunt doing most of the work while muttering to herself. Neighbors were helpful, especially Ida Morey. We ate at her place more than at ours. I was the envy of all the other kids because we had had a "tragedy". Still playtime continued but the days seemed to crawl by as we waited for Dad to arrive.

He came on the Fourth of July weekend. My mother and sister also came. After a quick inspection Dad was really upset. He couldn't understand how this could have happened. He began to make plans for various workmen to come and analyze the situation. Unfortunately, it being a holiday weekend, no one would come. To make the best of our plight it was decided we could all join in the festivities planned at the Yacht Club on Saturday.

On that afternoon we all went to the Yacht Club. Nearly the whole town was there. Kids were swimming, many adults were seated on the porch watching and gossiping.. My Mom and sister were out on the front beach swimming. Only the bigger kids and adults were allowed out there because it got deep quickly and the current was too strong. Nancy Jane, my sister, was three years older than me and never let me forget it. But I loved her anyway. Hot dogs and hamburgers were being cooked over the open fire behind the clubhouse and we were all given lemonade. My Aunt was on the side porch re-telling everyone, who would listen, about the storm and our flood. I teamed up with John Scardefield, one of my best friends, to go fishing off the Lime Dock. He had brought several lengths of string, a couple of bobbers and some hooks. We dug for worms behind Frederica Lawson's house in their compost heap. They were the best worms for bait besides manure worms. After getting some small branches for poles and good stones for sinkers we were all set. I had just got my hook in the water when Dad called:

Boy! (He always called me "Boy") come down here we are all going over to the town dock."

"No, that's okay. I want to stay with John and fish."

"Don't argue, come now."

"Can John come?"

"All right, but hurry."

John and I pulled up our lines, put them alongside the can of worms and stashed all under the back steps of the clubhouse. We joined Dad, Mr. Croke, Don Croke, Mr. Cantwell and his son, Donny. Walking around to the dock, I felt Donny give me a push every few feet. All the other kids were older by a year or two and Donny had never considered me worthwhile to even pay me any attention. When we got there, Don jumped off the dock and swam around calling John and Donny to join him. John, who was a good swimmer, was next in. Donny hesitated until his Dad pushed him in. Then Dad told me to jump but I hung back. The water was thirty feet deep at high tide and I had never been in deep water before. At the beach I had just learned to dog paddle a few feet before touching bottom. Dad kept telling me to jump but I was too timid. All at once he grabbed me and threw me over the dock. I sank like a rock. I was frightened and my mouth was full of water. Somehow I surfaced spluttering and wailing my arms around trying to keep above water. Dad and Mr. Cantwell were laughing but Mr. Croke yelled to Don to help me stay afloat. When he reached me, we both went under. The next thing I knew Mr. Croke was pushing me towards the dock. Dad had stopped laughing and was leaning over to grab me. I was pulled out but was I mad! I started to shake all over and kept spitting water out. It was hard to catch air. After a few minutes things calmed down. Dad then jumped in, swam back to the dock and told me to jump in beside him. I looked down to the water and couldn't seem to jump. John came along side and said he'd jump with me at the count of three. "One, two, three". He jumped and I followed. Dad got hold of me, told me to lie on my stomach and promised not to let go while I dog paddled. I finally did and reached the dock. I was helped out and told to jump once more. I did. This went on for five or six times and then we all got out and started back to the Club. Was I proud! I told everybody I had swam off the dock. Aunt Nell was furious with Dad and Mom only smiled. My sister made no comment. After staying at the Club for another hour or so we walked home. It was a big experience for me but to this day I cannot breathe properly when swimming even though I'm considered a fairly good swimmer.

That night I went to bed early. I remembered nothing until I heard Mr. Wickes out front with his horse drawn wagon delivering milk. He always made a fuss over me. Somehow, he made me feel older than I was. He didn't talk to me as if I were a little kid but as someone who understood that what he did was important. He had horses, cows, chickens, a plough, a big barn and all kinds of interesting guns. I jumped out of bed, put on my shorts and ran outside to his wagon but not before I picked up our gallon jug. He'd lift the big milk can down from the wagon, lean over and pour milk into the jug. It was my job to get the milk each morning. He kidded me for a little and then said he had heard I'd been swimming off the dock. He couldn't have said anything better.

My Aunt was in the kitchen fixing pancakes for all of us as I came back in. Nancy Jane was trying to be grown-up by helping but Mom and Dad hadn't showed yet. I put the milk jug in the icebox then took the sign for ice out and hung it on the front door. When I came in they were all at the kitchen table ready to eat. I was told to eat slowly, chew properly while I kept my mouth closed. Once the pancakes and sausage had been eaten, milk swallowed and my napkin put away we were told to wash thoroughly, clean our teeth and get ready for church. I hated my "Sunday go to church clothes!" They made me look like a "namby, pamby" little boy. When I was finally dressed it was still early so I asked if I could go down to Johnny Miller's and out on their fishing ramp to look at the water. I got the okay, ran down and walked out onto the pier. Johnny came out and joined me. He didn't go to church so had his normal clothes on. We stood talking and all of a sudden I was propelled off the pier into the shallow water and mud. I turned and looked up.

"Hey, you big sissy what are you doing in that mud? Look at you all dressed up and wallowing like a pig."

"Shut up Donny. What have I done to you?"

He just laughed and was joined in the ridicule by Johnny. I climbed out and took a swing at Donny but missed. He shoved me and down in the mud I went, flat on my back. Again I climbed out and ran down the pier. I knew I would be in trouble. When I ran in the kitchen door my Aunt and Dad were the only ones there. Dad started to laugh and Aunt Nell screamed. Mom came running down, grabbed me and rushed us upstairs saying what a naughty boy I was. She tore my clothes off, filled the bathtub, lifted me in, scrubbed like crazy and yanked me out. I was pushed into my room and dressed in my play clothes.

"Don't think you're not going to church, because you are. I don't care how you are dressed today because you have to ask God to forgive you and make you a better boy."

I couldn't believe it. I got to go to church in my old clothes. Anyway, why was I being called bad? It wasn't my fault. Off we went. Mom in her best outfit with her usual hat, Aunt Nell in the only dress I'd ever seen her go to church in, my sister all dolled up, even making me realize she was pretty and Dad in a dark blue suit, white shirt, tie, black shoes, derby hat and walking stick. I looked like I did every day of the week but Sunday. All the other members of the Parish greeted us. Everyone always stood outside the door until the service was ready. to pass around the latest gossip. I guess our appearance made up the usual congregation so we all trooped in. Our pew was the second from the front on the left hand side. Our family had been sitting in that spot since the church was built. God forbid anyone else from sitting there. After kneeling to say our prayers we all sat back. Mom looked at me and asked if I'd asked for God's forgiveness. I think the whole congregation heard. Then the old pump organ started. Miss Wickes, Charlie Wickes' sister (who was about seventy) started the processional hymn. John Scardefield entered from the basement steps dressed in a robe carrying the cross followed by the choir — most of the kids I played with — plus Mr. & Mrs. Van Walken. What an ensemble. The kids squeaked, Mrs. Van. gave us her best soprano and Mr. seemed to grunt the base. They had never managed harmony. Bringing up the rear was Reverend Rice. The procession and hymn over, we all knelt and listened or said the opening prayers, including the days' collect. I started to daydream. My sister nudged me to stand while the Reverend read the first lesson. Then there were more prayers followed by the second lesson. When that was over another hymn was tackled followed by the important part — the taking up of the collection. Mr. Lewis (I never did figure out where he lived, probably in the back country) walked to the front and Rev. Rice handed him the large silver platter. He went down the other side first collecting the offerings. Then he was on our side. My Aunt had given me a nickel to put in the plate and Mom gave my sister a dime. We dutifully dropped them in, I thinking of the candy it could buy. Dad put in five dollars and Aunt Nell put in her church envelope. Once Mr. Lewis got back in front of the alter, he handed the plate to the good Reverend who turned to the Cross and we all started to sing: "Praise God from whom all blessings flow etc." As this ended Rev. Rice moved to the lectern and gave all the announcements. At this point all children were expected to file out and go downstairs to Sunday School before the Reverend launched into his sermon. Down I went but Nancy Jane stayed upstairs because she wasn't a "regular". Hattie Brennen was our teacher. It wasn't a tough job because all we did was color pictures from the Bible while she tried to explain what they were all about. It seemed a long time to color.

9

We left church a little after eleven and walked home. Everyone changed except me. The adults grabbed a cup of tea and read the newspapers. I tried to interest my sister in playing tiddly winks but she had no interest. Sunday was always a quiet day when my folks were with us. I wasn't allowed to play with friends or go swimming. After a light lunch Dad did go for a walk with me up to see Uncle Le at the Grinnell estate. We looked at all the gardens for which he was responsible and heard for the first time that he was thinking of opening a Flower shop in Larchmont, N.Y. Dad didn't seem too interested. On our walk back to the house I was told that it might not be possible for my aunt and me to stay in our house during the winter because of the damage the water had done to the furnace and cisterns. I didn't take him seriously. After a big Sunday dinner we all sat on the front porch to watch the passing parade of evening walkers. Then I was sent to bed.

When I awoke in the morning I could hear my Aunt and Dad talking. Jumping out of bed I quickly dressed and went downstairs afraid I would be reprimanded for sleeping so late and neglecting my chores. All were there. Mom was cooking breakfast, NJ was sitting by the coal stove and Dad was in deep discussions with my AUNT. I heard Dad say:

"Nell, you and Charles cannot stay here when it starts to get cold. The water has damaged the furnace, the cisterns are not sanitary and the well water is marginally contaminated. I know you can get drinking and cooking water from the Morey's but it is no way to live through the winter. I'll try to have some of these things fixed but it's not right for the two of you to live this way. You will have to come to Scarsdale for the winter and Charles will have to go to school down there, I wish it was different but we have no other choice. I'll be up for you both by the end of September. Until then you can stay here."

There was no argument that I heard, so that was that. All I could think was that the end of September was a long way off. My memory is blurred over the next day and a half. Apparently, Dad arranged for someone to investigate the cellar problem, made provision for Aunt Nell and I to have someone for security in case other problems arose and made sure I understood what the future had in store for me. I couldn't believe I'd no longer be with my friends, which gave me a heavy feeling in my stomach. But then, I still had a couple of months before anything changed, so as far as I was concerned I had nothing to worry about — yet.

The next morning Dad, Mom and NJ got in the car and left for Scarsdale. As their car disappeared I asked my Aunt if I could go down to Ted Jennings' place. Getting the ok, I made a bee-line for his home. During the summer months he lived with his grandmother, Mrs. Schwartz. She owned one of the biggest places right along the river just northeast of the Yacht Club and the Lime Dock. Her property extended about seven acres to the railroad tracks. Most of the land was heavily wooded except along the shore where rock ledges dropped down to pebbly beaches with the exception of Sandy Bottom that was renowned for being a good swimming area, particularly for the older town people. Ted and I believed the whole area was our domain. Here we played Indian. When we tired of Indian play we decided to fish off the large rock ledge overlooking the river. The tide was right and we had good luck. We must have caught at least seven perch. All were thrown back because neither of us liked to eat any kind of fish. As we were getting tired of fishing, Ted's grandmother called and said it was time for me to go home. I left and ran to our house. My Aunt was fixing dinner so I was in time. The day was ending and my life seemed back to normal.

My next memory is of a Saturday a few weeks later. Aunt Nell said she had to go to Newburgh to see about her glasses. She had made arrangements for me to be taken care of by Edna Miller who was sixteen and did babysitting. I went down to her house as soon as my Aunt had caught the train to Beacon to get the Ferry to Newburgh. When I got there Edna was alone. Her parents, her brother and sisters had gone to Wappingers Falls. We started to play catch but she shortly got tired of it and told me to come indoors. I did and she grabbed me and starting calling me her little baby. She kept kissing me and mewing. The next thing I knew I had taken off her shirt and bra and started cuddling me to her breasts. This went on for quite some time and though I was embarrassed at first I came to enjoy it. In later years I came to understand how well- endowed she was. The afternoon seemed to pass quickly. When my Aunt returned, Edna made me promise not to say anything about what she had been doing.

My birthday came next. Aunt Nell baked a chocolate cake and gave me a new jump rope and an Indian headpiece. I spent the day with Ted Jennings strutting around in my new Indian feathers. We also went swimming at the Yacht Club where most of the other kids were. They all sang Happy Birthday to me and tried their best to give me my birthday spankings. It was another happy day. When I got home we had supper and then the cake. As we were eating it there was a knock on the front door. My Aunt opened it and there was Uncle Edgar shouting Happy Birthday to me. He gave me a new pocket knife. I was thrilled! Edgar was not really my uncle, he was my Aunt's longtime boyfriend. They had been going out together since she was eighteen. In April we had celebrated her forty-fifth birthday. Her suitor worked as a Postal Railway Inspector and traveled as far west as Chicago but spent most of his time in the New York City, Albany, Syracuse, and Buffalo corridor. After doing the dishes we all moved to the front porch. Sitting there listening to them I became very tired. I must have fallen asleep because when I woke it was very dark. I noticed Edgar had his arm around my aunt's shoulders. I couldn't remember seeing my aunt that close to anyone but me. He moved and came over and said:

"How about taking my flashlight and shinning it over to the Meat market's front door. Keep it low and you'll see something."

I took the light and did as he said. Sure enough cat's eyes shined back and I could see a large rat hanging from its' mouth. Edgar laughed:

"That's why the butcher keeps all those cats around. He'd be overrun with rats if he didn't."

At that I told my Aunt I never wanted to eat meat from that store again. It was past my bedtime so I had to say goodnight, kiss my Aunt and thank Edgar for the knife. In bed I couldn't sleep for hours thinking of all those rats.

September came and with it much cooler nights. I knew time was running out and we would soon be in Scarsdale. School started the day after Labor Day and I registered at "Crow Hill" as our school was affectionately called. There were two teachers, one for the upper school and one for the lower school. There was also a helper for kindergarten. John Scarderfield was in second grade, Jimmy Miller in first Don Croke in second and me in kindergarten. Ted Jennings had gone back to his home in Utica. My class consisted of six girls and four boys. Billy Gallagher, Fred Townsend (a black boy), George Decker and myself. We were all friends but not real pals. Our days consisted of drawing, listening to stories and then having to tell the teacher what the stories were about. It seemed they were stressing memory more than anything else. Unfortunately, I was taken out of that school within three weeks.

The last weekend in September Dad and Mom came up to help close the house. We finished packing, loaded the car and took off for Scarsdale. I couldn't believe I wouldn't be seeing my friends for months. I wasn't a happy traveler. It took nearly two hours to reach the Scarsdale home. I had been there many times but remembered little of it because I had been so young. The house sat on a small plot. It was stucco with wood trim painted a dark brown. It had a side porch enclosed with screening facing the driveway. A two car attached garage in back, a narrow flower garden and shrubs separated our yard from the house behind. By the garage was a small rock garden. Inside there was a living room, dining room, kitchen, eating alcove, maids room with lavatory and a fairly large hallway. Upstairs were three bedrooms and two baths. All of this sat over a large basement. It was a typical, small suburban home. The maid was still Iza. A heavy-set woman who had come from Scotland with her husband but who promptly left her. She was supporting herself by working as a maid to earn enough so she could earn passage back to her home. I liked her and she sure made a fuss over me. Still, I was near tears with homesickness for my river town.

13

CHAPTER 2

THINGS FELT SO different in Scarsdale. On that first day I took my
stuff up to my room, looked at the two beds and decided I'd like
the one at the far end of the room. Iza had made up both beds
and I wondered why. Shortly after starting to unpack, Mom came
into the room. Gave me a big hug and said she and Dad were
so glad to have me home. She also told me I would be starting
school Monday morning at Edgemont. She had bought me some
new clothes to wear. When she opened the bureau drawer and
showed me what she had bought, I was none too thrilled. It all
looked too fancy. I had to try everything on and show everyone
how I looked in them. Naturally, they all said I looked just fine
and so grown up. I wasn't convinced. However there was no
choice. The rest of the afternoon seemed to drag. Nancy came
home a little after five and she gave me a big hello and made me
feel happier. Dad had been out front cutting the grass and tidying
the gardens. When he came in, he washed and we all went into
the dining room for dinner. I can't remember what we had but I
do remember the bombshell that Mom announced:

"Next Friday MeMa is coming to stay with us until next spring
or early summer. Charles, she'll be sleeping in the other bed in
your room."

That was news. I didn't know if I liked the idea or not. She was
my Mom's mother and I remembered her as being a very warm
person but a bit dreamy.

After dinner we all went into the living room. Everyone sat
but I stretched out on the floor. Mom went to the piano (an old
upright) and started to play. It was wonderful! I had always thrilled
to her playing but had forgotten how great she made the music

15

sound. The piano was her "thing". She had been playing since she was a very young girl and was now widely recognized as an extremely gifted pianist. That first night in Scarsdale became sheer happiness as I listened. I didn't want to go to bed when I was told I must.

Lying in bed I started thinking about school. I was very nervous about going. The other kids had already started a few weeks earlier. I had no idea who would be in my class although I guessed Johnny McCullough, Roland Gesell, Eddie Lawler and Bill Smith might be. It seemed a long time since I had played with any of them. I missed my pals in New Hamburgh. With all these thoughts floating through my mind, I fell asleep.

Dad woke me in the morning. He was just off to work and wanted to wish me a good start at school. He patted me on the back as he was leaving and said:

"I want a full report on your day when I get home."

That made me extra nervous. I got up, washed, cleaned my teeth and went back to my room to dress. There was Mom with clothes laid out for me to put on. I dressed, looked in the mirror and saw a stranger looking back. What a sissy! I got all choked up and nearly started to cry. At breakfast, all were waiting. I was on display. Nancy gave a little giggle while the rest claimed I looked "adorable". They couldn't have used a worse word. Time came for us to leave. Mom said she would drive us, because it was my first day, even though it wasn't very far. She wanted to take me to my class. We arrived in good time. Nancy pushed my back and was off to her class. Mom walked me down the corridor to my classroom, opened the door and a very round, short woman turned and in a loud voice said:

"Look class, see who we have here, little Charlie Van Anden."

I could have dropped through the floor. All the kids seemed to turn in unison and stare. Mom pushed me forward and whispered:

"You'll be just fine. Nancy will come for you when it's time to come home."

She then left. Miss Hays — the round short woman who turned out to be the teacher — took my hand and led me to a seat in part of a circle where most of the other kids had sat down. Next to me was a blond headed boy by the name of Quentin and on the other side was a brown haired girl who told me she was Lyn. At about this time a buzzer went off and Miss Hays sat on the chair in the middle of the circle. The first day in my new school had started.

During the day I did find Johnny McCullough and Roland Gesell were both my classmates. They were friendly enough, which made the day easier. But my closest friend in kindergarten turned out to be Lyn Vandevere. She was funny, thoughtful to everyone and one of the smartest in class. She could even read some. The day was taken up by listening to stories, playing in the sand box, going on the slide in the classroom, running outside for recess, coloring in notebooks, taking a nap and chasing each other around the room. Nancy Jane didn't forget to pick me up at the end of the day and we walked home with Johnny McCullough. He lived behind us on the next street. Aunt Nell, Mom and Iza were waiting for us, anxious to hear all about my first day. I told them all about it and then my sister and I went outside. We played Hop Scotch with Mary Ann Liedecker, Herky Eaton and Don Suzzi. At five my sister and I were called in for supper. We had to eat in the little room off the kitchen unless it was a special occasion. Supper done, we played some games indoors until it was time for our baths. Mine was always first and then I was put to bed. On this night I was to draw or look through books and pictures until Dad came home. About quarter to seven I heard him coming up the stairs. We discussed my day which seemed to make him rather dismayed. He asked if any of us had been questioned on what had been read or asked for comments about the stories. When I told him no, he just shook his head. Before going to sleep, I heard my Aunt, Mom and Dad talking about the school. Apparently, they were not too impressed with my day. It was the first indication I had that they were not impressed with the quality of education being provided to either Nancy Jane or me.

The week went on without incident. I became re-acquainted with kids I knew and got to know many more. It was a happy class but even I realized there was no stress on learning. All that was required was for us to get on with one another and have a good time. Perhaps that was the intended lesson. I wasn't sure because I remembered "Crow Hill" and having to listen to stories and be questioned as to what the story was about and give reasons why we liked or disliked the characters portrayed. Simple, but it made us say what we thought about the story.

When I got home on Friday all was a bustle. Mema was arriving the next day. My room had been turned upside down, the windows washed and new bedspreads put on the beds. Mom was in a tizzy. Iza didn't know how to please her and Aunt Nell was trying to make herself invisible. That night my sister and I were put to bed early — even before Dad came home. Saturday dawned and I got up, quickly dressed and went downstairs. Iza was the only one there. She gave me breakfast — orange juice freshly squeezed (there was no frozen orange juice in those days nor containers of "Florida's Best), oatmeal cereal with milk and honey and the ever present glass of milk. Unlike New Hamburgh, in Scarsdale milk came in bottles delivered by milkmen. The top inch or so of the bottle was cream. Dad always liked to have that portion. Breakfast finished, I slipped out before the rest of the family came down. It was off to Johnny McCullough's. He met me at his front door. His Mom had an aversion of anyone but servants using the back door.

We had previously agreed we would go to Louie's pond. Louie lived way behind the houses across from Johnny's home. There was a path behind the Donaldson's that meandered through the woods to Louie's. He lived with his wife, Mary Jo, and his brother, Henry. The pond was about three acres in size. A stream running from the swamps to the East of their property fed it. Behind, four hundred yards or so, was one of the town dumps. Aside from these features, the area made you feel you were miles from civilization. The pond was a place that was always special. Besides, I thought Louie was one of the best adults I knew. He worked at the Fire Department and did odd jobs around town. No matter where we saw each other he always had time to talk to me. He was fairly tall, very muscular and his face was always split with a big smile. He was black.

On this day, as we arrived at the pond, Mary Jo called out and told us Louie was at the fire department but that Henry was down at his shack near the barn and he would love to see us. We ran down and knocked on the door. It was opened and Henry let us in. He was in the middle of stuffing a beaver. I can't remember how he did it but we were surely awed. He next brought out a large snake that he said he was going to preserve. At that we ran out and went to the pond. It was early fall so the pollywogs had long turned to frogs and the frogs were burying themselves into the mud preparing for the winter. We walked all around the pond but could see nothing that was unusual to attract our interest. Next we went to the small stream and started to make a dam. Our success was minimal. As we walked back towards Louie's, Mary Jo called out for us to come in and have some cocoa. In we went. It was delicious, particularly since she had put marsh mellows on top. We told her about Henry stuffing the beaver and that he was going to preserve a snake. She laughed and said:

"Don't you know? Henry is a taxidermist."

Johnny and I looked at each other and admitted we didn't know what that was. She explained which made us very impressed with Henry.

By now, it was time for lunch so we made our way back to Johnny's. When we got there, Mrs. McCullough said my Mom had called and wanted me home because my Aunt and Grandmother had arrived. Reluctantly, I took off for home. Aunt Eva was not one of my favorite people. She always gushed too much but you could tell she didn't mean a word. Besides, she thought she was so good looking and actually preened. Children to her were something you should avoid at all costs. As I walked into the house I could hear her false chatter. Entering the living room, MeMa jumped to her feet and held out her arms to me.

"Here is my precious boy! He is going to make the whole family proud when he is a big star in Hollywood".

I was stunned. Nevertheless, I ran to her and we had a big kiss and cuddle. Aunt Eva chimed in:

"Come, give me a kiss Darling".

It was all I could do to go to her.

"I hear you are sharing your room with MeMa. What a sweet boy. You two are so much alike and will love being together."

I had no idea how to respond so made an excuse to go into the kitchen. Iza just smiled:

"Don't worry honey. You and your Granma are going to get on fine."

Strangely enough, we did. I came to revere MeMa. She was a lonely soul who found in me someone she could talk to in her dreamy way and not be laughed at. We became fast friends.

Aunt Eva only stayed a few hours and left before Dad got home. [In those days men worked a half day on Saturdays.] After she had gone we were all sitting around in the living room and Mom looked knowingly at me and asked:

"What were you and Johnny doing this morning?"

I knew what was coming but had to tell them.

"Oh, we went down to Louie's pond and just fooled around."

The look she gave me stopped all conversation in the room.

"Charles, you know you are forbidden to go off through the woods to that pond. You'll fall in and drown. If you do that again I will confine you to our yard."

19

I started to protest and had just opened my mouth when she said:

"Don't you dare talk back! Just remember what I said."

It seemed so strange that I couldn't play in the woods and go to the pond for fear of getting hurt. At New Hamburgh I was allowed to run all over town, play around the river, have a tepee in the woods, cross railroad tracks, fish off ledges and do many other things without people worrying something would happen to me. Why was Scarsdale so different? It was the first time I realized the different attitudes of the two communities. I sure wanted to go back to my home along the river with my Aunt Nell.

Dinner with all of us there seemed crowded. Since it was a special day with the coming of MeMa, Nancy Jane and I were allowed to eat in the dining room. Our seating arrangement was established. At the foot of the table sat Dad, Mom at the head, Aunt Nell and Nancy Jane to the right of Dad and MeMa and I to his left. This format never changed over the years. My sister and I were made to sit up properly, hold our knife and fork correctly, chew with our mouths closed, eat everything put on our plates, refuse nothing because we might not like it, keep our napkins on our lap, never rest our elbows on the table, speak only when asked a question and sit there until all were excused. No exceptions were allowed. Actually, this was no different than the rules at New Hamburgh with Aunt Nell. Many years later I realized our table was the most informative time we spent as a family. So many subjects covered, opinions expressed and asked for, discussions turning to arguments which were never allowed to become loud, many laughs and a few embarrassing confessions. It is something that has become almost lost in today's life style.

After dinner I was allowed to stay up for an hour. As usual, we adjourned to the living room. That night MeMa asked if the radio could be turned on. It was and we listened to "Major Bowes Amateur Hour". That was a first for all of us except MeMa. I thought it a riot, especially when the performer got the gong. When the program was over, I went to my room and wondered if I'd hear my grandmother when she came to bed. I didn't because the next thing I knew it was morning. Sunday was for church. Iza served us a light breakfast and then we all dressed. I was surprised to see MeMa not getting ready. I asked Mom why and she said it was because my grandmother was not feeling too well. It soon became obvious MeMa never "felt well" on Sunday. No other explanation was ever given.

20

Church was at St. James the Less. A beautiful Episcopal Church built of stone. It was large, at least fifty times bigger than our church in New Hamburgh. We all, except MeMa , were driven there by Dad in our car. It was probably a one and a half mile trip. I had come to realize that very few people walked anywhere in Scarsdale. It seemed everyone in town had an automobile and some even two. As we walked into the church I was surprised how many people were in the congregation. There were three services each Sunday and all were very well attended. We went to the family service and today I was to enroll in the Sunday School. Children attended the first part of the service but filed out before the sermon. When that time came Nancy Jane and I left attended by Aunt Nell who was taking me to my class to make sure I enrolled properly. My sister was already enrolled in her class. Entering my classroom I recognized some of the kids from my kindergarten class. It made me feel a little better. There were more kids in that room than there were parishioners at our church overlooking my river. After enrolling, I went over and sat next to Tom Hewett and Jane Quackenbush, both from my school class. We did the usual coloring, cutting out and pasting Biblical figures onto sheets of paper. The time passed quickly and it was over before I made too much of a mess. Aunt Nell came for me. She seemed all in a flutter. She had been asked to become a teacher for the third grade. She had accepted. This made it a certainty we would be staying in Scarsdale all the school year. I guess I had been hoping we would go back to our home in the "country".

The days and weeks developed a normal pattern: school, playing with friends, church on Sundays, an occasional ride to some park or to the shore after lunch following church, all of which made me long for New Hamburgh. I began to notice changes in the relationship between family members. Mom was in control domestically. Aunt Nell had relinquished her authority over me and seemed quiet and not very happy. MeMa was always there, sewing, knitting or listening to the radio. Dad was without question the ultimate authority. Nancy Jane became closer to me. She and I seldom fought and if we did I was always blamed, or at least I thought so. Iza, cooked, cleaned, did the laundry and started to grumble more.

One day, early in November, the mood changed. My kinder-garten became a shambles. Miss Hays had asked all of us to sit down while she read another goofy story. Some of us were

21

allowed to sit on the seat in the bay window of the class. I sat with Quentin Smith on one side and Jane Quackenbush on the other. Shortly after Miss Hays started reading my seat became very warm and then I realized it was also very wet. I looked at Jane and she was very red in the face. I jumped up and water dripped onto my shoes. It was then I caught on. Jane had peed in her pants and it had all ran towards me.

"Oh, Jane" I shouted. "Why did you have to do that?"

She started to cry and Miss Hays came running over to us, grabbed Jane and rushed her to the bathroom, yelling at me to go into the boy's bathroom and try to clean up. I was soaked. Nothing I did got me dry. A few minutes later Miss Hays knocked on the door and asked me to come out. When she looked me over, she decided I'd have to go home. She also told Jane the same thing. Down to the principal's office we went. She explained to him what had happened. He had his secretary call our homes to have someone come for us. No one was at home at my place but Iza. She agreed to come and arrived in a few minutes. We walked home with her in laughter. Once there I quickly took my clothes off and had a shower. I didn't think I would ever feel clean. When I dressed and returned downstairs, Iza couldn't stop laughing. At that point I didn't see anything funny about it. Then I realized my good fortune, I was out of school for the day. When Mom, Aunt Nell and MeMa came home they also thought it was all very funny. When Nancy Jane got home I thought she'd split her sides with laughter. That evening Dad also had a good chuckle over my day. I finally saw the humor as well but couldn't help but think of Jane and what her folks had said to her. Perhaps they laughed too. The next day when I entered class, Jane was already there. She came up to me and said she was sorry. I was surprised and pleased that she had enough gumption to do so as soon as she saw me. That incident marked the beginning of a good friendship.

The weeks rolled on and finally it was the long Thanksgiving weekend. Dad had promised we would go to New Hamburgh on the Saturday. We did. It was wonderful! I immediately went over to John Scardefields and found him home. He and his older brother were just leaving for the Yacht Club. Henry, his brother, was twelve and old enough to have his own 22 rifle. They were going to the Club for target shooting. John would throw a can into the river and Henry would fire his rifle to hit and sink the can. He was a good shot. He then let John shoot. John was an even better shot. I asked if I could have a turn but was refused. While we were there several other older boys joined Henry with their own rifles. Everyone agreed John was the best shot. I made up my mind that when I was old enough I'd ask Dad if I could have my own 22. On the way home in the car I broached the subject. What an argument ensued! My mother and aunt were adamant I'd never own a gun. Dad said he would certainly get me one when I was old enough and responsible. The rest of the ride home was constant arguing between the women and my Dad. It got so bad the rest of the day there was dead silence between my parents. A day that started out so promising turned out to be very uncomfortable. That night as I went to bed MeMa told me:

"Charles, don't be so much in a hurry to grow up. You are always pushing your Mom and Dad to let you do things too soon. Slow down, you have so much,"

Looking back, I think that was the most serious bit of advice my grandmother ever tried to give me. Normally, she just went with the flow.

Christmas came quickly. I remember that one because Santa gave me a pilot's cap with goggles just like the one worn by Charles Lindburgh. I wore it constantly for months, if not years. Johnny McCullough also got one. We were sure we would grow up to be famous pilots.

The rest of the year in kindergarten passed and not many more memories exist. There was the excitement of the squirrel in the hollow of an oak tree in the playground which nipped my fingers as I tried to poke it in its' lair. This caused Miss Hays to rush me to the nurse, certain I would die from rabies. I survived. My infatuation with Lyn Vandevere continued. Johnny McCullough became my closest friend, particularly after we went sledding one winter afternoon down the hill behind our property. We went too fast and couldn't stop before we hit the steel fence at the bottom. His foot got stuck in the mesh. I couldn't pull him free. After racing to his house to tell his mom, she called the police and fire department. They arrived with sirens screaming, much to my delight. It took 45 minutes for them to get his foot free. It had become all swollen. Days passed before he could walk properly. When school ended, Aunt Nell and I were allowed to go back to New Hamburgh.

CHAPTER 3

DRIVING FROM HUGHSONVILLE the river soon came into view. My heart started to thump with joy. We crossed Wappingers Creek, then the bridge over the railroad tracks, passed blocked Stone street and our home was in view. At last, I was back where all felt right. Our house looked wonderful! Entering, it smelled musty but as soon as we opened the shutters, windows and doors, that good Hudson River air cleansed all. We weren't settled before John Scardefield was knocking on the back door. Outside I barged. and the two of us ran down to the Yacht Club to play by the river. Soon Johnny Miller joined us. Don Croke, Billy Gallagher, Frederica Lawson and Billy Ruf drifted in as well. The rest of the day was filled with laughter and it seemed I had never been away. The summer of 1933 had begun. It was to be one of the most unusual periods of my young life.

Somehow, things had changed. More adults were home every day. Strangers were all along the railroad tracks. Most looked dirty. A few looked downright mean. I soon learned farmers were patrolling their fields and some even locking their barns. Several times a week men would knock on our back door and beg for food. Many nights I heard people using our hand pump out back. Aunt Nell seemed nervous and the whole town appeared on edge. It wasn't until "Uncle Edgar" spoke to me one evening while we were out on the front porch that I learned quite a few men in town had been laid off from their jobs. The Stone Crusher, the Railroad and the Bleachery had all drastically cut their work forces. He said a lot of people all over the country were out of work, hungry and very unhappy. It sounded awful but it made very little impression on me. I was happy. My friends seemed

25

happy. Fish were still biting. Ted Jennings had just returned for the summer and our Indian camp was going to be better than ever. But, best of all, Ted and I had just found an old rowboat that had drifted onto his grandmother's property. We were determined to fix it up and even rig it so we could sail.

The next two weeks we spent nearly all our time caulking the boat's seams, attempting to raise the boat's sides a little higher with wood found along the river and trying to figure out how to re-install oar locks. We also wanted to fashion a keel on the bottom. Our project came to intrigue some of the men in town and one day Captain Robinson stopped by and helped us figure out solutions to our problems. These solved and completed, we decided to find a round small tree to cut down to make a mast, step it and give it proper support. We were given much help in doing this. Aunt Nell made a sail for us out of a sheet. She fastened metal rings that were given to us by the local foundry to the sheet. Installing it on the mast we realized we had not thought of a boom. Here again Captain Robinson helped us out. By the first part of August we were ready to launch. We had even painted the boat an ugly green from old cans found in Teds' grandmother's basement. On the appointed launch date, nearly half the town turned out to watch. Several men helped move the boat to the Yacht Club beach. Ted and I then pushed and shoved as hard as we could to get it into the water. It floated! One of the men, Bill Ferris, had given us some old oars. We jumped in with the oars and started to row. We seemed to go in circles but we were thrilled. The rest of the day we spent rowing, learning how to go straight. That night Aunt Nell told me how proud she was of Ted and I for sticking to it and finishing our "dream" boat. I went to bed early, exhausted and very happy.

The next few days were heaven. We started sailing. We had promised to stay in the small bay by the club but it soon seemed very cramped. As we learned, with much advice from people along shore, we gained confidence, which only made the small bay seem even smaller. Captain Robinson lived in a house in front of the cove between The Millard Lumber Company and Rabbit Island. The cove was fifteen times the size of the small bay upon which we had been learning. He suggested he tow the boat over there so we had more room to maneuver. He said he would only do it if my aunt gave permission. He had one other requirement: we must wear life jackets. Neither of us had any but several men in town found some for us. Aunt Nell reluctantly agreed to the plan. We started sailing on the cove and that became the beginning of my love for sailing.

For the next five or six days we forgot about being Indians or playing with other friends. We spent nearly every minute with our boat. On a Friday before my parents were to come up, Ted and I raced to the cove to take our craft out. It wasn't there! We searched all over the riverfront but no boat was found. We were heartbroken. The whole town turned out to search but everyone came up empty handed. It had obviously been stolen. The police were advised but it did no good. Our boat had gone. My Dad and Mom never did see the boat but they sure heard a lot about it. The experience was one of great joy that turned into huge disappointment. Dad tried to tell me that life sometimes played such cruel tricks but you had to buck up and go on. Perhaps he was right, but that didn't ease the real hurt which Ted and I felt. Looking back, it was, I think, the first real lesson of my happy go lucky young life.

Two weeks later I had the whole town in an uproar. One morning I awoke early — about 5:00 AM — and decided to go outside. Walking across the street towards the meat market I heard someone call my name. Looking down the street I saw Billy Ruf. He waved to me and came up the road. Billy was three years older and we had never been close friends because of the age difference. On this morning he asked if I'd like to go fishing with him. It sounded good to me. He said he would meet me in about fifteen minutes after he had collected his fishing pole and suggested I get mine. Down to the basement of the house I ran. Picked up one of Dad's poles, rummaged around for fishing hooks, sinkers and bobbers and ran out to meet Billy. As we met he said we should dig for worms behind the Post Office. Sure enough we found a lot of good ones. I thought we would go down to Johnny Millers pier to fish but he said he knew of a better place down by the railroad draw bridge on the Wappingers creek side. Seeing it was so early I knew Aunt Nell would not be up so decided not to wake her to say where I was going. Off we went.

As we walked along the railroad, a long freight train passed us. We noticed several men hanging on the metal struts underneath some of the freight cars. Billy told me these were Hobos — men out of work — using this method to travel. I thought it would be great to ride that way. Just before we reached the drawbridge we went down the bank to the shore of the Creek. Someone had stacked rocks to make a half circle and had been using it as a fireplace. We settled down to fish. The tide was coming in so the fish were biting. Within the first hour we had caught a dozen fish, eight perch and four catfish. We were having great fun! By ten o'clock the tide had turned and all we started to catch were eels. We decided to forget fishing. Billy had another plan.

"Let's swim out to those old barges and see what's inside them."

I told him I wasn't that good a swimmer yet but he assured me I could hang on to a large log he'd found on the shore and he would push me out. All I had to do was hang on tight. Not wanting to be seen as a baby, I agreed. We made it. As I scrambled up the side I heard voices. Billy was up next and then he heard the voices. I started to climb back down when two heads appeared out of one of the hatchways.

"Hey, boys. Stop right there."

My stomach seemed to turn upside down! I was scared. Billy just looked at them and said"

"Why should we? What are you doing here anyway? You're sure not from around here."

One of the men climbed out of the hatch. He was as skinny as a rail with a dirty, scraggly beard. His nose seemed to hang crooked over his mustache. I became more nervous. Soon a short, friendly looking man in rumpled clothes also climbed out of the hatch. His appearance eased my fear. The short guy said:

"We have been watching you fish. Seems you've caught some pretty good ones. Let's cook them up and eat."

Billy said: "We have nothing to cook them in."

"All we need is a few of those branches from those bushes along the shore." the short guy replied.

Much to my amazement, Billy agreed to the idea. The next thing I knew we were climbing down the side of the barge. I clung to the log and Billy and the short guy pushed me ashore. The bearded man followed. Wading out of the water I could hear him coughing and wheezing. He sounded awful. Billy found a board, took out his knife and started cleaning the fish. I just watched, wondering what he had gotten us into. I wasn't too sure if these men were safe to be around. If only I could run away. But I doubted I could. The short guy walked down the shoreline to the bushes and brought back sticks about three feet long. When Billy finished cleaning the fish he used his knife to sharpen the sticks, while short guy started a fire in the fireplace we had seen earlier. At this point Billy asked the men what their names were. Short guy answered:

"I'm Roy and this here fellow is Clem."

Not much more was said until the fire had really started to burn. Clem kept coughing and spitting a yellow glob out of his mouth, which didn't make me very anxious to eat fish. I didn't like to eat fish anyway. The fire hot enough, Roy said it was time to start cooking. We skewered the fish and held the sticks over the fire. I was told to keep turning mine as they were doing. In about ten minutes, Roy said he thought the fish were ready. We let them cool a bit and then started eating. I couldn't get much down but Billy ate two and Clem and Roy had all the rest. As I watched I became aware of sirens screaming in the background. Roy said he guessed there must be a fire somewhere. We thought no more of the ruckus.

Billy and Roy kept talking. Clem curled up on the ground and just kept coughing and all I wanted to do was run home. Finally, Billy and Roy stopped talking. Billy came over to me and said:

"Roy has asked me to get him some bread and vegetables and any soda available. These guys are Hobos like those we saw riding the rails. They have no work or homes. I've told him we'll go get them what they want. Clem is real sick. Roy is worried about him. Come on let's go."

Wow, was I glad to be getting away from there!

When we got to Main Street, there were three police cars in front of my house. The fire engine was down by the war memorial overlooking the river with men running all around. Rowboats were out on the river with men peering over their sides. Billy said:

"I wonder what's up? You go ask your aunt if you can have some bread and vegetables and I'll ask my mom the same. Meet me back here as quick as you can."

I ran to our back door, opened it and rushed in. At that, Aunt Nell, who was sitting at the kitchen table, let out a terrible scream, followed by a very loud:

"Charles, where have you been? When I woke this morning you were gone. I couldn't find you anywhere."

I realized she was yelling at me and crying at the same time. She then got up and grabbed me, turned me around and started to spank me hard.

"You bad boy! You are going to be the death of me. I have had the police and firemen looking all over town for you. They are even now out on the river looking for your dead body. How could you do this to me? What will your father and mother say? They will never let us live here anymore. I could keep spanking you with all my strength until you are black and blue!"

She then turned me around and started to hug and kiss me, crying all the time. I felt terrible. It was hard to believe I had caused so much trouble and that my aunt was in such a state. The scene was interrupted when two policemen entered the house. One was saying:

"We still have no trace---Oh my, what's this? Is this the little boy we are looking for?"

My aunt just nodded, still crying. The other policeman turned around and went outside. The next thing I heard was his shouting that I had been found and was okay. Then I noticed Ida Morey standing in the doorway to the dining room. She was also in tears. She was my aunt's best friend and I guess had been over to keep vigil with her.

After a while, all calmed down. I explained what I had been doing and who had been with me. It was then I remembered why we had come home. I told them about the two hobos and that we had come home to get them food. Ida seemed to take charge. She left and went down to Mrs. Ruf's to see what Billy was up to and to organize some kind of food gathering for these men. I had to remain in the house the rest of the day. Aunt Nell kept alternating between scolding and loving me until it was my bedtime.

On Labor Day weekend Dad and Mom came up to help close the house and take Aunt Nell and me back to Scarsdale. There was an end of summer picnic at the Yacht Club that was a disappointment. It rained and indoors it was too crowded. We left early.

The next day we returned to Scarsdale. While driving home I kept wondering why my parents had not said anything to me about my getting the town in an uproar. I knew a lot of people at the picnic had commented on that day to my folks. Strange. Not even Aunt Nell had said anything to them in front of me. I began to worry more. When we had unpacked, said hi to Iza and my sister, it was time for supper. It was unusual but we were all going to eat in the dining room. After grace and being served, Dad turned to me and said:

"Boy, right after supper you and I are going to the basement for a discussion."

It sure was hard to sit through that meal!

Dinner finished, down to the basement we went. Dad had a spot behind the cellar stairs where he had a card table set up with two chairs. One chair faced in and the other was along one side. Two file cabinets were against the wall and a small table lamp illuminated everything. Such was his "office" at home.

"Boy, sit down. I have heard all about your escapade with Billy Ruf. How you could be so naughty I can't understand. You know you can't do as you please. Other people have to be considered, particularly your family. Aunt Nell was frightened near to death. Her responsibility in taking care of you is great. She dotes on you. Yet you, apparently, don't understand your obligation. As a little boy you cannot do things or go places without telling her or others, who may be taking care of you, where you will be or what you are planning to do. Your mother and I have discussed how you should be punished and have decided to confine you to our property for a month. During that period, no friends will be allowed to play with you. Iza and your Mom will find jobs for you to do after school and there will be no radio programs for you and it's in to bed at six o'clock every night. We are seriously considering not allowing you to go back to New Hamburgh next summer. You are beyond spanking at this point but if you do not behave from now on the belt will be laid on hard."

The way he looked at me made me shiver. He was always good at making me feel small and unworthy. I tried to say I was sorry and ashamed of frightening Aunt Nell but he cut me short and told me to go to bed. No one even said goodnight to me. Sleep came eventually, however, not before I shed a lot of tears.

The month passed. Dad did not talk to me the whole time. Mom only told me what small jobs I had to do but entered in to no general chitchat. My sister seemed to avoid me, Aunt Nell managed to sneak me a hug now and again and halfway through the punishment MeMa returned. She paid no attention to the friction in the home and treated me with her usual dreamy, loving way. It did take longer than a month for things to return to normalcy. It was just too hard to restore the easy banter and happy spirit of the past. It was one of the most effective punishments I ever received from my family. It awoke me to the realization that good relationships required consideration of the responsibilities of all concerned.

We did go back to New Hamburgh for Thanksgiving. The feeling I felt when we drove up to the house was one of great satisfaction and contentment. Those feelings never diminished, I belonged. It wasn't fifteen minutes from our arrival before John Scardefield was knocking on our door. He and Johnny

Miller wanted me to go down to the Yacht Club with them. I remembered to ask my folks for permission and then ran with my friends to the club. A whole group was there, doing the usual Thanksgiving rifle shooting into the river to see who could hit the most targets. Again I was deemed too young to participate. It was just great to be back.

The rest of the school year in Scarsdale just drifted along. I was in Miss Hepburns' first grade class. Johnny McCullough, Roland Gesell, Ed Lawler and other boys from my kindergarten were in my class as well as a number of the girls, including my favorite — Lyn. I loved Miss. Hepburn as a teacher but for the first time became aware that a lot of the kids in my class were smarter than me. It seemed to take me longer to catch on to arithmetic and reading. In gym I excelled. I was the fastest runner, could climb the rope higher and faster, could throw and catch a ball better and did gymnastics with ease. These attributes led me to friendships with other athletically inclined guys. It became obvious the class started to divide into friendship groups. Those who were studious seemed to hang together, the sports minded became close and then there was the small group that floated between the other two. The girls, as a whole, seemed to notice the sports minded guys more than the studious. How the girls separated themselves into factions I had not figured out. I still thought Lyn was the best. We were still close friends. She tried her best to help me with the math and reading. It was a good thing she did or I think I'd still be in first grade.

During the winter it became very cold. At first there was no snow but later in February we had about fifteen inches. In early January, Dad took us all back to New Hamburgh so we could skate on the river. It was black ice that had frozen all the way across, was nearly sixteen inches thick and was smoother than normal. [Ice Breakers were not sent up the Hudson until 1939 or 1940.] I had learned to skate the year before on Louis' pond so was anxious to see how far I could skate on the river. To my amazement, all the kids seemed to carry umbrellas. They would skate out to the center, open their umbrellas with their backs to the wind and be blown fast across the ice. I soon got an umbrella from the house and joined in the fun. But the memorable thing about that day was having my first ride on a Hudson River Ice Boat. They were large, heavy and very fast. I sailed in Mr. Wicks' "Puff". Three of us were in the cockpit — Mr. Wicks, John Scardefield and myself — and out on the port runner was Sammy

Shay. I couldn't believe how fast we went. We actually went faster than one of the express trains that ran along the tracks by the river. Also on the ice were three other boats: "Icicle", "Jack Frost" and "Whiff". After I had my ride, all four boats had a race. I can't remember who won but I have never forgotten the beauty of those flying boats and that magic day.

Chapter 4

By the end of the school year it still had not been decided whether or not Aunt Nell and I would be going to New Hamburgh for the summer. I knew she had told Dad she was going and hoped he would allow me to be with her. The house actually belonged jointly between Dad, Aunt Nell and my Uncle Le. The weekend after the last day of school, Dad drove my aunt up and I was left behind. I was crushed. When he came back all he would say was that we would discuss my summer later in the week. About Thursday he brought the subject up just before I went to bed.

"Charles, we have decided you can go up with Aunt Nell but this year your sister will be going also."

At that my sister said:

"I'm not going! I hate it there. The people are so awful and the kids are so stupid and dirty. Why can't I stay in Scarsdale? All my friends are here."

"Because, your mother and I have a very busy summer and will be away a lot. Iza has told us she is leaving to go back to Scotland and there will be no one here to take care of you. One of the things we will be doing over the next month or so is trying to get a replacement for her. If that happens we may let you come home early."

That seemed to settle that. I was happy and sad all at once. I was thrilled to be going back to New Hamburgh but very upset over Iza's leaving. She had been with us since I was two and seemed part of the family. When Saturday came it was time to say goodbye to Iza. She gave both my sister and me big hugs and kisses as we got into the car. She promised to write and never stop loving us. As we drove off I had an awful empty feeling. The emptiness left as soon as the New Hamburgh house appeared. To me this was home.

The summer started off with trouble and fear. The town had three cases of Polio. My aunt, like all other adults, feared many more children would come down with the sickness. Most of us kids were not allowed to go swimming. Large groups were avoided and we were never allowed to eat at someone else's home. Russell Morey, Ida and Conklin's son, died of the disease three weeks after we returned to town. The other two children with the sickness recovered but Clarence — one of the black kids in town — was left with paralysis in his right leg. He had to walk with a brace. No others in town became infected. Many other communities were fighting the same epidemic. Just before my birthday in August we learned that my cousin, Glad, who lived on Long Island, had contracted it and his face was partially paralyzed. Other friends, who lived in the Bronx, had two of their children come down with it and the oldest boy was severely crippled. He never walked again.

Aside from the polio epidemic, the summer was the usual happy time for me. Swimming was eventually allowed, boating, fishing, playing at being big Indian chiefs and other pursuits consumed the weeks. On the day of my birthday, Paul Huested knocked on our door about ten in the morning. He ran the Railway Express Agency across the street. He said he had a large crate for me. When I got over to his office he helped me open it. It was my birthday present from Mom and Dad — A brand new bicycle — bright red. I was thrilled. Other kids had let me ride theirs but I never had one of my own. Jumping on it, I rode to John Scardefields to show him, then down to Ted Jennings. John wasn't that impressed but Ted immediately got his out and we spent the rest of the day riding all around town. That evening, Aunt Nell gave me a present and a birthday card sent to me by Iza. It was the first any of us had heard from her. She said she was happy to be home in Scotland but missed me. I missed her too but more impressed over receiving a card all the way from Scotland.

The rest of the summer flew by.

On returning to Scarsdale after Labor Day, I discovered Iza's replacement had already settled in. She was a tall, regal black woman by the name of "Willie", the best cook we ever had, an immaculate housekeeper and possessed a great disposition. I immediately became enthralled with her

Ten or twelve weeks later, I ruined everything when I caught scarlet fever. "Willie" had to leave our home for fear of becoming infected. I was sick for about three weeks, after which everything in my room had to be burned. The worst result was that when Mom called "Willie" to come back, she informed us she could not because she had taken a new job. She needed a steady income. We were all devastated. Shortly, a new girl was hired — Lillian. She was white, lazy, sullen and just plain awful. She lasted two months. Next to fill the position was Margaret. She was dumpy, unattractive, lazy, unkempt and black as the ace of spades. She was always on the verge of being let go. She stayed with us for four and a half years. She and I became good friends. She spoiled me. She became an ally. In her eyes I could do no wrong even though that seemed to be my strong point.

I was in the second grade. Miss Flowers was my teacher. She was a very attractive blond but I didn't learn much from her. Unfortunately, she became my third grade teacher as well. The school year crept along after I returned from my bout with scarlet fever. In the late fall I did distinguish myself by setting Crane's woods on fire. Don Sutzi and I had gone hiking in the woods and he brought along some matches. Stopping to prepare a small campsite for a short rest, we decided a fire would be nice. After he had started a small one, I wanted to start my own. He gave me the matches and I lit some leaves and twigs. Before we knew it the two little fires had joined. We tried to stamp them out but the breeze spread them faster than we could stamp. The fire grew bigger and bigger. We ran all the way home, Don to his house and me to my basement. Here I proceeded to play with my fire truck which I had been given the previous Christmas. I heard the fire whistle and knew someone had seen the conflagration and reported it. I stayed in the basement. Several hours later I heard Margaret talking to someone. It was Louie. He came down the basement steps and called:

"Charles, I know you are down here. We have to talk."

I knew I was caught. He told me he had suspected that I had set the fire because he had seen me running in the woods behind his house coming from the direction of Crane's woods. In tears and trembling, I confessed. He talked to me sternly about how dangerous it was to play with matches and then said he wanted to take me to the fire station as soon as he got my father's per-mission. I knew if he did that my Dad would learn of my starting the fire but agreed anyway. I was in trouble. When Dad learned from Louie what had happened I was punished by being confined again. Louie did get permission to take me to the firehouse. That occurred a week later. The chief gave me a long lecture, showed me pictures of other fires which had destroyed homes and of people who had been burned by fires. I was sickened with what I saw. Louie then showed me all over the firehouse and let me sit in one of the fire trucks while he backed it into the garage. He then walked me home.

Winter passed, school crept along and my scholastic knowledge barely budged. For me the best part of the day started when school was let out. I did learn a new word: incorrigible. It was applied to me often. As the end of my second grade school year approached, for the first time a track and field day was planned. The day arrived with the school divided into two teams — the reds and blues. The reds selected me to compete in two events, the sixty- yard dash and the broad jump for grades two thru four. I was thrilled to be asked. As the start time approached, my nerves were tingling and I could hardly stand still. The dash was held first. Twenty- four students had been entered. Three separate races were to be held on the first go around and then the first two finishers from each race were to run in the final contest. I was to run in the third section. The starter gun banged and off we went. All the runners seemed in front of me. My sister started yelling for me to go faster and I doubled my efforts. Second place was my finish. I was mad at myself for starting so poorly. Mr. McGlathery, the gym teacher, came over to me and said:

"Charles, you can do better. No one in grades two through four can run as fast as you. If you calm down, you can win."

I felt better but was not too sure he was right. At that point, Lyn Vandevere walked up and said:

"Charlie, I know you are going to beat them all."

To my amazement, in front of all my other friends, she planted a kiss on my cheek. I could have dropped through the ground. All of a sudden all I could hear was a chorus:

"Charlie and Lyn are in love. Charlie and Lyn are in love."

I didn't know whether to shout at them to shut up or to ignore them. Mr. McGlathery saved me when he announced the start of the final race. It turned out to be an easy run. I won by three yards.

An hour later, the broad jump competition for the younger group started. I think there were seventeen selected to enter. I knew I could run and jump pretty far but doubted I could win.

As usual, Lyn disagreed with my pessimism and kept telling me I could win. When it was all over I had placed fifth. But Lyn only saw the good side. She pointed out I had beaten all the second graders and all but two of the third. No wonder I thought of her as one of my best friends!

Six days after the track and field meet, I was back in New Hamburgh with my aunt. It was as if I had not been away all winter. But changes there were. John Scardefield had started working on the DelPaso Farm. He was there from 7:00 AM until 4:00PM. That essentially changed our relationship. He felt much older than me and started to spend his free time with those of his own age or older. We were still good friends but involved with different people. Some evenings we played catch or tossed a football around but it was not the same. Ted Jennings still stayed with his grandmother and we continued to play together a lot. He had been given a proper tent that we set up along the shore on his grandmother's property. It was about 150 yards from his house. This became our summer campsite. Aunt Nell gave me permission to sleep there two or three nights a week. We fished often, played Indian hunters, swam and rowed his family boat up and down the river close in to shore. Sometime around the third week in July, we were fishing off the rock ledge on a point of land on his property. We noticed a man rowing a boat towards us. He kept yelling something we couldn't understand. As he got closer he shipped his oars and stood up. We soon realized he was swearing at us. Our response was laughter. He then bent down and rose with a rifle in his hands. Up to his shoulder he raised it and bullets hit the rock upon which we were standing. We dropped our fishing poles and jumped behind the ledge. The man kept shooting and yelling. We were petrified. This must have gone on for five or ten minutes before the man started rowing off towards Sandy Bottom. When we felt safe, we ran to Ted's house and told his grandmother what had happened. She called the police. They came and searched all around. It was nine o'clock that evening before they caught the guy. He had gone fast asleep in the woods across the railroad tracks. He apparently had been drunk after drinking heavily since being laid off from work at the Stone Crusher further up the river. We never did learn what happened to him. For a week I wasn't allowed to sleep at our campsite.

My birthday came as usual. I can't remember what presents I received or whether Aunt Nell baked me a cake. All I can remember is that I had a card from Lyn. She was moving to Los Angeles,

California. Her Dad was going to work for one of the movie studios. It was all I could do not to cry. Not only was she moving but said they would be gone before I returned. The summer had been ruined.

Right after Labor Day I was back in Scarsdale. School started the following Wednesday. All the kids in my third grade class were talking about Lyn's moving to California. She had been the most popular and was missed terribly.

Our class was different this year. Many of our old classmates had been assigned to another teacher and a lot of new faces had been assigned to Miss. Flowers. Almost immediately Johnny Fearing, a newcomer, and I formed a liking for one another. He was funny, a good athlete, a fair student and considerate of all. A group formed around us, Bill Smith, Bumpy Callahan, Dave Welling, Ed. Lovett and Keith Norman. Our main interest was sports. My old friends, Johnny McCullough, Roland Gesell, Ted Miswaw, Bill Levitt, Bob Engelhardt and Tony Pakarsky were still friends but they had started to associate with other groups. Once again, I couldn't help but notice that these breakdowns seemed to be caused by different outlooks and interests. I wondered why it was so difficult to bridge these groups. I tried hard to do so but with minimal success. An outcome of this situation was the arrival of "slam books" which I had heard of but now experienced first hand. From the start I hated them. They were so mean and always hurt those who craved to have friends but didn't seem to know how to go about gaining them. Our group decided not to participate.

In October, Dad purchased a grand piano for my mother She was thrilled. Music became an even bigger part of our family life. Four weeks later she surprised us by announcing it had been arranged for me to start violin lessons. I was dumbfounded. In my mind, nothing epitomized sissy boys more than those that played violins. No amount of arguing deterred my Mom's determination to have another musician in the family. My sister had been taking piano lessons for two years and even I could tell that talent had evaded her. My lessons were to be every Tuesday afternoon after school. All had been arranged. A Mr. Kordgewhan was to be my instructor. He was a violinist with a New York City Symphony orchestra. I pleaded with Mom to cancel the lessons to no avail. I enlisted Aunt Nell in efforts to discourage my mother but a worse advocate could not have been found. Dad did not even come to my rescue. The prodigy had no escape.

On the appointed day of my first lesson Mr. Kordgewhan arrived with a violin my mother had already selected. He took it out of its' case, tuned it up, put resin on the bow and played a jaunty tune, laughed and said:

"Charles, see that is easy. You'll be doing little tunes like that in no time. All you have to do is to pay attention to what I tell you, practice every day, play the scales over and over so your fingers become flexible, learn to keep your ear tuned to the proper notes and keep in time." With that, he acted as if he had stirred my enthusiasm. He hadn't. All I could do was stare at him. He was a funny looking man, very tall, quite stooped, wore thick glasses and talked with a foreign accent. His nose seemed to spread all over his face and it was very red. I didn't know whether to laugh or cry. He then handed me the violin and had me try to tune it by turning the pegs while plucking the strings. He then put a green velvet chin rest on the bottom of the instrument, had me place the violin under my chin, holding it between that and my shoulder without using my hands to hold the other end. My left hand was then grabbed and placed so my fingers curled around the stock so they could touch the strings. He had me do this a number of times. Then he took the violin from me and handed me the bow. He had loosened it. I was instructed to tighten the hairs on the bow and run them over a block of resin. When I had finished he returned the violin to me, had me place it under my chin, hold the stock properly and run the bow over the strings. The sound was awful. We then went through a series of placing my fingers at various positions on the strings while drawing the bow over the touched string. I thought the lesson would never end. It finally did. As he was leaving he told us I would do just fine as long as I practiced. He also suggested we purchase a music stand. I felt trapped.

Every Tuesday he showed up. Six days of the week I had to practice. I did improve but I tried to keep the lessons a secret from my friends. No such luck. Sometime around Christmas I was exposed. Johnny McCullough came looking for me one Tuesday afternoon and heard me squeaking away. The next day, it was all over school and the neighborhood. Surprisingly, it did not cause me as much embarrassment as feared. Just the same, the violin and I never really became properly acquainted. I took lessons for five years, played in the school orchestra, gave some recitals but thankfully quit playing at the end of seventh grade. By the time I graduated from High School I couldn't play much

41

at all. My family should have saved their money. Perhaps, that is wrong. I did learn to appreciate really good music but just could not produce it myself. I know my mother was disappointed.

Besides this venture into musical stardom, school was kinder to me. It was probably the result of Miss Flowers' apparent disinterest in teaching. We all seemed to receive roughly similar grades. No pressure was ever evidenced in making us apply greater effort to reading, writing or arithmetic. We just drifted along. Her consuming interest was her boyfriend who seemed to be at school as much as the students. Under this relaxed atmosphere "puppy love" blossomed among a large segment of the class. Johnny Fearing and Pam McCrae were inseparable. Bill Smith and Patsy Blackwell were a duo as well as Bumpy Callahan and Nancy Nichols. Johnny McCullough and many others were not interested in any girl but girls tried to gain their attention. My interest was riveted on a new girl, Madeline Harding. I was smitten with her from the start. She was a pretty blonde with a radiant smile. We became close friends and were soon teased by our classmates. In retrospect, it was a fairly happy school year. Contributing to this was our increased involvement in sports. From football to soccer to basketball to baseball to track we competed. The girls always came to watch us show off.

Fortunately, it was a year in which I avoided trouble. For the first time, my scholastic average was not a major source of discussion at our dinner table. The most excitement came the first week in May. Eddie Lauer, who had lived four houses down the street from us, had moved to Florida over the Christmas recess. We had never been real pals but were friendly enough. Then, out of the blue, I received a package from him that May. Upon opening it, I found a wooden box with the words: "Baby Alligator Inside". Holes had been punched in its' lid and the outside wrapping had been a mesh, which allowed air to circulate inside. Gingerly opening the top, I found the baby alligator crawling sleepily inside. I called my Aunt to come see. She did and quickly told me it was the cruelest package she had ever seen. My Mom heard us excitedly talking so came to see what was happening. She took one look and said:

"Outside with it!"

Her tone of voice made it clear there was no alternative.

What to do with Eddie's present? Then I thought of Louie's pond. I called Johnny McCullough to tell him of my new pet and my idea. He was soon at our house. Off to the pond we went.

We made a big ditch by the water and then made a small trench from the water to the ditch. We hoped this would not provide a direct access to the main pond. In went the alligator. He happily swam around while we tried to feed him worms and bugs. He wouldn't eat. We then decided to leave him alone for a few hours. When we returned, no alligator could be found. Johnny suggested we build a raft. Finding old boards we put them together with nails and a hammer lent to us by Louie's wife. We then went to the dump further behind the house and scavenged for some cans with screw tops. Six were found. These were fastened to the bottom of the raft by rope. Our vessel completed, we flipped it over into the water. It floated. An argument ensued as to who would get on the raft first. Johnny won by the "one potato, two potato, three potato, four" method. We pushed the raft over to Louie's pier with a large pole and then Johnny jumped aboard. The raft tipped, went partly under water and Johnny fell. It was deeper than we thought. With his feet stuck in the mud, the water was above his nose. He struggled and went deeper. I jumped in and swam to him, pushing his body as hard as I could. He wouldn't budge. I started yelling and thankfully, Henry, Louie's brother heard. He came running and jumped in, grabbed Johnny and pulled him out. He had been so still, I thought he had drowned, but he soon began to throw up water as Henry was hitting his back. In a few minutes he seemed okay, but neither of us could stop shaking. Henry took us into their house. Mary Jo took one look at us and made us strip down to nothing. Towels were thrown around us, our clothes put in the sink to soak and we were told to get into their bathtub. We were soon clean. She made us hot chocolate and started to dry our washed clothes in the oven. While we waited for them to dry, she and Henry told us not to tell our parents what had happened. They were both afraid they would be blamed for allowing us to play around their pond and hold it against Louie, jeopardizing his job as our gardener. I couldn't see their reasoning but was glad our families would never learn of our adventure. We kept quiet. When Louie heard of our near disaster, he made us promise only to come to the pond after we had told Mary Jo that we were there and that under no circumstances were we to use the raft again. We so promised.

We stayed shy of the pond for about a week. I was worried about the alligator. We finally returned, notified Mary Jo and Henry we were there and then combed the banks looking for our pet. We did so many times but never saw the alligator again. I came to realize Eddie's gift wasn't such a hot idea. I felt guilty and sorry that I was responsible for its' demise. For some reason, it bothered me for months.

The summer of 1935 was different than any I had experienced before. New Hamburgh was not as happy a town as in the past. Unemployment had come to many more men. A greater number of men seemed to be traveling the rails as Hobos and the frequency of backdoor beggars increased. An air of caution prevailed. Smiles were fewer. Fishing became a necessity, not a sport, for many. On the trip from Scarsdale we had driven on a road that took us past a CC camp. There men were hired by the Federal Government to build highways and given food and shelter while working on the various projects. Those men never seemed happy. Rather, they seemed lost or in a daze. The commercial traffic on the river was not as active. Fewer ships came to the town dock to either load or unload. Our Yacht Club was not very active and the local stores were struggling to stay in business. I became aware of these things not so much by personal observation but by overhearing the adults talking.

Still, it was great to be back. Many of the older kids were helping local farmers and not hanging around town as in previous years. I asked John Scardefield why so many of his friends were working while men were left without jobs. He said it was because the farmers could use young people at far less a cost than hiring the older men. It didn't make much sense to me. Ted Jennings was back from Utica staying with his grandmother and Billy Gallagher, Johnny Miller and Frederica Lawson were still available to hang out with so the summer wasn't too bad for all the doom and gloom.

The canoe became my summer passion. Dad had had a canoe for years and although I had often paddled with him, or some other adult, this was the first year I was allowed to take the canoe out by myself. At first, I was restricted to the cove or close in to shore. But by the middle of the summer, when Dad came up for a few days, he told me I was good enough to be able to go wherever I liked. Aunt Nell had a fit! She said she didn't want the responsibility and worry of me going all over the river while she was in charge of me. A compromise was reached. I could go anywhere but only if I took a friend who also knew how to paddle. That confined my canoe activity to late in the day. The only friend good enough was John Scardefield. He and I spent at least four or five early evenings a week exploring the river from

Newburg Bay to the stone crusher — a span of nearly six miles. One evening early in August, unexpected excitement arrived. Exploring the cove behind Danskammer Point we heard a very loud grinding noise followed by shouts for help. We paddled quickly toward the commotion. As we nosed around the point, we saw a power- boat firmly aground on the rocks with three men and a woman stumbling around. John said:

"They are as drunk as can be. Look at them. One guy is completely naked and the woman only has her panties on. I don't think we should get involved with them."

As we started to paddle away one of the men shouted at us:

"Hey you fellows, come over here and give us some help."

John shouted back: "No way. We have to get going."

The man: "Come on. We need help. We are from up river and need to re-float this boat to get back."

"You aren't going to float that boat. It is stove in at the bow and we can't get all of you in our canoe. I'll tell you what we'll do. We will go around to the brickyard, behind this point, and have someone there get you help or come for you. We have to get going."

"Okay. Just promise to get help."

While this conversation took place we had maneuvered closer to where they were. We could plainly see the naked couple. My eyes must have bulged out of my face. I had never seen anything like that woman before. I guess the naked man could see our interest because he started to shield the woman with his back to us. John said:

"Charles, I'll bet this is the first time you have seen anything like what's before your eyes. Do you know what they were probably doing before they crashed? They were having some kind of sex orgy and not paying attention to where the boat was going."

I had to ask: "What's a sex orgy?"

John started to laugh loudly: "You are so damn innocent it's unbelievable."

I felt embarrassed and confused. We started paddling and made our way to the Brickyard. As we approached, one of the watchmen called to us asking what we wanted. We told him about the grounded boat, the four people involved and that they needed assistance. He assured us he would call one of the rescue squads and get the help needed. Heading back to New Hamburgh we passed the stranded foursome and shouted to them that help was on its' way. I tried to see the naked people again but they had found their clothes. Paddling home I again asked John to explain what a sex orgy was. He just kept laughing. When I finally got home I told Aunt Nell all about our adventure. When I got to the part about the sex orgy I thought she was going to pass out. All she said was:

"Never you mind. Go upstairs, clean up and come down for supper."

That was the end of that. However, I didn't stop thinking about it.

Shortly after this event, I noticed Ted Jennings seemed more subdued than normal. I soon discovered the reason. He had been told his grandmother was selling her home and that he and his folks were moving in the fall to Michigan. He would no longer return to New Hamburgh for the summer. We decided as a last project together we would try to build a sailboat from scratch. We combed the banks of the river for suitable lumber. We finally collected enough and started. Problems immediately arose. None of the lumber was true so that the seams in the hull were narrow in spots and too wide in others. Attempting to saw each piece was time consuming. He started to get impatient and for the first time since we had known each other his temper became all too obvious. After two weeks or so we had the hull nearly finished. Captain Robinson, as before, guided us in our efforts. I thought the boat was shaping up pretty well but one day all changed. As we were fashioning a brace for one of the seats, Ted's plane slipped. He dropped it, picked up a heavy hammer and started to smash everything we had done to pieces. All I did was watch him and wonder what had gotten in to him. The boat in a shambles, he dropped the hammer and ran in to his house. He never said a word to me. Dazed, I tried to put pieces together but realized it was beyond repair. Upset and dismayed, I walked home. Aunt Nell took one look at me and said:

"What's wrong? I've never seen you so quiet. Did you and Ted have an argument?"

I looked at her, shook my head and softly said:

"Ted just smashed our boat all to pieces. He never said a word to me. He just walked away. I don't understand. He has never done anything like that.

"Charles, don't fret about it. You can start another boat. Ted is a good friend of yours. You have always had fun together. He doesn't have any other friends but you. Do you realize that? He has never been accepted like you. You're friends with everyone.

46

That's your nature. Ted has always been a loner except for you. He's an only child, been spoiled — not that you haven't been — and is now upset because they are moving and there will be no more summers in New Hamburgh, Try to forgive him. Knowing you, you'll find a lot of other things to do. Now Buck-up."

It took me a couple of days to get over it. Three days later, I saw Ted standing in his front yard. I went over and said:

"Hi."

He looked at me and burst into tears. "Charles, I'm sorry. I'm so ashamed. I know you were intent on building that boat. I just don't see the point anymore. I'll never be back here again. I don't want to move. Please forgive me. You're the best friend I have."

I stood there, looked at his unhappy expression and said:

"Come on, let's see if our tepee is all right."

Off we ran. The rest of the summer we played together a lot but at times it felt awkward.

The summer breezed along. John Scardefield and I still canoed many an early evening. We spent time crabbing in late August. It was one of the most prolific crab seasons in years. I guess because we had very little rain and the river became more brackish. Labor Day came and my Aunt and I were soon closing the house and on our way back to Scarsdale. It was tough saying goodbye to Ted. I never saw or heard from him again.

CHAPTER 5

Fourth grade started with a bang. Miss Stern was our teacher. Her name fitted her personality. She seldom smiled, was fairly tall and very thin. Her dark hair was pulled into a bun and her skin was blotchy. When speaking, the sounds that came forth were grating. With all of this, she was undoubtedly the best grammar school teacher I ever had. She was fair, helpful and always prepared. It took weeks to get accustomed to her but once I did my grades started to improve dramatically.

Later in the month I was offered Greg Scofield's Saturday Evening Post's delivery route. He had let his route dwindle to fourteen customers and the route manager gave me the opportunity to take it over. I was ecstatic. Within a week my route numbered twenty-six customers. Johnny McCullough had been offered Jeff Fenstermacher's route so we became fierce competitors. I got the idea to go to the Scarsdale railroad station to hawk the magazine to commuters coming home from work. The number of magazines sold per week quickly grew to over sixty. They sold for five cents per copy and I believe I was allowed one cent for each sale plus points good for merchandise from a catalogue. I thought I was in clover! Johnny soon caught on to how I was selling so many. He quickly started selling at the other end of the station platform. It was an election year. Roosevelt was running for a second term and the Republicans had nominated Alf Landon to run against him. Mrs. McCullough was very active in the Republican Party and soon solicited Johnny and me to pass out Alf Landon "Sunflower" pins to commuters while selling our magazines. All during October and early November, I would stand at the top of the stairs leading from the platform, shouting:

"Saturday Evening Post, Five cents. Take a "Sunflower" pin and vote for Alf Landon." At first I was fearful it would hurt business but it didn't.

On my home delivery route, I learned to get the money before turning over the magazine. Some customers wanted to pay once a month but often it became necessary to chase after the money. One such account was the O'Dells. They lived on a street two blocks away from my house. I loved to make a delivery there. I'd ring the front door bell and soon Mrs. O'Dell would open it. Her little black Scotty would jump all around in excitement. She always wore a loose fitting Kimono, bend down to quiet or play with her little dog and the kimono would open widely and her big boobs would hang out and bounce around. I would stammer for the money, turn beet red and keep my eyes fastened on the scene. I seldom got the money but it was always a great day. This situation lasted until late March. One week in that month, the door opened and there stood Mr. O'Dell. I asked for all the back money. He reluctantly paid but told me to stop the delivery. By the end of April they had moved. I learned later that they had separated.

Business climbed. I was up to one hundred magazines a week and sometimes more. I kept upping the number of issues I'd take delivery of in confidence of selling them. I would usually spend two evenings a week at the railroad station. On the second evening, one man always came up from the 7:20 train, ask me how many copies I had and buy the three or four I had left. As I took in more issues I'd be left with a higher number. One week, on the second night, the usual friendly man asked how many I had left. When I told him six, he walked off. Having gone thirty feet or so, he turned around:

"Son, I have watched you sell these magazines ever since you started. I thought it wonderful of you to have such gumption but now you are trying to play me for a sucker. I don't like that. I'm finished buying from you."

He then walked off. I had learned a great lesson and to this day appreciate that man. He was right. I was playing him for a sucker. I hope I have never done that again to anyone.

A few days later things changed. Uncle Le, who owned a flower shop in Larchmont, N.Y. went into bankruptcy. He had to move to the house in New Hamburgh. To my dismay, Aunt Nell decided to go back with them and share the house. I thought I might be allowed to join them but Dad quickly squashed that idea.

The school year was going fairly well. I was actually learning. My interest in reading was stimulated and I devoured book after book. Most were adventure stories. My violin playing placed me in the school orchestra. Why they accepted me is a mystery. At a number of performances they had me direct the orchestra from the podium. I still think they did this so my playing didn't grate on the ears of the audience.

My mother was determined to expose me to as much good music as she could. As a result, I was enrolled in a group from school that attended the Walter Damrosch concert series at Carnegie Hall during the winter months. Nine or ten from our school participated. Johnny Fearing and I were two from our class who were involved. Our group had a box on the mezzanine level directly over the orchestra. Johnny and I occupied the front row seats. The kettledrums were directly underneath. We enjoyed watching them perform. The music was wonderful and Mr. Damrosch always explained the pieces they were playing. It made the music come alive. After attending three or four of these performances, Johnny started to get restless and conjure up mischief. One Saturday, he brought a pocketful of crayons. Halfway through the second number, out came the crayons. Johnny broke them in pieces and proceeded to drop them over the rail aiming at the kettledrums. The first few times he missed. He finally got the range and "bong" went the drum when it should have been quiet. The drummer looked all around and we started laughing. A few minutes passed and John scored again. We thought it a riot. He handed me some pieces and we synchronized our drops. "Bong", "Bong" went the drums. It was all we could do to contain ourselves. In a couple of minutes we started to lean over the rail again. WHAM. WHAM. Our collars were grabbed from behind. We were yanked to our feet, hustled out of the box, dragged downstairs and shoved into a security office. Trouble had arrived! Two muscular security guards stood before us and one said:

"Young men, you are without a doubt the worst boys to ever come to these performances. Punishment will be arranged and you will no longer be permitted to attend".

At that point, the door was opened and in rushed Mr. Dunsmore, our music teacher.

"Boys, you are a disgrace to the school and to your families. How you could be so irresponsible I'll never understand. You have jeopardized our ability to bring students to these grand affairs. We have all been asked to leave. How you will be punished, I can't say at this time but let me assure you it will be severe. Now collect your things, behave yourselves and meet me here with the other students as quickly as possible. We will all catch the train home."

Johnny and I did as we were told. During the trip back all ignored us. Arriving at the school, we found our furious parents waiting. My mother was near tears and Dad was blistering. Johnny's parents seemed in a similar state. I dreaded reaching home.

"Boy, go down to the basement. I'll be right there."

Thirty seconds later, he was.

"Drop your pants!"

He had a leather belt in his hand and proceeded to whip me good and hard. How many times I can't remember but I do know I was sore for over a week and hated to have to sit down. That was not all of my punishment. I was grounded after school for a month. The real punishment occurred at school. The Monday following the escapade, the whole student body was called to the auditorium. Johnny and I were paraded onto the stage. Mr.Moyle, the principal, spoke of our crime and outlined our punishment. For the next six weeks we were to remain after school for two hours. During that time we were to help the janitors by washing blackboards, sweeping floors, emptying garbage and doing any tasks they could find for us to do. In addition we were to wear dunce caps at all times and no students were allowed to talk to us for any reason. We were to be humiliated. It turned out to be an extremely tough six weeks. Mr. Zabriski, the head janitor, was unrelenting in making sure we were kept at it. The students really did ostracize us and other parents made it obvious we were "persona non gratis".

When the six weeks ended we learned that our parents had reimbursed parents of those kids who had been dragged out of the performance. We were told we would have to work shoveling snow, washing cars, cutting grass when spring came and doing anything we could find to raise money to pay our parents back. We did but it made the fourth grade year unpleasant and unforgettable. [The one exception to the punishment routine was the decision to allow me to continue with the Saturday Evening Post sales effort.]

Over the Easter recess, Dad and I helped Uncle Lee clear the land on the "hill" overlooking the river. The property was next to Mr. Wick's farm. My father had arranged to lease it for five years with an option to buy or to continue a renegotiated rental. We didn't go up every day but did six days of the recess. It was hard work. Trees had to be cut down, the brush stacked and then burned. The hardest part was digging out the stumps and roots. The work was going so slowly, Dad hired Bill Ferris to give us a hand. He was glad of the work because he had been laid off from the railroad. I had known Bill forever. He was about 5'10", had dark black hair, a swarthy complexion and was tough as nails. He was married and already had three children. His wife looked like an Indian squaw and had a mouth on her that could curl a parson's hair. At first he treated me as a spoiled, soft, rich kid. I was determined to gain his respect. I admired him for his strength, good attitude, eagerness to keep at it and an uncanny ability to make something difficult, simple. We didn't finish the job that spring but Bill did by early June. During the recess period I was allowed to spend one night in New Hamburgh at the house. It turned out to be a very uncomfortable time. Within hours of being in the house it was very clear that Aunt Nell and Aunt Gertie were not getting along too well. They seemed to argue over everything. Uncle Lee said very little and it became obvious my presence in some way aggravated the situation. For the first time, "my town" lost some of its' appeal. It was great to see my friends but it was a relief when it was time to depart.

When Dad came back he quickly sensed my unhappiness.

"Boy, Why so glum? Didn't you have a good time?"

"Yeah, but it was strange to be in the house with two aunts and an uncle. In the past, Aunt Nell and I always got on and did things. We kind of knew what and where each other were. We always got along fine. With Aunt Gertie and Uncle Lee there, it changed the whole atmosphere. I guess, I was just not comfortable."

No more was said

After Easter, school became more normal. The Carnegie Hall fiasco had faded somewhat and all thoughts turned to getting passing grades, preparing for the end of school track & field meet, playing baseball and showing off to the girls.

Two major things then occurred. First, Dad surprised all of us by buying a catboat twelve feet in length, which he promptly named "Nancy Jane" after my sister. He had joined the Horseshoe Harbor Yacht Club in Larchmont so he could keep it moored there. I was excited to start sailing her.

The other momentous event happened at a cookout at the Davies. Dana Davies was my sister's best friend. She had two brothers, Don, the oldest and Steve, one year older than me. I had always liked Steve but we had never done much together. On arrival, we started to toss a baseball back and forth to break the ice. Talking, we found we had much in common. Both of us loved sports, disliked school, hankered to own our own rifles and were interested in the opposite gender. As time slipped by, while Mr. Davies was making a big deal out of barbecuing , it was obvious Steve and I would be friends.

The barbecue was a big success. Much teasing and raucous laughter proved everyone was having a good time. When desert was finished, Mr. Davies and my Dad stood up and asked for everyone's attention. We all gathered around in anticipation. Mr. Davies started:

"Dana and Nancy Jane, we have enrolled the two of you at Camp Cowasset in Cape Cod. Steve and Charles, the two of you are going to sailing camp at Wampanoag, also on the Cape. Don, you have been signed up for a special astronomy course at Tabor Academy in Marion, Massachusetts."

To say the least, we were all stunned. Dana and Nancy Jane started whispering to each other, Don looked pleased but Steve shouted:

"I'm not going! I have never sailed and have no interest in going to a stupid camp."

Mr. Davies quickly responded:

"You are enrolled, you are going and there will be no further discussion."

At that, Dad looked at me and dared me to say anything. Knowing the time was not right to cross him, I kept my thoughts to myself. Steve nudged me and said:

"Let's go have a catch."

We went out front and started throwing the ball back and forth.

"Charles, we have to get out of this. The last thing I want to do is go away to camp. My friends and I have plans for the summer and learning to sail at some creepy camp is not one of them. If it were fishing and canoeing it would be better but I have never sailed, don't want to sail and have no interest in doing it. I'd probably get seasick as well."

He kept muttering as we continued to throw the ball. I started to think a summer of sailing wouldn't be that bad. It would beat staying in Scarsdale and there would probably be a lot of other things to do at the camp. Our catch ended when the barbeque was officially over. We said our goodbyes and thanks and went home. Later, going up to my room, Dad called:

"Boy, you are going to Wampanoag. You'll have a great summer. Camp provides all the things you like. I'm sure Steve will find it fun also. We'll be driving up on the 26th of June. The Davies will be driving up with us."

Entering my room, my grandmother came in right behind me. Looking at me, she said:

"Charles, you are such a lucky boy. Most children don't have 1/10th of what your family gives you. Go and enjoy the summer. I know you will love it more than any of the other boys. You have so much enthusiasm for the outdoors. The time will fly bye and you won't want it to end. Just remember, we all love you."

She certainly made me feel better. I have to admit, she always did. She might have been a dreamy person but she sure knew how to express love and warmth. For that I have always been grateful.

School drew to a close the middle of June. The track and field day was fun and very kind to me. This year I entered the sixty-yard dash, the broad jump and for the first time the high jump. I won the first two and received a fourth in the latter. The most important result of the year was the marks obtained. I passed everything and even made the third honor roll. My family thought I should have done better but at least there were no punishments imposed. Miss Sterns had been my savior.

We sailed the twelve- foot catboat several weekends. The first time, as the launch took us out to our mooring, I was surprised how small and clunky it looked. After we had all climbed aboard we took the sail cover off, raised the sail and then I was told to drop the mooring. The wind was fairly light as we tacked out. Dad sailed her for about an hour and then let Nancy Jane take the tiller. It was another fifteen minutes or so before it became my turn. The wind started to pick up and I was thrilled. We zipped along and had to lower the centerboard all the way. Heeling way over, it was hard to hold the mainsheet. Dad told me to cleat the line. I told him no, that when Ted and I had the boat on the river, Captain Robinson had told us never to tie down the mainsheet on a small boat because a strong burst of wind could capsize it. Dad was adamant. We sailed with a cleated main. We didn't capsize and it was a fun day. Each time out increased my enthusiasm for sailing. I was now actually looking forward to camp.

The drive to camp was long. It took two days. Arriving at Wampanoag. Miss. Taylor, the owner, greeted us. She was a woman in her sixties. Grey hair, glasses, skinny, in a long black dress and very "proper". She had never married. She had hired Mr. Graves to be the head counselor. He was a very muscular man, of average height, strong in voice and very much in charge. He had sailed around the world as a mate on the vessel "Yankee".

After signing in at the office in Miss. Taylor's gray clapboard house, we drove through the grounds of the Camp to the tent site. It was a large grassy area surrounded by pine trees and shrub oaks. Twenty-five tents were on wooden platforms. Each tent was twenty to twenty-five feet from the next. Four metal bunks were in most. Some had three. At the foot of each bed was room for a trunk. A small walkway separated these from two long benches. That was the extent of our accommodations. I was introduced to my counselor, Mr. Everett. He was a college student at MIT. I liked him immediately. He was friendly, with a quick wit and helpful in getting me settled. I was assigned to a tent with three bunks. Being the first camper to arrive, the bunk on the outside became mine. Steve was placed in a tent with four bunks eight sites away. His counselor was a Dartmouth student by the name of Mr. Garrison. After being settled, our folks left taking my sister and Dana to their camp. There was no time to miss our parents. We were given a tour of the whole camp. It was all overwhelming.

As the day progressed most of the campers arrived. By dinner I had met my tent mates: Jack Eastham, from Pennsylvania and Johnny Sheppard from Virginia. I liked them both immediately. By summer's end we had become the best of friends. I can't ever remember having an argument with either of them. Ours was a happy tent. Unfortunately, Steve was not so lucky.

The summer flew by. It was paradise! One, I sailed a lot, winning most of the races in the inner bay which resulted in my being allowed to sail and race with the senior campers in Cape Cod Knockabouts on Buzzards Bay. I was the first junior camper to ever be given that privilege. Two, I won both the junior archery and rifle championships. Three, Jack Eastham and I were selected to join the seniors on an eight day canoe/camping trip on the lakes in New Hampshire, which was fabulous. Four, I was awarded the Camp Spirit medal for being the best camper of the year. I loved every minute of every day.

Camp over, I was picked up by Mom and Dad. The previous day they had retrieved my sister from Camp Cowasset. Nancy

Jane and I were told we were going to Aunt Eva and Uncle Walter's home in Beach Bluff, Massachusetts to stay with them for ten days. That was a shock to both of us. Our folks said they were going to Nantucket to vacation. As we drove to Beach Bluff I couldn't help but dread the next week or so. On arrival, we were greeted with the usual sickening display of false joy from my Aunt. Fortunately, MeMa was there. Things started to look at least bearable. Since their house was small, my parents did not spend the night. It was early to bed for Nancy Jane and me. The unfinished attic was my room and N.J .was to share a room with MeMa.

The next morning we had a quick breakfast prepared by my grandmother and then Aunt Eva piled us into her car and drove over to her friends, the Websters. They had two children. Paul, who was a year older than me and Grace, two years younger than me, and five years younger than my sister. They had been expecting us and had arranged for bicycles. We rode around for a half hour or so and then Aunt Eva said goodbye. She told us she would be back for us at suppertime. N.J. and I looked at one another and I could see she was upset. Paul suggested we ride to Marblehead that was a mile and a half from his house. Off we went. My sister rode alongside and whispered she wanted to go back to Aunt Eva's. I didn't see how we could do that because we had been told to stay at the Webster's. She did spend the rest of the day with us but that was the only day she did. On the other hand, I found a lot to do and thought Marblehead beautiful. At one boat yard, I started talking to a man who seemed friendly. It was hard to understand his accent but we soon learned he was a Dutchman. His name was Henry Bayh and owned the yard. He had only been in this country nine years but loved it. For some reason, I told him my name. He said:

"That sounds Dutch to me. Was your father from Holland?"

I told him, no, my family came over before the seventeen hundreds. He then showed us all through the boat yard and pointed out some of the yachts he was proud to have there. That was the beginning of eight or nine days of pure joy.. Every day, Paul and I would race to Henry Bayh's Boatyard first thing in the morning. We started helping him by bailing out some of the boats tied to his dock. We would help his customers put things on or off their boats and ask Mr. Bayh if there were other things we could do. After about the third day he asked if we would like to take one of his small boats out for a sail in the harbor. We jumped at the chance. For the rest of my time there we had the run of the harbor with one of his boats.

One evening, as we were sitting at the old fort near the entrance to the harbor with Nancy Jane, Grace and Mrs. Webster, we saw a beautiful sailboat approach, drop its' sails and anchor. A spectator sitting by said:

"That's the Endeavour 2nd, the British boat that is challenging in the America's Cup."

Paul jumped up and said"

"Let's go!"

"What do you mean?"

"We are going to get a boat from Bayh's and row out to see that yacht."

"Okay, let's go."

At that Mrs. Webster said:

"I don't know what you two think you are doing. You must be back before dark and I don't see how you can row out there and be back in time."

"Don't worry Mom, we will and can." said Paul.

Off we ran, found one of Bayh's rowboats and Paul started rowing out to Endeavour 2nd. On the way he said:

"Charles, I have an idea. We can get on that boat. You know you are taken for Freddie Bartholomew by a lot of people. He's British. I'm going to tell the men on that boat you are Freddie and want to look the boat over."

"Are you kidding? They will never fall for that. I don't look like that sissy anyway!"

By now we were close to our destination. To my horror, Paul shouted to the men on the boat and told the big lie. They started laughing at us and told us to go away. Paul wouldn't and kept assuring them I was the real Freddie. One of the men said:

"All right, you lads, come on closer and let us see the big movie star."

Over Paul rowed. As we got near the fellow said:

"Do you really want to come aboard?"

We both shouted:

"Yes, Please!"

"Okay, give us a line so we can tie you fast."

Shortly, we were scrambling aboard. They were all laughing but were very nice. We got a tour of the whole boat. It was beyond anything I had ever seen. I couldn't believe where I was standing. We stayed for about fifteen minutes. Paul was assuring them all that I really was Freddie B. To this day I don't know if they believed us or not but I doubt it. In any event, it was the highlight of the summer. When we got back to my sister and the Webster's, they said they had seen us board and wanted to hear all about our adventure. We could hardly stop talking. When we got to Aunt Eva's, I don't think she believed a word of our story. But it really did happen.

Two days later my folks came to pick us up to go home. Since there wasn't room at Aunt Eva's they spent the night at an Inn on the Marblehead harbor. I had told them all about Endeavour 2nd and Henry Bayh. Before leaving for the long drive back, Dad wanted to meet Henry and thank him for being so nice to Paul and me. The two men took to each other immediately. We stayed longer than we should have. As we were getting into the car, Henry called out:

"Charles, hope you come back next year. It was fun to have you around."

All I could think was how long it would be until it would be August. I sure hoped I would be able to come back.

CHAPTER 6

A FEW DAYS before school was to start, more excitement came. One morning when I went outside I saw Spencer Brent throwing stones at two beautiful Irish Setters. I ran over to his yard screaming for him to stop. He just looked at me and continued throwing. I walked over to the dogs, reached gently out and grabbed their collars. Spencer kept shouting at me to get away claiming the dogs were after him and needed to be chased away. I didn't believe him and continued to hold on to the dogs. He stopped throwing and the dogs began to wag their tails. I walked them back to my house, took them in our back door and went down to the basement. Leaving them there, I went up to the kitchen and got them a bowl of water. They drank it gratefully. My sister heard all the commotion and came to the basement. I asked if she had ever seen them before. She said she hadn't. We then looked at their collars and found tags with a telephone number on them. I went upstairs and called the number. When I told the person who answered that we had found two Irish Setters and had them in our basement, she immediately said:

"Oh, thank God. We thought we had lost them. They have been gone for two days and they have never done that before."

I gave the lady our address and told her we would keep them until they came for them. About forty- five minutes later, a large, black limousine drove up our small drive. A nice looking black man, wearing a chauffeur's cap, got out. I met him at the side porch door. He said he was from the Hellmann's and that he was there to collect their two dogs. I took him to the basement and the dogs jumped all over him. We each took one upstairs and out to the limo. As the man was getting back in, he said:

"Mrs. Hellmann can't thank you enough. There has been an award posted for these animals, so she'll be sending you the forty dollars."

I said: "Gee, I had no idea there was an award. I'm just glad the dogs are going back to their owners."

He asked for my full name and waved as he drove off. To this day, I'm still waiting for the reward. The Hellmann's turned out to be the Hellmann's of the mayonnaise company. I still think their product the best.

When school started, I found that Miss Sterns was my fifth grade teacher. I was happy she had matriculated with us. There were not many new faces in our class with the exception of one that to this day sticks in my mind with questions. His name was Ralph Guenneri. You couldn't help but notice him. He smelled. He wore overalls, had dark, curly hair, was covered in pimples and had very crooked teeth. Overalls were not allowed in our school. Dress code for boys from kindergarten to sixth grade was shorts up to the first week in October, worn with a clean shirt. Then knickers were worn until the middle of April. Ralph claimed all he had was overalls. His mother must have convinced the principal that was true because he never did wear anything else. He was not only strange he seemed to be angry all the time. Johnny Fearing and I tried to be friendly but made no inroads. His home was just around the corner from my house, a little closer to the school. They had moved in two weeks before school started. No one had seen much of them since their arrival. It got so that he became a loner, which in itself made all of us uncomfortable. As the months went by, he was just there in the background.

My violin lessons started again a week after school began. My mom was determined to make a musician out of me. A conflict erupted the second Sunday of September. The Reverend Chalmers at St. James the Less talked to me after Sunday school. He asked if I would join the church football team. Practice was every Tuesday and Thursday from 3:30PM until 5:00PM and the five games scheduled would be on Friday afternoon. I was thrilled! The team was for boys ten through twelve years old. To join I needed my parent's permission, football pants, stockings, shoulder pads and a blue jersey. I so wanted to play but was fearful my folks would not give permission nor buy the equipment. On the way home from church, I asked.

My Mom had a quick response: "You know you cannot."

"Why not? I want to so much and I'll use some of the money I have saved from the Saturday Evening Post sales to help buy the equipment and each week I'll give you what I make from the week's sales."

"No. You have violin practice every Tuesday afternoon."

"I don't want to play the darn violin anyway."

"Charles, Stop it. I don't want to hear any more about it. At that, silence pervaded the car. I could see no way I could get Mom to change her mind. Rev. Chalmers had asked me to let him know by the next evening. He had even given me his home telephone number.

After an awkward lunch, I started to go outside to find something to take my mind off my disappointment. As I was leaving, Dad called out:

"Boy, stay in for a few minutes. I'm going for a walk up to the woods on Fort Hill and I'd like you to join me."

That was different. Dad and I seldom did anything together. Don't know why, just never did. I answered:

"Okay. I'll be outback tossing the ball against the garage. Call me when you are ready."

In a half hour or so, Dad called and off we went. On the way we passed the house where Lyn Vandevere had lived, which made me think of her and wonder what she was doing and how she liked California. As we entered the woods we had to climb over a stone wall. Dad started talking about the area and how it had been the spot where the revolutionary soldiers under General Washington had fought the British. The skirmish had become known as the Battle of White Plains. The Americans had lost and retreated to West Point on the Hudson River. I could imagine it all. We seemed far from civilization so that probably made the history lesson more real.

He then changed the subject.

"Boy, I know you want to play football for St. James but you do have a violin lesson on that day, you also get delivery of your packet of Saturday Evening Posts right after the lesson, then start the route delivery before going to the railroad station to sell more. That schedule always brings you home late for supper and then there is your homework. That is a lot to cram into one afternoon. I have asked your mother to speak to Mr. Kordgewahn about changing your lesson to Wednesday but that still leaves your responsibility with the Post. Perhaps you should give that up. What do you think?"

"Dad, I really want to play football. It would be great if Mom could get my violin lesson changed but I don't want to give up my Post route and sales. Perhaps I can get Johnny to receive my delivery. I should be home from football practice by quarter to six. That would give me time enough to get to the station. After that I could do my home deliveries."

"What about your homework? I think your priorities are mixed up. You are trying to do too much."

"Perhaps Don Sutsi would take over my route for those five or six weeks. I know he wants to take over my route and sales when I no longer want to do it."

"That's a thought. See what you can work out. We'll talk about this tomorrow evening. Is that fair enough?"

"It sure is and thanks Dad."

At that, the subject was dropped. We spent another hour or more on our hike. Returning home, Dad told my Mom of our discussion. She wasn't pleased but grudgingly went along. I still remember that walk as the closest time my Dad and I ever spent together.

The next day I asked Don and he enthusiastically agreed, as I knew he would. One hurdle was over. Now Mom had to get the violin lesson changed. That evening, I called Rev. Chalmers and told him I thought I would be able to play but couldn't confirm that until tomorrow evening. He said, he hoped it would work out for me.

School went slowly that Tuesday. The hours just dragged until the final buzzer. I ran home eager to see my instructor. He wasn't there yet. He finally showed and for the first time I really tried to pay attention and play the very best. My eagerness did not go unnoticed. The lesson over, Mom came in and broached the subject upper most in my mind. Looking annoyed, Mr. Kordgewahn said

"I knew something was different today. You are certainly an interesting boy. At times, I think we are wasting our time and in other moments I'm not so sure. If you would only practice more, perhaps our efforts would pay dividends. Let's make a bargain. If you promise to concentrate and work harder, I'll try to accommodate you. Next week, I can come on Wednesday. The following week I can't, nor the Wednesday following but then I can come for one more Wednesday. After that it must be Tuesdays. I have other pupils who must be considered. The few lessons you miss will not matter if you practice."

I turned to my Mom:

"Does this mean I can play football?"

"Yes, but thank Mt. Kordgewahn and practice as he has requested."

I did. However, all I could think of was football stardom. It was to be a rude awakening.

The first Tuesday practice was held behind the Scarsdale High School. There must have been thirty or more boys present. The Rev. Chalmers divided us in to three teams. Much to my disappointment, I was placed in the third group and told to play left tackle. My weight was probably 60 pounds. Every other lineman weighed at least 90 pounds. The backfield was made up of older boys who soon made me realize they thought me a joke. Our coaches were older teenagers. After warming up with exercises and running in place to loosen up, the linemen were gathered together and told how to crouch down on the line. Then we were told to run 15 yards and try to throw a block on those selected to act as opposing linemen. When my turn came I followed instructions, ran as hard as I could and then threw myself at the guy I was to block. He was waiting for me. As I flew towards him, he must have raised his knee, which caught me in the side. I was nearly knocked cold. Someone dragged me off to the side. In a few minutes, it was my turn again. I ran more slowly, gingerly tried to throw the block and missed completely. It was obvious, a lineman I wasn't. The only game I played in was against Harvey School. After the kick-off, we lined up against the other team. I was surprised to find opposite me, Ronnie Erskine. I had known him for four or five years. At one time he had lived on our block. As we crouched down on the line, he whispered to me:

"Charlie, let's just lean against one another after the ball is hiked, Okay?"

I nodded my assent and that's what we did the whole game. On that highly competitive note, the season ended.

Shortly after football season, Mom had another surprise for me. She had enrolled me in Miss. Covington's Dance class. Attending Covington's was known as the first step into Westchester County society. She not only taught dancing but manners and proper etiquette. Boys had to wear blue suits, white shirts, ties, black patent shoes and white gloves! Girls had to wear long dresses, jewelry, low high heel patent leather shoes but I don't believe they had to wear gloves. Only the boys had sweaty hands. I couldn't believe my mother had done this to me. I almost ran away. No argument deterred the inevitable.

The first day was everything I imagined. Miss Covington was rather short and rotund. She wore a long off-white dress and held a "cricket" clicker in her hand, which she used to gain attention. Class opened with a long introduction detailing the necessity for learning the proper way to conduct oneself, particularly with the opposite sex. Politeness was a must and the duty of males was to treat the other gender with respect and consideration. We were taught the proper way to use a handkerchief and that it should always be white. When asking a girl to dance it was necessary to approach her formally, bow from the waist and say:

"May I have the honor of this dance?"

If accepted, your arm was to be extended gently towards her, upon which she would place her hand as you escorted her to the dance floor. We had to practice this routine time and time again.

The first dance learned was the waltz. It took me ages to get that right. My feet would become entangled and they always seemed to find my partner's. We must have spent three or four sessions on that dance alone. The fox trot was next. That was easier. The way you held your partner was different for each dance and never should your bodies come in contact. Oh, it was fun. I went to the classes for two years and I believe each lesson found me paired with Amy Lu, the heaviest girl in class. I never figured out why. One thing I do know is that dancing became something I tried to avoid.

This was the first year I became aware of a larger world. At the dinner table Dad would discuss the Ethiopian war where the Italians, under Mussolini, had invaded that poor country, ran into determined opposition by people still living as in past centuries. Haille Salassie, the Ethiopian leader, became a hero. I read much of what was being reported. Concurrently, the Spanish Civil War was raging. My father became fearful of fascism, hated General Franco and the war. He also talked of Adolph Hitler and the Germans and claimed the world was going crazy. This further stimulated my interest. At school, the teachers started giving us assignments on world affairs. Dad became further concerned with what I was bringing home from our school. As bad as Fascism was, he feared communism would be the greater threat to the United States. It was all above me but it did start my interest. The Sino-Japanese war was also in full swing. Reading of all the atrocities was scary but fascinating stuff. This interest in all the wars shifted our time from playing cowboys and Indians to war games. Reflecting this shift was the large battles we began to play out on the fields and around the barns of Bill Harden's home. Twenty to twenty-five kids became involved. We made cannons from large pipes, used BB guns, without the BBs, and used Bags of lime, found in the barns, to throw towards each other's trenches to simulate bombs and gun smoke. These battles went on intermittently for weeks. Little did we know that many playing would end up fighting for real in five or six years. But then, we were all just kids.

It snowed three days before Christmas. The snowfall was over 14" deep. This caused a problem. Every Christmas Eve there was a carol sing at the pond. Over a hundred people would come, hold candles while singing and leave wishing all a "Merry Christmas". My Mom always played a pump organ that had to be brought down to a spot along the shore. Getting the organ there this year was a problem so I was told to enlist a group of guys to shovel a large place off so all could gather around for the sing. Eight of us did the job in a little less than three hours. Ralph Gustav's father used his truck to bring the organ down. The carol singing tradition had been saved. It turned out to be the nicest ever held. Mom played beautifully, even though it was near zero degrees. As we all sang "Silent Night" in the flickering candle light, a permanent picture was printed in my mind. Few Christmas eves have ever matched that night.

The day after Christmas we all, except MeMa, piled in our car and drove to New Hamburgh. For me, that made the season perfect. After hugging Aunt Nell and warmly greeting Uncle Lee and Aunt Gertie, I was off to John Scardefield's. His mother told me he was up above the Gallagher's home sledding. I ran all the way. Nearly every kid in town was there. John shouted for me to join him on his sled. Piling on behind, we were off. Down the hill we shot. We spent most of the day sledding. It was so good to be back. This was my real home and these were my best friends. I remember thinking: "I bet no one here even knew of a dancing school".

When we returned to Scarsdale we found MeMa in bed not feeling well. Mom said I would have to share my sister's room until my grandmother was better. Nancy Jane was not very happy over the arrangement. Going to bed it seemed strange to me also. About a week later my parents announced they had decided to convert the attic into a bedroom for me. We went up the narrow stairs and looked the space over. It was T shaped with windows at the bottom of the T. There was no other entrance or exit other than the narrow stairs. This worried Mom but Dad said he'd provide a rope to throw out the window to climb down in case of fire. Construction started the following weekend. Mr. Al Reed, who worked in the maintenance department at the New York Life Insurance Company, was to do the work while Dad helped. Mr. Reed needed the extra money. He had eight children and found it difficult to make ends meet. It took until May before it was finished. Once moved in, I was delighted. It was furnished with an old iron bed with a lumpy mattress taken from the house in New Hamburgh. There was a bookcase, a makeshift desk and two old carpets obtained at the Salvation Army store. A sink was in one corner but there was no toilet or bath. I decorated it with pictures of the Hudson River, a West Point Pennant, My father's Naval sword from the World War, pictures of friends in New Hamburgh and my BB gun hung over the closet door. A few days after settling in, I went up and saw "Varga Girl" pictures tacked up along one wall. These turned out to be a gift from my sister.

Easter recess came just in time. Studies at school were not going to my parent's satisfaction. They were constantly telling me I was spending too much time on extra- curricular activities and neglecting homework. My answer was simple. I'd give up the violin and dancing class. Mentioning that only aggravated the situation. Something had to give and it ended up being my Saturday Evening Post sales. I turned it all over to Don Sutzi. It had been fun selling that magazine and the home route and station sales taught me many things that proved valuable in later life.

Uncle Le was told I would not be helping him over the recess period. Instead I was to spend each day studying in an effort to improve my performance in class. I wanted to go back to Camp Wampanoag for the summer but Dad said I'd go only if my marks warranted such an outcome. It was an unusual period for me. I had no reprieve.

My marks did improve but my mark in Art remained below flunking. Miss Bowers was the teacher. She was a character. Tall, bosomy, very dark, black hair flecked with gray, sandals ever present on her big feet, no lipstick or make-up and a few sprouting hairs on her chin. She wore smocks every day but even I could tell she could draw and paint. All my efforts to show artistic ability met with scoffs. I was determined and tried all kinds of pictures of the Hudson River. Most were awful but my last project for the year was a picture of the River at Danskammer Point. It turned out so well, Miss Bowers put it up in the school hallway. I passed with a 68. My other marks had also improved so camp had been saved.

When the school year ended, I spent ten happy days in Scarsdale before going to Camp. Several times we sailed the "Nancy Jane". One Saturday afternoon, my sister and Dad went out alone. They came back wet and with my sister in tears. After dropping the mooring, they sailed out of the small harbor and found the wind stronger than they anticipated. As usual my Dad tied down the main sheet. Further out, they were hit by a strong gust of wind. Over they went. The experience frightened my sister terribly and when Dad walked in the house and saw me, he sure looked chagrined. On hearing their story, I didn't dare say a thing. That evening, at dinner, not much conversation took place until Dad looked up and said:

"Charles, I guess Captain Robinson knew what he was talking about. The wind was really stiff out there so I tied the mainsheet to the cleat. When we started to heel over too far I couldn't unfasten the line. We just kept going further over until we were all the way over. We were lucky one of us didn't drown. I guess I learned a lesson because of my stubbornness."

Shortly after this, I went back to Camp Wampanoag. Mr. Everett was my counselor again. Steve and I were in the same tent. Jack Eastham and Johnny Sheppard were the other two, in what seemed our crowded accommodations. We all got along great. The summer turned out to be even more fun than the previous year. Almost all our sailing was done outside in Buzzards Bay. We raced at least twice a week. By the end of the summer I was tied in points with Bill Eastham, Jack's older brother. Three races were held to determine the winner. Bill and I could choose two others to be our crew. Jack was in my boat and I had asked Steve to be the second. He still didn't have much interest in sailing but agreed. We ended up winning but only because Steve turned out to be the best spinnaker handler. We were all thrilled with the victory. I think Steve bragged about the three races for the next five years even though he never set foot in a sailboat again.

The summer had flown by. Once again I had the opportunity to go on the canoe trip. It proved a great time and on different lakes than we had been on before. The portages were much longer but the water was so clear it was possible to see the fish and turtles swimming near the bottom. I wish we could have stayed longer.

At the dinner marking the end of camp, I was awarded my second camp spirit medal. I was happy to get it but felt very awkward. Many of the others were certainly just as worthy. It was the only time in the history of the camp that a boy had won it two years in a row. I did think that winning might result in pleasing my parents. It turned out I was wrong. My penchant for trouble was still with me.

It was to be another end of summer visit to Beach Bluff. Aunt Eva and Uncle Walter had been conned in to looking after us while Mom and Dad had their vacation. This time it was to be Martha's Vineyard. I was eager to go because I enjoyed Paul and loved knocking about Henry Bayh's boat yard. No sooner had we been dropped off than I was on my way to Paul's. Down to the boat yard we bicycled. I think Mr. Bayh was as glad to see us as I was he. We spent the rest of that short afternoon just fooling around the harbor. The fourth day dawned bright and breezy. Sailing once through the harbor, we dared each other to sneak out to the outer bay. Henry had made it very clear we could only sail within his view but we figured the first part of the bay would still meet that requirement. Our sailboat came alive out there. Heeling way over, we raced toward Beverly. Forty-five minutes later we had come about and sped across the waves on a direction that would take us just past the outreaches of Marblehead Neck. It was so exhilarating we failed to come about and return to the harbor. Out to the ocean we went. Three miles later we noticed the wind slowly dropping. We decided to head back in. On the reach back to the outer bay the wind shifted and dropped further. Within fifteen minutes it had died completely. Shore seemed far away. Looking out to sea we noticed a white bank of fog drifting towards us. To make matters worse, the tide had changed and seemed to be pushing us further out. We started to scull. Progress was slow. Soon we were enveloped in fog. With no motor, I resorted to paddling with my hands as Paul sculled more vigorously. We had lost sense of direction and had no idea where we were headed. Dampness pressed in and our fear mounted. We could hear nothing but the water softly lapping against the hull and occasionally a distant foghorn. I couldn't stop shivering and I noticed Paul having the same problem. We decided to shout every few minutes in lieu of having no horn. For hours we did this to no avail. Finally, Darkness arrived. We kept talking to one another in an effort to ward off crying. Two frightened kids had no idea where they were. I knew if we survived, trouble loomed large and yet we so wanted to get back to our families and secure surroundings. I kept wondering what Henry Bayh was thinking. It probably meant the end of his friendliness to us. Time took forever to move. Now and again we thought we heard surf breaking on a beach. Towards the middle of the night, I heard a large boat off our port. We yelled and called as loud as we could but nothing happened. The late August night was cool and the wet from the fog seeped into our bones. We were now shaking from fear and the cold dampness. Early morning finally arrived and with it a small breeze. But we had no idea which way to sail. Instead, we tried to keep the bow pointed into the slight wind, hoping to stay as stationary as possible. In the improving light, we hoped for the sun to rise and perhaps burn off the fog. It seemed to be thinning. No sounds reached our ears until suddenly we heard seagulls. Our spirits started to rise. In a short while we saw the seagulls. The fog really was thinning. Another hour or so passed and then we heard a powerboat coming towards us. Shortly we saw it and stood up waving our arms and shouting loudly. It kept going. They never noticed us. The sound of their motor faded and our hopes took a nosedive. The shore was still not visible. We had no idea in which direction to look. We scanned the white horizon for signs of the rising sun. We thought we saw brightness off our starboard side. Then the fog just slipped away and we could see the sun. That was east, so we knew we shouldn't sail that way if we wanted to reach the shore. We adjusted our sails and headed west. The wind was so light we barely moved but we were regaining some confidence. Our discussion turned to what would happen when we were found. It was obvious to both of us that we were in serious trouble with everyone but no matter how much trouble was in store, we wanted to get home. When the sun was about 15 degrees in the sky, we heard another powerboat in the distance. It became clear it was headed in our direction. We finally saw it. In another twenty minutes it was close enough to hail. They veered directly for us. It slowed, then cut its' engine and came alongside.

"Are you two boys all right? All boats in the area are on the lookout for you. The Coast Guard has posted a general alert. Throw us a line and we will tow you towards Marblehead. We'll turn you over to them once we find them. I believe they have one of your Dad's and one uncle aboard the boat in charge of the search and rescue operation. They sure will be glad to see you safe and sound."

71

I tossed them the line. When it was cleated fast, they started their engine and our tow to safety began. Paul and I were happy and scared. God alone knew what was in store for us.

When the Coast Guard boat came in to view, our rescuers transferred our line to them, said "Goodbye, Good luck" and left. We were ordered aboard in a very brusque manner. Uncle Walter and Mr. Webster were there. They both started yelling at us and threatening to have us horsewhipped and severely punished. I was told my folks had been notified and were on their way here from Martha's Vineyard to take me in hand. Mr. Webster told us Henry Bayh was beside himself in anger and that the newspapers had been on the story of our escapade but had been called off. They would not be allowed to interview us because that would only blow the whole thing into a tale of adventure and might gain sympathy for us, which was nonsense. We had been totally irresponsible and deserved punishment not sympathy. Paul and I were not able to say much in our defense. That we were okay and very sorry was no satisfaction. We had acted selfishly and were wrong. The Coast Guard made my uncle and Mr. Webster sign some papers and then said goodbye to us as they let us off at the town dock. Henry was not there.

Off we went, Paul with his Dad and Uncle Walter with me. On arriving in Beach Bluff, I was greeted by my sister who threw her arms around me and whispered:

"You have really cooked your goose this time."

Then MeMa threw her arms around me, showering me with kisses and telling me how much she loved me.

Aunt Eva just looked at me and said:

"You are a very wicked, wicked boy! This is the last time you will ever stay with us. You are nothing but trouble and always have been".

That was the way things stood until Mom and Dad arrived. They each hugged me and then proceeded to give me a tongue lashing. It was very clear I was in deep, deep trouble. We stayed in Beach Bluff another three days. No one showed me sympathy or spoke much to me. I tried to make myself scarce to avoid any lectures on my unforgivable actions. On our last day, Dad took me down to see Henry Bayh. That went better than expected. He told me how very disappointed he was in Paul and me for not obeying the rules he had set for us but that he was glad we were safe. He hoped we had learned a great deal from the experience but we would probably realize it more and more over time. When we parted, he shook my hand and said:

"Charlie, you will always be one of my favorite young men. You will have some very hard situations develop because of your impetuous nature and enthusiasm but I'm sure you are going to turn out fine."

That is the last I ever saw him. I have never forgotten his words or his great kindness to me. He is still a bright star of my past.

Chapter 7

School started the Tuesday after returning home. I was entering the sixth grade. For the first time my teacher was a man, Mr. Silversmith. He was new to the school. As the days passed, it became obvious he was one of the better teachers. He was very strict and from day one established his authority. Being popular was not important but that we all learned was a passion with him. Standing about 5'4", rotund, dark, slicked down hair, large flapping ears, a nose and eyes almost hidden by bushy eyebrows, he was anything but a commanding figure. He always wore elevated shoes, a light blue suit with a blue shirt and a darker blue tie. We all thought he looked comical. When he spoke he started at a very low volume, increased the volume as he went along and then dropped the volume almost to a whisper near the finish of his point. It certainly made us strain to catch what he was saying. At least it did after we got over our dismay.

His real forte' was current affairs. As he talked of what was happening in the world he spoke of the terrain, climate and economic base of the region under discussion and referred to the history of the people and country involved. He made it all relevant and most of our class enthusiastically participated. This became my strongest subject and opened my mind to things other than my immediate surroundings and pleasures. I look back on his class as one of the best in my young life.

Our class only had four or five new faces, two of which sat either side of me. Harry Turner was not an extrovert but he was a very good student. I don't believe he ever missed being at the top of the honor roll. It took him more than half the year to become friendly with anyone. He sat on my right. Aileen, Zugsmith on the other hand, never seemed to stop talking. Most of the time what she said made very little sense. It was just talking for talking's sake. She tried her best to make friends with other girls but I don't think she ever succeeded. She came to be called: "motor mouth." She sat on my left.

We were just beginning to get in to the swing of things when September 21st came and grabbed everyone's attention. The great hurricane of 1938 struck Long Island and New England. It was a disaster. Over 600 people died, homes and whole communities were leveled. The storm brushed Scarsdale. I remember standing on the street in front of our home leaning into the high wind at a forty-five degree angle. Standing up straight was impossible. The wind would just blow you over. Many years later I often sailed into the harbor behind Napatree, Rhode Island and anchor for the night. The barrier beach had vacation homes before the hurricane but none were left. Each time I anchored I thought of that storm and prayed it would not strike again.

School resumed and old "motor mouth" was full of stories about the hurricane. I doubt any of them were true. Mr. Silversmith had to sternly admonish her from going on at such length with the gory stories she would relate. The third week in October the hurricane was pushed aside by a new event of greater interest.

The last period of school on the Friday of that week, we all became conscious of noisy activity outside somewhere near the school. When we were excused at three, we all rushed to see what was happening. Running down the street and turning the corner on Sealy Place we saw about five police cars, three fire engines and many men running around. We also smelled a pungent odor. The police stopped us as we tried to get closer. Many of them had their guns drawn. Looking down the street we saw fire engines pumping liquid out of the Guernneri house. Everyone wanted to know what it was but the police would not enlighten us. In a few minutes, we saw three men and a woman in handcuffs being escorted by policemen to a "Paddy Wagon" parked in front of the house. In they were pushed, the door closed and the wagon driven off with sirens blaring. None of us had ever seen such excitement. The police finally got us to disperse.

Johnny McCullough, Roland Gesell, Don Sutzi and I walked to the Sutzi's home. All we could talk about was the police activity. In a little while Don's brother, Kenny, came in. He told us the police had raided the Guennari place because they had discovered the family had been operating a large distilling operation in their basement. What we had seen being pumped out was the liquor from the stills. The smell, as the liquid was running into the sewer, was similar to the stink that always surrounded Ralph G. when he walked into class. The weekend was consumed with conversation concerning the illegal operation which had been going on in our small neighborhood. I think it was the only time I can remember the whole school being anxious to return to school on Monday. Surely, we would get all the details then.

Everybody arrived early on that Monday. Ralph never showed. In fact, no one ever heard of him again. He had made no friends, his family had never made friends in town and the police were saying very little of what had actually happened and how they were tipped off. The Scarsdale Enquirer published a very short article about the "disturbance" but I can never remember hearing of, or reading about, what happened or what had become of the family members. Rumors abounded about how the Guenneri's were associated with the Mafia but that is all it was — rumors. Next door neighbor, "Motor Mouth", tried to make people believe she knew a lot more but that she was sworn to secrecy. No one believed her. I think Scarsdale wanted to push the whole thing under the rug. It was an embarrassment and below their dignity. Only the best people populated Scarsdale!

Normalcy soon returned.

Dancing school was still going strong and I was foiled in not dropping out. Every week would see me dressed up, white gloves and all. This year Miss Covington seemed to always select me as her partner in demonstrating the various steps. I know I was plain awful! A new twist was added this year. Not by Miss Covington but by a group of mothers with children in the class. They had decided there should be formal parties at least once a month for the students. Groups of six girls and six boys would be invited to various homes for dinner parties. All had to dress formally, arrive for soft drinks and hors d'oeuvres, the boys required to escort a girl to the table, hold her chair while she was being seated and then sit properly beside her after all the girls had been seated. Maids and butlers would then serve us a full course dinner and we would be instructed how to eat properly and converse in subjects of a genteel nature. After desert we would repair to the living room for more polite conversation and sometimes dancing. I disliked these sessions with a passion! It became obvious to me that we were being taught to speak of things in such a way as to offend no one, develop no opinions truly of our own and to accept life as centering around "our own sort". I longed for New Hamburgh. There people were real, expressed their views with conviction no matter what others thought, worked hard for what they had — which was far less than what Scarsdale people had — and appreciated others regardless of their opinions. The give and take of life was better and stronger.

While on the subject of dancing and parties, I should mention that this was the first year I was invited to "The Westchester Cotillion" at the Scarsdale Golf Club. Miss Covington actually ran it. Sometime between Christmas and New Years it was held. We started with those inane dinner parties, then chauffeured to the club for dancing followed by a light evening snack (called a "repast") at 11:00PM, followed by two or three more dance numbers before we were chauffeured home. I believe I only danced once and that was because Miss Covington spotted me standing around the sidelines. She dragged over the ugliest girl there and prompted me to ask the young lady to dance. I was mortified. When it ended, I rudely disappeared. Three years later I met that ugly duckling at another cotillion. She had turned into an attractive girl with the fullest figure at the dance. I asked her for the pleasure of a dance and was turned down abruptly. At the age of seventeen we met again and actually became good friends. She was John Fearing's girlfriend.

There had been no football at St. James the Less that year. Rev. Chalmers had left to become the rector at another church and no other minister had the interest in perpetuating the team. Football became pick- up games at school or in the neighborhood. We only played tackle football. Touch football was considered a sissy game. One weekend in October Dad took us to West Point to see Army play Columbia. I was a staunch Army fan. The Academy being on the banks of the Hudson River assured my support. It was a good game but Columbia won. The deciding factor was their Quarterback, Sid Luckman. He was outstanding that day. I believe the winning points were a field goal kicked by Luckman. He dropped kicked the ball right thru the uprights at the end of the last quarter. This so inspired me that I spent many hours during the following weeks learning to drop kick.

The second Tuesday in November was an election day and when my folks went to the school to vote I went with them to use the goal posts to practice. Soon, Ronnie Erskine and his younger sister, Shirley joined me. We must have spent hours drop kicking the ball. Shirley proved to be better than both of us. This increased my determination to become more proficient, so more of my time was spent practicing. This effort paid off at a future time. However, the biggest benefit of these sessions was the good friendship that developed with the Erskine's.

The day before Thanksgiving, Dad asked me to go to New Hamburgh with him to help Uncle Le move some equipment around on the hill where he had his large commercial garden. I hadn't been there for months and was surprised how good it all looked. Bill Ferris had done a great job in finishing the clearing of the land. It made the property look huge. Because we were so busy on the hill I was unable to get down in town to see any of my friends. I wanted to stay overnight but that was refused. For some reason Dad seemed to want me to bypass the town. I knew we were to come back up the next day for the big dinner at Uncle Le's so it seemed strange he wouldn't let me stay. On the way back to Scarsdale we stopped in Beacon at a hardware store. When we walked in we went to the back counter where all the rifles and shotguns were kept. To my surprise, Dad told me to pick out a 22 single shot rifle. I was dumbfounded and elated all at once. The Savage 22 was my selection. Driving the rest of the way home he told me he had bought it for me because, in spite of my disastrous sailing adventure, he and Mom were proud of my accomplishments at Camp and the winning of my second camp spirit medal. He also said he expected me to keep the woodchuck population down on the hill. However, he couldn't refrain from telling me he expected me to stay out of trouble and do better at my studies. Sleep came hard that night. I was too excited to drift off.

The next day we were back in New Hamburgh. Walking into the house I knew something had changed. Aunt Nell was not there. I quickly learned that she and Aunt Gertie had had a terrible row and Aunt Nell had moved out of the house to the little house across the street next to the meat market. Everything felt so awkward. I knew my special aunt must have seen us arrive but I couldn't run over to her as I wanted. The Thanksgiving dinner was delicious but as soon as I was excused from the table, I was off to the Yacht Club with my rifle. Sure enough, John Scardefield and a lot of other friends were there with their rifles shooting at the tin cans they were throwing in the river. I joined in the sport. For so many years I had longed to be able to join this activity. On this day I learned the thrill of satisfying a long time desire. It was a great feeling of growing up.

Upon leaving the shooting, I took a circuitous route to the back door of Aunt Nell's little home. Before I could knock, the door flew open. She grabbed and hugged me so hard while tears ran down her face.

"I knew you would come. I so miss you. This is a home for you anytime you want to come. How was dinner? I saw Nancy Jane. Will she come see me? Oh, it's all such a mess. I don't expect you to take sides. Be nice and thoughtful to your Uncle and Aunt. I know they care for you. Don't worry about me. I'm happy with my own place and I love my job at the Post Office."

We talked for more than an hour before I felt it necessary to go back across the street. It was all a new situation and I wondered how I would handle it. Things did work out satisfactorily but my two aunts and uncle never spoke to each other the rest of their lives.

Driving home that night no one spoke of the break up and my aunt's move. I was upset that none of the others had gone over to see my Aunt. I felt terrible for her. She owned one third of the house Uncle Le and Aunt Gertie were living in and Dad owned two thirds. When my uncle had gone into bankruptcy he sold his third to my Dad for cash to live upon. I also learned later that Dad was paying all the upkeep costs as well as the heat. I loved that house but guessed I'd never feel at home there again. The world is full of surprises.

CHAPTER 8

JUST BEFORE CHRISTMAS my bicycle broke down. I thought I could fix it myself. On first try, I failed. Johnny McCullough then suggested we go to a bicycle repair shop and watch them fix bikes. Off we went to Garth Road where there was such a shop. We hung around for several days watching the mechanics. After witnessing many a repair job we thought we knew enough to work on mine. We stripped the gearbox down on my coaster break, replaced some of the bearings, greased it well, adjusted the pedal mechanism and put all back together. It worked! We then cleaned and polished the bike. When we finished, it looked like new. As we were doing all this, other kids kept coming around to watch. Seeing our success, some asked us to work on theirs. After doing a few we decided to stop fixing them for free. We made twenty or more signs announcing the "McVan Bike Shop". My address and telephone number were incorporated on the signs. We posted the signs on telephone poles all over town. At first we had no business but in a week or so we started getting customers. Most bikes we could fix and we certainly shined those fixed to look great. Business kept increasing, the phone kept ringing and my family became annoyed. I guess we weren't charging enough because so many customers were leaving their bikes with us and Dad couldn't get the car in the garage. All came to a screeching end when Dad forbade us from accepting any more business. We had become tired of the business anyway. It was consuming too much of our time. However we did make some pretty good money.

At Christmas I was given a book, "I Married Adventure", by Osa Johnson. I became enthralled with the story and so did Johnny. It told of Martin Johnson and his wife, Osa, exploring and photographing the jungles, people and animals of deepest Africa. I had recently finished reading a series of adventure stories set in the wilds of that region and this new book brought it all into reality. We became so enthused we decided to become photographers like Johnson. With money made from our bicycle business we each bought cameras. I purchased a second hand German 35mm Mier Triplan, 3.5 lens camera. Johnny got a Kodak with a 2.5 lens. We started taking pictures all over town. Paying for development became so costly we decided to use the rest of our bike money to purchase equipment and chemicals to develop our own. A portion of my attic room was made into a makeshift darkroom by covering the windows near the sink. It took us awhile but we learned how to develop and print and improved our quality steadily. The 1939 New York World's Fair soon opened. We went as often as possible and took our cameras with us. The photographs we took became better and better but Johnny proved to be the much superior photographer. He had an artistic knack, which I never achieved. Our money was running out and we could envision not being able to buy film and developing supplies. It was decided we had to establish a photo processing business in hopes of making money.

McVan Bike Shop was resurrected and changed to McVan Photo Company. Signs were posted on all school bulletin boards and on telephone poles around town. We soon had kids asking us to take pictures of their girlfriends or boyfriends. Business really started to pick up. We put a drop box at school for exposed film to be developed. The business kept growing and my schoolwork kept suffering.. As usual my priorities were upside down as I kept marketing our services and finding new outlets to attract customers. We made enough money to buy a top quality enlarger and better developing containers as well as items to crop and overlay pictures in unusual mounts. Business became so good we had money left over to fritter away, for which I seemed to have a special talent. My family became concerned. They started threatening to send me away to a military school. So far they were only threatening. Even so, I knew they could fulfill their threats.

School ended in mid- June. My marks were better than expected. The comments from the teachers were very flattering concerning my citizenship. Mr. Silversmith even praised my interest in world affairs and current events. His one disgruntlement was my lack of thoroughness with my homework. I did learn a lot from him. He stirred my interest in the larger world. Hitler,

Mussolini, the Far East and European lack of backbone fascinated me as well as the U.S. political scene. Best of all I went through a school year without a major disciplinary infraction!

Dad had sold the "Nancy Jane" catboat over the winter. He had heard of a 19ft. sailboat called a Lightning that was for sale in Greenwich, Connecticut. It was second hand, one year old and the owner had become ill and wanted to sell quickly. We drove up to look at it in March. I was smitten with it. On the way home I begged him to buy it. He finally said he would but only if I would use part of my money I had earned to help. I quickly said: "Yes!" The purchase was made in April and it was decided Dad and I would sail it down to the Horseshoe Harbor Yacht Club over the Memorial Day weekend. We figured it would take at most five hours. When the day came it was very hot, very little wind and extremely hazy. We left the mooring in Greenwich around 9:00AM. Horseshoe Harbor came into view a little after seven that evening. Dad was burnt to a crisp, was disgusted with the lunch Mom had packed for us. — one cream cheese and jelly sandwich each, a thermos of milk holding about two glassfuls and three crackers. I loved cream cheese and jelly but my father couldn't stand it. All in all, it was a very unhappy trip. The boat was fine and we decided to keep the name: "SISU". Over the summer we sailed the boat several times but another big event took place that changed my life.

One weekend in early April, Dad said I had to go to New Hamburgh with him to help Uncle Le on the hill. I knew there was much to do but hoped I'd get a chance to take the canoe out on the river after we had finished our work. An idea crept into my mind. I hadn't seen Steve Davies for months and thought it was about time we got together. If I could ask him to come with us, perhaps Dad would say okay and then there would be a greater chance for us to get out in the canoe. I asked and Dad said it would be fine as long as Steve would give us a hand on the hill. I called Steve and he enthusiastically accepted. We left bright and early Saturday morning and drove directly to the hill. We worked all morning and the first part of the afternoon. I then asked if Steve and I could go out in the canoe. To my surprise, Dad said we could and that he'd come along. By three we were paddling out to Diamond Reef. Looking shoreward, Steve said:

"Hey, Mr. V, can we paddle over to that island? I'd love to see it."

Dad replied: "I haven't been there in years. Let's go".

83

Off we paddled. Beaching the canoe, we explored the whole island. I had been there many times. It was about an acre in size. A large one- room cabin stood on the highest point with a spectacular view down the river to Danskammer Point and Newburgh, six miles further down. Its' fireplace was large and made of stone. On its' western shore was an outhouse which hung slightly over the water at high tide. The rest of the island was overgrown with shrubs and trees. One big oak tree stood on the southern point dominating the rocky shore receiving the lapping water. Steve said:

Mr. V., you should buy this place."

Dad just smiled and said: "That would be something, wouldn't it?"

I chimed in: "Dad, why don't you buy this? It's obvious nobody seems to use it any more. I haven't seen any boats moored here in years and I can't remember when the last time I saw anyone actually on the island."

There was dead silence. A few minutes later, we started poking around and teasing each other on how we could fix the place up. As we pushed the canoe off the island, Dad quietly said:

"Perhaps I'll give the Reynolds a call. I think they still own it."

I couldn't believe my ears but I kept my mouth shut. To push him would only make him find reasons not to contact them. Driving home we talked of other things and soon the idea seemed to melt away.

The Thursday after bringing "SISU" down I was late for dinner. Dad had arrived home early and they had started the meal before I came in. I thought I'd be in trouble but my father seemed in a fine mood. Apologizing for being late, I took my chair. As soon as I was served, Dad said:

"I have an announcement."

My mother smiled and Dad proceeded:

"I have rented the island in New Hamburgh. Charles and "Monk", you and your mother will spend the summer there. I'll be up on weekends and maybe for a week's vacation in August. There will be much to do to get the place livable and I expect both of you to do all the chores given you without any grumbling. So what do you have to say?"

I blurted out: "Fantastic! When do we go up?"

My sister said: "I hate that town. Why do we have to go there? I can stay here with Dana. I know her family will let me."

"Young Lady, You are going and I don't want to hear any more about it. It will be a good experience for all of us. New Hamburgh has its' good points as well as Scarsdale."

Mom broke in and said:

"Let's stop any negative comments. It will be good for all of us and hopefully bring us all closer together."

Not much more was said that I can remember but I for one was a happy young boy.

CHAPTER 9

A WEEK LATER saw us driving up with our car loaded. We stopped at Captain DeWit Robinson's boat ramp where we proceeded to load two of his rowboats with stuff from our car. It took about five trips to unload everything. Bill Ferris had previously swept the cabin clean but not to my Mom's satisfaction. All was stacked on the cabinets that lined the western wall under the picture window. I was enlisted to scrub the whole floor with soap and water. Only when that was completed and dried were we allowed to put anything on the floor. That done, it was over to Uncle Le's to get the four metal bunks we were to sleep on. Rowing them over was tricky because the wind had increased and the waves bounced the boat all around. I was fearful the bunks would slide over the side. No mishap occurred. After the beds had been made it was time to cook dinner. A fire in the fireplace was started and we prepared for our first meal in our new home. It may not have been the best meal I'd ever eaten but it sure tasted good. A card table and four folding chairs was the center of our festive meal.

As darkness approached, we built up the fire and lit the large hanging oil lamp. Sitting there watching the flickering flames spreading shadows around the room, Dad turned to me and said:

"Boy, there is much to do and I expect you to be responsible for the lion share of the chores. We have no electricity, water, stoves, closets, bathroom or heat, other than the fireplace. We need an icebox. You and I will bring the one from the house over town tomorrow. I've ordered a refrigerator to be delivered to Uncle Le Monday morning. He then laid out the long list of chores for me.

The schedule he outlined did not deviate for the next five years. I got so used to the routine it became unsettling when it stopped.

That night we tried to sleep inside but it became so stuffy we decided to move the cots out on the covered front porch. In the morning we dressed for church. It was a panic the four of us using the wash stand outside the backdoor. I was continually back and forth to the river fetching water. (It wasn't long before we realized we had to swim in the river with soap to keep clean.) Rowing to shore we must have looked a sight in our best Sunday clothes. I thought it comical and couldn't resist splashing my sister . It was not appreciated. It was wonderful to be back. Aunt Nell sat with us in our pew. The world seemed to be righting itself.

In the afternoon, Dad and I picked up the icebox, carried it to the run and loaded it onto a rowboat. Reaching our destination we carried the box to the side of the back door, leveled it up and braced it. We had also brought some ice so we were in business with some kind of food preservation. Mom and my sister immediately asked me to row them ashore so they could go shopping. Dropping them off and rowing back, I kept thinking I would be awfully busy rowing back and forth to shore. If I didn't do it they would be stranded. When I was on the hill they'd really be isolated. I mentioned that to Dad and he said he had already considered that and somehow we would have to build a bridge. I thought he was kidding.

That evening after supper Nancy.Jane suggested we play cards. I had never liked card games but with poor lighting, no radio and nothing else to do it was agreed cards would be fun. We started with Gin Rummy and finished with Bridge. When it was over I had proved my ineptness. Slipping in to bed, I had no sooner fallen to sleep then I heard my Mom shouting at my father:

"Reg, I think there is a spider crawling on me. Turn the flashlight on."

On the light came, followed by a scream:

"There are four crawling all over the bed! Get them off! Kill them!"

Dad and I both jumped out of bed and my sister started to cry.

"Boy, get the flit spray."

"Where is it?"

"I think in the box by the back door."

Running to the box I heard my mother say:

"I'm sleeping inside. It's not only spiders but mosquitoes."

Coming back out with the flit, I pumped it at her bed and then Dad said:

"Help me in with her bed."

In we pushed it. No sooner done than my sister asked for hers to be pushed inside. Things finally settled down with the two of them inside and the two males outside. In the morning, it was decided we would have to buy netting to put over our beds. Mom and N.J. went shopping and came back with eight frames for netting that could be attached to the metal cots, over which, the netting could be draped and then tucked under the mattresses. While they were gone, Dad and I transported a kerosene two-burner stove, four oil lamps, two with reflectors, several chairs and three tables from the house in town to the island. We arranged all as we thought looked best but when the ladies walked in they weren't satisfied. We spent an hour or more moving things all around until they were satisfied. After supper Dad said he had to go to work in the morning and he'd be back late Friday night. He explained again what my duties were and impressed upon me that he didn't want to have any bad reports when he returned. Going to sleep that night, we were all on the porch under our mosquito netting. Everyone was happier. Before dropping off I watched a tug boat, towing several barges down the river, listened to the freight cars being pulled by steam engines up the railroad tracks and watched the blinking light from the small lighthouse at Danskammer point. Waves were gently splashing against our shore and to their sound I fell asleep.

When Dad came home for the weekend, we started discussing what we should do with "SISU". It was still on a mooring at the Horseshoe Harbor Yacht Club in Larchmont, N.Y. I immediately asked if I could sail it around. That suggestion went over like a lead balloon. After discouraging his idea of selling the boat, it was decided to have it hauled out of the water and have it shipped to the island. By the middle of August it finally came. We moored it off our western shore. I was thrilled to see it but only got an opportunity to sail two or three times before the summer ended. From the middle of July, Bill Ferris and I had been involved in another major project — building a bridge from the island to shore. My mother and sister refused to stay on the island without some sensible way to get off.

A footbridge had been decided upon. The span was 138 feet from where it was to be anchored on the island to where it was to tie in to the shore. The problem was that shore was the railroad bed of the New York Central Railway. Before we could start we had to obtain their permission. It took three weeks and much negotiating by Dad to receive their blessing. When it did come, there was a large rental fee involved. That almost scratched the deal. Dad agreed only when he received their ok for him to drive our car on the land beside the railway tracks and park it next to our proposed bridge. The deal consummated, we started building. Every day until completion, I worked on the hill in the morning and spent the afternoons constructing the bridge. It was a tremendous learning experience and the cementing of my relationship with Bill. We finished the third week in August and as we were putting our tools away Bill put his arm on my shoulder and said:

"Charles, for a twelve year old, spoiled, rich kid you are a good worker. When your Dad said you were to help me, I thought: "Hell, this is going to be great, I'll be babysitting a young boy. But it turned out to be great, a real help. I have to say, you're okay."

I didn't know how to respond, so just smiled and put away the tools..

With much joy, my Mom and sister were the first to walk across the bridge. That evening, it was decided it had to be painted. The job was done- primarily- by Bill. The rest of the summer rushed by and I was soon on my way back to Scarsdale. I wasn't looking forward to it. That world was totally different.

CHAPTER 10

MY SEVENTH GRADE year started with a new teacher, Miss. McAllister. She was in her mid- twenties, a stunner, with dark hair, big breastworks, a slim waist and fabulous legs. All the male students were "gaga". She was our homeroom teacher as well as our English instructor. Her main interest was as the school drama coach. As luck would have it, Johnny Fearing and I were assigned desks on either side of hers. Front row with the best view in the house. How good a teacher she was became questionable. English started with a review of diagramming sentences which, it is obvious, I never mastered. My eyes, as well as my mind, kept wandering. Johnny had the same difficulty. Our grades soon reflected this. As the weeks rolled by we came to notice she had a most peculiar habit. Often, while stressing an important point, she would pull the top of her tight fitting sweater out with one hand and with the other, reach down her front holding a pencil and scratch her breasts. It was most distracting but we loved it!

The only other thing I can remember about her class was learning a poem and reciting it to the class. I chose John Maisfield's: "Sea Fever". Learning that poem was the only time throughout my schooling when one of my parents helped me with my homework. My Mom coached me. On the day of my recitation I performed well enough to receive Miss. McAllister's praise. She must have taken pity on me because it was the first time she had noticed me as a student. Previously, she had tried to get me to join the Drama group for one of the plays she was directing. I had refused at once which did not endear me to her. My grandmother was most upset when she learned of my refusal. She had tried her best to interest me in acting. I never had the

91

slightest interest but she, somehow, saw me as Shirley Temple's partner. I left all those thoughts to Herky Eaton who lived down the street. He actually ran away from home to go to Hollywood to find Shirley. The police caught up with him on a train headed west to Chicago. That was a laugh and a half.

Of all subjects I had to take, Social Studies or current affairs was still my favorite. There was so much going on in the world that fascinated and/or disturbed me. Adolph Hitler had invaded Poland and World War II had started just as we were returning to school. I had followed all of this by listening to Lowell Thomas and Gabriel Heater, news commentators, breathlessly reporting over the radio. Our family was certain the U.S. would support England and France in their assistance to Poland. My grandmother had been born in New Zealand and my mother in Tasmania. They had not come to this country until Mom was sixteen and thus felt very close to Great Britain. I had always been aware of that. In 1937, when Edward VII had abdicated, I had been dragged out of bed to listen to his speech giving up the throne. England, in our household, was our sister nation. I found it amazing there was so much sentiment for America to stay neutral. In school I quickly learned that our/my view was in the minority. So many believed we should mind our own business and get on with all the blessings of our continent. This occasioned many a heated discussion in class. My teacher was still Mr. Silversmith and he would egg me on. I began to keep a large map of Europe with map pins to show the unbelievable German advances. This was hung in my upstairs bedroom. It seemed every day the pins were moving. One day, Mr. Silversmith told me to get a world map because much was happening in the Far East. He was certain we were headed for war. I believe this outspoken opinion lost him his teaching job before the school year had ended. Today it is hard to understand how strong feelings were felt. When he was let go, I was saddened and when I told my folks they were dumbfounded. Even though he was no longer my teacher, I ended up with a high mark in the subject.

Academically, the year started off well for me. Athletically, it was also good but extracurricular activities soon caused many problems. I had given up my magazine route the previous June. On my returning from the summer in New Hamburgh, Johnny McCullough quickly came over to my house with all the news about McVan Photo Company. He had been doing business on and off all summer and had made over $160 dollars. Things looked promising so we decided to expand coverage to other schools in town. We must have made fifteen posters to place on bulletin boards in those schools. As soon as we were ready we went around putting them up. It didn't take long before my phone was ringing. Principals of those schools angrily asked us to take them down immediately. Under no circumstances were we getting their permission to run our business out of their facilities. Our principal, Mr. Moyle, soon called us into his office. He had been told of our intended expansion. He was not pleased and told us to take the posters down from our school as well. We tried to get him to recant but he refused. We were forced to change our method of advertising. We enlisted three of our friends to solicit business. We would pay ten cents for each job obtained. To cover that cost we raised our price twenty cents. Since we were well established and our results looked more professional we thought we could get the extra money. Business did pick up but it required more of our time to make on time deliveries. I learned another business truth. All sales people are not equal. Out of the three hired, one was very good — the others performed irregularly and constantly had reasons why our price structure should be changed. It was a good lesson.

Between photography, violin lessons, dancing school, sports and homework something had to give. Johnny was a much quicker student, he was no longer taking violin lessons and he never attended dancing school. To help me he offered to do 75% of the photo work if I'd agree he could have 75% of the profits. I agreed. It was the beginning of my phasing out of our little business. To be honest, he had all the artistic talent and I really wanted to spend more time with sports.

At Christmas I received two presents that I have cherished to this day. One was the book: "Four Years In Paradise" by Osa Johnson. This was a sequel to her first book mentioned before. The second gift was another book: "Seven Seas on a Shoestring" by Dwight Long. This was an account of his sailing alone around the world. I reveled in both books. It was difficult for me to decide if I wanted to be an explorer of darkest Africa or sail a boat around the world. Hours were spent researching the African continent. I stopped being obvious about it when Carol Stern, a member of my class, said out loud:

"You only want to study Africa so you can look at those pictures of naked women."

That did it. I switched to studying charts of sailing routes that would take me around the world. If nothing else, both interests gave me good geography lessons. The sailing adventure dream lasted the longest.

In the new year of 1940, Louie took a job as a garbage man for the town. One day when I was down at his house he made the job sound like a fun thing to do. I begged to be allowed to work with him one day. He'd just laugh and say my folks wouldn't approve. I kept asking. He kept laughing. Then in early March he said:

"Okay, the other helper on the truck is off sick this week. I'll sneak you on. I don't think the driver will tell anyone."

On Friday, about 5:00AM, he came for me. We walked to the garbage truck parking lot and jumped on the truck. For the next six hours we collected in a section of town I didn't know very well. I thought garbage collecting was a blast! We had a great time together, picked up a lot of smelly stuff, became very pungent ourselves but finished up at the town dump. After unloading we went back to his home at the pond. He washed up, while Mary Jo made me some hot chocolate with marsh mallows. I left his house about three thirty and went home. No one was there but Margaret. Because it was a schoolteacher's workshop day there had been no school. My Mom had taken MeMa shopping and N.J. was still at her private school. As I walked in the house, Margaret took one whiff and told me I stank worse than a skunk. She pushed me in her bathroom and told me to wash thoroughly and give my clothes to her. I did as told. That evening at dinner, Dad asked how I liked being a garbage man. I told him it was fun and that Louie and I had had a great time together. To which he answered:

"I'm glad you liked it. The way you are going at school, that's all you will ever become."

I knew he meant it.

The following Monday, Louie came to the house about 5:30PM. He was in trouble and so was I. The Union boss had found out about my being on the truck. He was threatening to fire Louie and suing my father for allowing me to interfere with union rules. I could tell from Louie's demeanor it was a serious matter. I told him I would discuss it with my Dad when he got home. I did and he was none too pleased. Over the next week, Louie and my Dad worked things out with the Union and Town so no one was fired and the incident dropped. Once again, Dad told me I had an aptitude for trouble. I will say it was an eye opening experience. As much fun as I had, I still knew I didn't want to become a garbage man. I also knew Louie found me unusual, to say the least.

Shortly after this it was back to New Hamburgh on most Saturdays to help Uncle Le prepare for the new season. This spring, he had decided to expand the garden. Plowing and harrowing became necessary. We borrowed Charlie Wick's horse and plow. Bill Ferris started but I had to take my turn as well. It took me days to learn how to do it properly and to make straight furrows. Besides we expanded the number of cloth sheds, and Dad decided to plant a large — over 2 acres- vegetable garden. He also planted an orchard, a strawberry patch, raspberry plants and blueberry bushes plus an area for five bee hives. I thought he was getting overly enthusiastic. However, little did I know what he had in mind.

Not long after these Saturday work days, disaster struck.

Three weeks before the end of school, we were all excited about the Red/Blue field day and track Meet. I had already signed up for the sixty- yard and the one hundred yard dash, the high jump and broad jump. A new competition was being added this year — the shot put. None of us had ever done it before. Mr. Mac had bought some round shot for throwing but also had collected some round rocks of various weights for us to practice with as we spun around and heaved them down a measured path. I had no interest in entering the competition but several of my friends persuaded me to practice with them. One afternoon we were out heaving away when a group of girls, led by Nancy Nichols, came over to watch. They stood on either side of the measured path. When my second turn came, I had an eight- pound rock in my hand. I spun around and threw the stone high and as far as I could. As I released it, I saw Aileen, old "motor mouth", jump to run across the path. The rock arched and fell towards her running legs and hit her foot and ankle with a sickening thud. I was horrified. She screamed shrilly and continuously. Everyone came running. I hurried to her, knelt down crying:

"Why did you move and cross over? I'm so sorry, I'm so sorry, oh , what can I do?"

By then, Mr. Mac had arrived. Someone ran to call an ambulance. All the girls were crying and my friends were telling everybody it wasn't my fault. Aileen was put on a stretcher, taken to the parking lot and the ambulance finally came. I didn't know what to do. I tried to explain it all to Mr. Mac. But he seemed as rattled as me. Nancy came to me and said she knew it wasn't my fault and she would tell everyone it was just a tragic mistake. We were then all told to go home. I did and as soon as I entered the house told Mom what had happened. She was horrified and just kept saying:

"Oh. Charles. Oh. Charles. Why do you always get yourself in trouble? Wait until your father hears about this."

When he did get home, he heard all about it. Mr. Zugsmith called and said he was going to sue. Aileen would be in the hospital for at least a week and then home in bed for two to three weeks. Dad was really shaken. I had to repeat over and over exactly what happened, who was there and how badly did I think her injury really was. I couldn't answer the latter but did provide all the other information. School the rest of that week went by in a fog. On Friday, Aileen came home. I was told to immediately call her family and ask to visit them all. I went down alone. Knocking on her front door, my legs were shaking so much I could hardly stand. When it was opened, there stood Mr. Zugsmith. He shook his head and refused to shake my hand. He ushered me upstairs to Aileen's room and there I made my apologies. It was all I could do not to cry. I really was sorry and wished with all my heart that I had never tried to shot put. It was a very awkward time. Mrs. Zugsmith just kept asking me why I had hurt her little girl. I tried to explain how it all happened but they didn't seem to believe me. I left wondering what would happen next.

I learned Saturday morning. Dad and Mom drove me to Salisbury, Connecticut to meet with Mr. Quaile, the Headmaster of Salisbury School. We had a lengthy interview, discussed all my misadventures, school grades and extra- curricular activities. He showed us all around campus and then took us back to his office. I was enrolled on the spot. I would enter the second form the day after Labor Day. The decision was made without any input from me. My family was tired of coping with my struggle to mature. It was their hope the school would set me on the right track. As we were leaving, Mr. Quaile shook my hand and said:

"Charles, I look forward to having you as a member of our student body. I'm sure you will fit in well and once you adjust to our way of life you will love it here. Most boys do. I would like you to read a book over the summer. It is `Captain Horatio Hornblower' by C.S. Forester. It's a story; from what I've learned about you, that will be a thrilling read. Have a wonderful summer."

The trip home was quiet. I admitted to myself that the school reminded me of camp and Mr. Quaile seemed like a good man. That night, as I was going to bed, Dad said:

"Boy, I certainly hope this does you a lot of good. Something has to happen."

Two weeks later school ended. My report card stunned the entire family. I had made the honor roll. Equally important were the comments by the teachers. Such as: "A delight to have in class.", "Charles has worked hard this year and the results prove it.", "He'll never be an artist but he accomplished much this year." and "His attitudes and friendliness make him a candidate for the good citizenship award." The latter I did not receive. That comment must have been written before the last tragic event. My swan song at Scarsdale schools certainly turned out better than I had hoped. The summer was ahead and then a whole different educational experience.

CHAPTER 11

ONE WEEK TRANSPIRED between the end of school and going to the Island. During that period, I devoured "Captain Horatio Hornblower". It was by far the best and most exciting book I had ever read. It was right down my alley. The read was interrupted only once when a group of us went to Play Land. When I was finishing the book I can remember sitting on our porch and picking up the "New York Sun" and being brought down to earth reading the terrible but heroic stories about the Dunkirk evacuation of allied troops from France, which had taken place a few weeks before. The accompanying pictures showed desperate soldiers, clinging to boats of all sizes, being dragged from the beach. My map of Europe, hanging on my room wall had few pins left on that continent. War, all of a sudden, seemed very real. Yet our country remained deeply divided over whether or not we should become involved. Franklin D. Roosevelt was running on a platform, that if re-elected to a third term, he would keep us out of war. It was difficult for me to understand. That day was the last where the "Westchester Mystique" was part of my daily education. After packing the car on Saturday morning, we drove to New Hamburgh for the summer.

The days seemed to fly by. Work on the hill took more and more of my time. The expansion ensured that more weeds would have to be pulled and my uncle seemed to need more of my help. Instead of quitting work at one, I now ate lunch on the hill — usually sandwiches and iced tea — and quit around three. This change was not too bad because most of my friends in town were working even longer hours. Many late afternoons, I sailed "SiSu" up and down the river pretending to be captain of a Man of War maneuvering into battle. I came to know every inch of the river from Cold Spring to Poughkeepsie. The harder the wind blew, the happier the sail. Evenings usually found me in the canoe paddling all over looking to the sky to spot the first star. Then I would impatiently wait for the bats to appear. They would dive, quickly turn, swoop up high and dive again to catch their evening meal of insects. I could almost feel at one with the river and the heavens. In those days it was easy to see the "milky way", which always made me realize how insignificant my existence really was. Some evenings found me instead, hunting woodchucks on the hill. No matter how many I killed, more would come to feast on our garden. Truthfully, I hated to kill them but if I didn't we wouldn't have had any vegetables or flowers. I was so soft- hearted I would bury each one I shot and say a quiet prayer as I shoveled dirt over their fury, still bodies.

As the weeks passed, more and more of the older guys in town were enlisting in the Navy, Marines or Army. It was surprising how different the attitude toward the distant war was between my town and Scarsdale. The riverside town was very aware of the raging war overseas and almost everyone believed it only time before the U.S. became involved. A going away party was usually held at the firehouse for a departing enlistee. Normally, only the older guys and adults would be invited but I did go to one. That was after the war had started for us to see and wish Jack Bezane all the best for his stint in the Army. I had become friendly with him while spending a weekend cleaning out a silo at the DelBaso farm. As hard as the work had been, we had a good time doing it and got paid much more than I was getting paid on the hill. I was pleased to be invited.

September came too quickly. We left the island four days before Labor Day and then spent a frantic week preparing for the new school. Dad took me to New York City to visit Rogers Peet, the men's clothing store. His tailor/salesman fitted me with all the clothes I was required to have. Instead of a farmer/sailor, I felt like little Lord Fauntleroy. One thing for sure, the store swallowed a lot of my Dad's money.

On departure day, my stomach seemed all in a flutter. Before getting in the car, I had a sentimental hug and kiss with Margaret. I knew it would be the last I saw of her. She was leaving my folk's employ. They had decided to try to manage without her services. I was to be away, my sister was at her school and I'm sure my father wanted to cut expenses. Nonetheless, I had become very fond of her and knew she had always been good to me. I hope she understood how much I appreciated all her kindness. As we parted, she looked me straight in the eyes and said:

"You's a lucky white boy. Remember me and others not so fortunate, you're special, understand?"

Her comment has always stayed with me.

Getting out of the car at Salisbury, we were greeted by two older boys dressed in gray slacks, white shirts, red stripped ties, blue blazers with an emblem over the left breast pocket, polished dark brown shoes with a hint of gray socks showing between shoes and pants. One was tall and the other of medium height but very muscular. I was at once intimidated. The muscular one was the Head Prefect and the tall fellow was the Prefect of South Dorm. I was taken to South Dorm and shown to a room with two beds, a desk with chairs on either side, one bureau, a mirror above it and a small wastebasket. My trunk was placed at the foot of my bed. My roommate had not arrived, so I chose the bed closest the window. While starting to unpack, Bob Girvin, the Prefect, left to be quickly replaced by Mr. Watson. He was the Master of South Dorm. He also turned out to be the History Master. Besides his regular clothes, he was wearing a black gown. I soon learned that all Masters wore black gowns unless they were on the athletic field or in the gym. After welcoming me he advised us of all the rules of the Dorm. They seemed never ending. Somewhat settled, we went downstairs to see the Head Master, Mr. Quaile. He welcomed us warmly and immediately asked if I had read "Captain Horatio Hornblower". He had not forgotten he had recommended it to me. When I said I had and really liked it, the meeting ended. We could see other boys and their parents waiting to be welcomed also. Walking outside, we went to the gym, the athletic field and some of the classrooms and then back to the car. Mom kissed me, Dad shook my hand and they got in and drove off but not before telling me to stay out of trouble. I stood alone and desperately wished to be along the Hudson.

When I got back to my room, Norman McLeod was there. He was to be my roommate. We introduced ourselves and then I said hello to his parents. They were from Pittsburgh, Pa. but also had a summer place in Old Lyme, Connecticut. My first reaction to him was: what a "pip-squeak". He was about 4'8", didn't weigh more than ninety-five pounds, with very thin light brown hair, an angular face and a prominent nose stuck on a pimply complexion. His voice was reedy and he was obviously very shy. No one could have been more different compared to my friends along the river. I didn't know what to make of it all and wondered what rooming with him would be like. As it turned out, he was a very nice guy with a great sense of humor. He had been sheltered all his life and I don't believe had ever been in trouble nor done anything but what his parents asked. I quickly learned he had no friends at home, was an only child and was non — adventurous. Our rooming situation worked out ok but he relied on me too much. One thing for sure, he turned out to be the better student.

After Norman's parents had left, I suggested we explore the whole campus and try to meet some of the others. We had already met some on our dorm but most of them were still unpacking and getting settled. As we walked out of the study hall back door we bumped into two other students. One of them looked familiar. I stuck my hand out and said:

"Hi, I'm Charlie Van Anden, who are you guys? This fellow is my roommate, Norman McLeod."

"Good Lord, I didn't know you were coming to Salisbury. I'm Berks Erskine, Ron's older brother. I remember you. You, Ron and Shirley used to spend a lot of time at Edgemont drop- kicking. Are you good at it?"

"I don't know that I'm that good but I do enjoy both punting and drop kicking. In fact, I love the game of football. Hey, is Ron here too?"

"No, he'll probably come next year. He's still at Harvey School."

"Yea, I remember he went there. When I played for St. James Church I was the right tackle and when we played Harvey School he was their left tackle, so we played opposite each other. All we did was lean against one another once the ball was hiked. He saw no point in our roughing one another up. I guess we weren't really into football in those days."

"Oh, excuse me. This is Chuck Palmer. He is the Prefect on my dorm in Payson Hall. He's one of our better players".

We shook hands again and then Norm and I continued to explore. I couldn't help but think, I was glad to see a face that I recognized. It made me feel more at ease.

For dinner that night, a buffet was served in the dining room. It was the only night of the school year when we didn't sit properly at tables. Right after dinner it was back to the dorm for a meeting with Mr. Watson. The format of the school calendar was explained and all the rules and regulations outlined.

The next morning, right after Chapel, a general meeting was held in the Study Hall. Mr. Quaile addressed the students. He welcomed all, laid down some additional rules, talked about the honor code, which he would enforce strictly and advised of the non-smoking policy for students. Each student was required to go to his office sometime over the next three days, knock on his door, walk in upon being given permission, look him directly in the eye, shake his hand and promise not to smoke and obey all rules during the school year. If a student violated that pledge, he would immediately be dismissed without recourse. On that note, the first study hall meeting ended. The school year had officially begun. It had been an overwhelming first few days. A new life had arrived.

My first class was English. Mr. Keur was the instructor. He talked with a soft foreign accent, was a large man of medium height, with a rather rotund appearance. Straight, light brown hair swept across his forehead above penetrating blue eyes that seemed to pierce your defenses. He had been born in Holland and moved to New York City with his family when he was twelve. As a teenager, he studied hard, wanting desperately to become Americanized. Yale University offered him a scholarship and he graduated with honors. He was now thirty-one and impatient to find the woman of his dreams. His frustration was taken out on his pupils. He quickly made mince- meat of me. He gave no quarter and relentlessly pursued the exposure of my lack of the basics. I had never been confronted with such an onslaught. I wanted to sink through the floor and hide from his probing. It was obvious the other students in class enjoyed my misery being confident in the knowledge they were far ahead of me. When the bell rang, it was like a reprieve. Out the door I trotted, down the hall to History.

Mr. Watson was the instructor but things proved no better. Instead of recent history or current affairs, we were to study ancient Greek and Egyptian history. He considered himself an expert in the field. I had hoped he would be easier on me because he was the master of my dorm. I was mistaken. Nearly all in the class were from his floor. He was a little man with a deep voice, eyes that peeped from behind thick glasses and completely devoid of humor. By the end of the hour I was lost somewhere around the Parthenon. When the assignment was handed out I thought it must be for the term. No such luck, it was due by the next class. Each succeeding subject followed the same pattern except Latin.

Mr. Tappert was the teacher. Looking at him, you just knew he lived and breathed the near forgotten language. He also was a man of small stature and somehow seemed to turn into himself. He did have a sense of humor but it was very strange. We all believed the ancient language he taught perfectly mirrored his looks. His thin, swarthy face with eyes that always seemed squeezed together as if trying to bring life to the printed word made him look the classic man of the historic language he was teaching. It was obvious he was enamored with his subject but his enthusiasm never lit a fire under me. The first morning had convinced me I was in the wrong school.

The afternoon proved better. I was put on the third squad football team. After warming up exercises, throwing the ball around and kicking, while Coach Myers watched, we were then assigned temporary positions. I was placed in the backfield as a running back. For two and a half hours we practiced: tackling, blocking, running, passing and catching the ball and defending against opposing plays. It was the most structured football practice in which I had ever participated. I loved it! This was the typical format of all afternoons unless we had a game against another school. Study hall always came too soon. After dinner and more study, the lights would go out and sleep come rapidly. In this routine, school marched on.

Sunday turned out to be more fun than expected. After Church and lunch we had free time until the five o'clock study hall. Everett Yeaw, Norman McLeod, John Horchner and I hiked out to the woods behind the football field to see the log cabins students had built in previous years. They were about three quarters of a mile in the woods. When we reached them we were amazed. The cabins were fantastic. Most were twenty by fifteen feet in size. Stone fireplaces were built along one wall. Some had wood- burning stoves as well. Some had two windows but most had one. Each cabin was maintained by a group of students. You had to be asked to join a group before you had the privilege of using it. None had been built in eight years. I was determined to change that. It wasn't until the next year before a group of us started. I'll get into that when the time comes. The trip out to see them was one of the highlights of my first full week.

Our school was situated in a beautiful location. It was in the center of the Berkshire Mountains perched on a hill looking southwest to a range of mountains that appeared to rise from beautiful fertile valleys. Pillars of smoke could often be seen rising from chimneys of typical New England farms, surrounded by gorgeous stonewalls that marked their rocky acreage. The views beckoned most of us to come and enjoy their possibilities. Over the five years I was in residence, I explored a great deal of the area. Fall, winter or spring had different features to enthrall those who loved the outdoors. To this day, it is a special place.

The second week in October changed my initiation into this new environment. Rising one morning I felt rather funny. At breakfast, the food had no appeal so I returned to our room to make my bed and clean up. Sweeping the floor, I had to bend over to reach under the bed. A horrific pain struck my right side. I found it almost impossible to straighten up. Clutching the bed, I heard Norman come in the room. He took one look at me and ran, shouting for Mr. Watson. Soon, they both returned and tried to stretch me out on the bed. I cried out and Ev. Yeaw came in to see what was happening. The three of them tried to pick me up and nearly dropped me on the floor. Ev. and Mr. Watson then helped me to shuffle to the infirmary. Miss Barber, the nurse, felt me all over, said I was feverish, put me to bed and called Dr. Peterson. Two hours later he arrived. After checking me thoroughly, he was sure I must have eaten something that had turned my stomach into knots. He told the nurse to keep me in the infirmary for two or three days under close observation. I was given some aspirin for the fever and told to rest. Soon the pain had eased a little and I drifted in and out of sleep.

By early afternoon, I was awoken with much pain and a high fever. Dr. Peterson was called again but the nurse was informed he had gone out of town for the weekend. She then wrapped me in blankets and tried to sweat the fever out. By nine thirty that night I was in agony and partially delirious. The pain was so bad I could not straighten my legs. The nurse then called Mr. Quaile to ask what she should do. He immediately came running over, took one look at me, picked me up in his arms, walked out to his car, put me on the back seat and drove like mad to the Sharon, Ct. hospital. I was rushed in to the emergency room. A nurse examined me and immediately asked an intern to call a surgeon. She was certain I had appendicitis. The only doctor they could locate was the local coroner. He said he would operate if he had to but would prefer someone more qualified if they could find one. In any advent, he would not do it unless he had my family's permission. They called my home in Scarsdale but the only one there was my sister. Mom and Dad had gone to upstate New York to see a Colgate football game. My sister acted quickly. She called Dr. Wooley in Poughkeepsie. She was one of my mother's closest friends and had been our doctor when we were very young. She was wonderful and immediately called the Sharon Hospital to talk with the coroner — Dr. Norris. After discussing the situation, she agreed to have him proceed. I was wheeled into the operating room, saw the bright lights overhead, felt something go over my nose and mouth and woke up three hours later in a strange room. As my eyes opened and focused, a beautiful apparition appeared, it was a very pretty young lady in a nurses' uniform. Her name was Miss Nulligan.

Chapter 12

MY RECOVERY SEEMED to be coming along quickly and Miss Nulligan became a wonder in my eyes. The day after the operation I was eating some light food. The second day I was up and about although confined to my room. Then everything started to go wrong. The third morning the fever had returned and my stomach started to swell and hurt. They tried everything to reduce the fever but to no avail. By nightfall, the pain in my side became unbearable and I was soaked in sweat. My folks arrived all upset they had been away and out of touch until returning to Scarsdale. When they entered the room I was delirious which really shocked them. My temperature was 106 + degrees and I was gasping for breath. All that night I remained out of it and by morning the doctors became fearful for my survival. Dr. Wooley had been in to see me right after the operation and had warned the other doctors to keep a close watch on me. She feared infection. My condition became more uncomfortable and I became unconscious. Dr. Peterson had returned and told my Dad he was not comfortable with the treatment the other doctors were pursuing. They were contemplating opening me up again to see what was going on. He was adamantly opposed. His recommendation was that all medication should be stopped and my body left to fight for survival on its' own. Dad was in a quandary. He came in to my room when I slipped back into consciousness for a few minutes. He stood by my bed and said:

"Boy, they believe you are going to die. Dr. Peterson wants to stop all medication and not operate again. He believes you are having a very bad reaction to the medication. The other doctors disagree but I think the old Doc may be right. We are going to let

you fight this out on your own. You will have to fight hard but I
know how tough you are and you can lick this."

He and Mom both kissed me and left the room. Miss Nulligan
reached down, gathered me in her arms and whispered that she
loved me dearly and knew I was going to be all right. I clutched
her and drifted back into "never land". The medication was
stopped that night. By noon the next day my fever had broken,
the pain had lessened and Miss Nulligan was still there. When
Mom and Dad came in they were thrilled. Dad said:

"I knew the whole time you would pull through".

Mom just held me and cried. They kept me in the hospital for
another ten days to make sure there was no relapse. Each day I
became stronger. Miss Nulligan stayed until I was discharged. She
never took a day off. She was plain wonderful!

Doc Peterson had been right. The sulfur drug they were
treating me with caused a terrible reaction. The moment it was
withdrawn, I started improving. To this day I avoid any sulfur-
laden medicines.

I returned to Scarsdale to recuperate. That took another ten
days or so. Everybody seemed to come and visit. Aunt Nell did
and I learned she had been at the hospital when I had been
delirious but no one had ever told me. My world seemed to be
slowly righting itself. My sister had been a brick through it all.
She certainly showed she could make the right decisions. The
whole experience was a good lesson. It made me appreciate and
understand others better and certainly taught me the fragility of
life. I knew I had been lucky.

Two weeks before Thanksgiving I returned to school. The next
six months saw wide swings in my behavior. What an awful pill
I must have been. At school, I was greeted with change. Norman
McLeod had a new roommate — Tom Hewett. Apparently, Norm
found rooming alone uncomfortable. Tom and Ev Young had not
been getting along too well so Mr. Watson moved Tom into my
old room and switched my stuff into Evs. It was a much better
arrangement. Yeaw was more my type. He liked sports, the outdoors, hated studying and was a lot of fun to be around. We got
on famously. He was taller than me, heavier, very muscular, of
ruddy complexion, sandy hair and best of all, a poor student. Our
room became a gathering place for dissidents and cut-ups.

Returning to classes it was obvious much ground had been
covered which left me far behind. Verbal sympathy was abundant but expectations were for me to work harder and to catch

up. The assignments were staggering. Mr. Keur calmly informed the class he supposed "Charlie" would just have to devote more of his leisure time to study. The only master who showed any sympathy was Mr. Myers, the head of athletics and our math teacher. He agreed to spend an hour or two on Sunday afternoons to explain and tutor me on what I had missed. That made me nervous because he had a reputation of being very demanding and a stickler for clear and neat papers. Mr. Tappert merely told me to use Christmas vacation to catch up. In all, the next few months portended to be dreadfully unpleasant. As the days slid by, I became very discouraged. Looking for escape, I started hanging around with guys who were notorious trouble — makers. They befriended me quickly and almost every evening after study time they would gravitate to our room. Magazines like "The Police Gazette" and pulp fiction, of the risqué kind, were funneled to us, expanding our imagination. Soon they started talking about running away and hiding out in one of the larger cities. They hoped we might be able to hook up with some of the gangs described in the "Police Gazette". It all sounded so adventurous and a good alternative to the never-ending pressure of school. Plans were made as to how we would escape.

The week after Thanksgiving was selected for the implementation. We each promised to bring back a small, easily disguised bag for clothes and the largest sum of money we could scrape up. Most nights, Ev and I would stay awake talking over the various scenarios we visualized of our exciting future. These became rather lurid and definitely far-fetched. Naturally, schoolwork took a back seat because we were so sure our lives could do without such outdated stuff.

When the Thanksgiving break came, I caught the train at Millerton, N.Y. for the trip to Scarsdale. Mom had agreed to meet me at the railroad station. At dinner that night, I was questioned all about how things were going, what I had been doing to catch up with class work and how I liked the school. Somehow, a good picture was painted.

Going to bed that night, my sister stopped me as I was opening the door to the stairs to my room. She smiled and said:

"You sounded a bit evasive tonight. How are things really going?"

"Pretty good but the courses are really tough and because of being away so long I'm way behind."

"Can't you get help?"

109

"The only Master who has offered has been Mr. Myers and he seems to make everything more confusing".

"Why don't you ask one of the Prefects to help?" I'll bet a number of them would."

"Yeah, maybe. I guess it will work out somehow."

"Don't do anything stupid. You have a tendency to go off on your own and jump before really thinking things through."

"I won't. Goodnight."

Getting in to bed, I couldn't help but wonder if somehow I had given her a hint of our plans. Sleep came slowly as I worried.

The next morning we left early for New Hamburgh and the usual Thanksgiving meal at Uncle Le's. As usual, it was delicious but as soon as I could be excused I was off to the Yacht Club with my rifle. Hardly anyone was there. Perhaps there were five or six and most were younger. John Scardefield soon showed and we had a good time catching up on all we had been doing. He'd heard about my operation and asked to see my scar. I proudly showed it to him. The scar was five inches long and still rather red and ugly. He was dumbfounded, said an appendectomy incision was usually two inches or less. He sure sounded like an authority. It was the first time I became aware of his fascination with all things medical. Until he died, at the age of 76, he was always telling others about his or unusual medical encounters. He should have gone to medical school but didn't.

We spent an hour or so target shooting but it didn't hold our interest as it had in the past. Everything seemed different. Walking back to John's he told me the river would no longer be allowed to freeze over from shore to shore. Icebreakers were going to keep a channel open at least as far as Poughkeepsie and maybe as far as Albany. The government wanted to keep shipping moving twelve months a year. Consequently ice boating would stop on the river. I couldn't believe it but he was proven right.

Leaving him at his house I went over to Aunt Nell's. She was as pleased as ever to see me. When I was leaving I got up enough nerve to ask if she could give me ten dollars or so. She naturally said yes, how about twenty. Sheepishly, I took it and gave her a big hug. No questions were asked as to why I wanted the money. I told her I'd pay her back. I then returned to Uncle Le's and we were soon off to Scarsdale.

I then went to visit Johnny McCullough ostensibly to see how McVan Photo Company was doing. Business was still pretty good but not as strong as it had been with the two of us working. He said he wished I were home to help in bringing in more customers. I finally got around to asking how much money we had. He said over $80. I then asked if he would mind my taking thirty dollars. To my surprise he asked if it could be a loan because he wanted to buy more equipment. I told him fine but I wouldn't be able to return it until spring. He wasn't too happy but gave me the thirty. I hung around most of the day giving him a hand with developing and printing. When I got back home I looked in the storage area of the attic for a small bag. There was one but it seemed awful small but had to suffice.

The next day, after church, I caught the train back to school. Arriving just before dinner all my unhappiness and worries returned. After eating, Charlie MacDonald, Bill Keeley and Ev joined me in our room. They were still enthusiastic about our big "breakout". When "lights out" was called I climbed into bed and nervously wondered what it would be like to be on my own in company with three other unhappy guys. Sleep had trouble finding me.

The week marched along. Wednesday, after "lights out", I asked Ev what he thought of Charlie and Bill. He responded:

"They sure are a lot of fun."

It was not the answer I was hoping to receive. I said:

"I think they are a little off their rocker. Their language is the most gross I have ever heard out of the mouth of any of my friends. Sometimes I think they want to be gangsters."

"Are you having second thoughts about going with them Saturday night?"

"Naw, I guess not. It's just a feeling I have. I don't trust them very much."

"You're not chickening out are you?"

"No, I'll go. This school has me in the dumps. I can't seem to make any headway. Every class seems beyond me and none of the Masters seem interested in whether I get through or not. I guess I'm a little scared of not making it and if I don't I'll really be in the garbage can with my folks. But I'm not so sure I'll stick with Charlie and Bill once we are on the road."

"Well, I'm going but I'd rather stick with you than those guys."

Silence followed. Morning finally came and classes started off with further histrionics. Mr. Keur asked me a question on our assignment of the day. My answer was so convoluted he couldn't restrain himself. He grabbed his desk, picked it up a good foot, slammed it on the floor and shouted:

"Mr.Van, I have heard some answers in my time but never one so wrong and so mixed up. YOU HAVE NOT BEEN PUTTING YOUR MIND TO YOUR STUDIES! Now, take a deep breath and try, please try, to give me an answer that has relevance to this course!"

I sat speechless. The Saturday night escape became a must. The class ended with the other students embarrassed for me, looking the other way and saying nothing. I felt like skipping out right then. Somehow, I made it through the rest of the classes.

Saturday arrived. Classes as usual were held in the morning. The football season had ended so the sport on this day was soccer. I couldn't seem to get my heart in the game. I tried to fake studying before dinner and after that was over went back to my room, acting as if I was really pounding the books. In fact, Ev and I furtively started packing. Before "lights out", I knocked on Charlie's door to give him the signal we were ready. We had decided 12:30AM would be the best time to slip out. Charlie and Bill were to sneak in to our room and then we were going to use our window, which was closer to the down spout, to ease out and start traversing the roof on our way to the spout and the ground below. My mind was racing. I couldn't stop shaking and the minutes seemed to crawl bye. Finally, 12:25 came and in came our fellow conspirators. Charlie was out the window first, Bill second, followed by Ev. and then I slithered out quietly closing the window. When we were all on the ground, off to the woods we ran, stooping low to minimize our silhouette. My mind kept flashing images of Aunt Nell, Mom, Dad, NJ, Miss Nulligan and friends. Circling behind the Head Masters house on our way to the lower road, my pace slackened. I couldn't help but think: "What am I doing? Am I crazy? I know this is wrong. Don't I have the guts to make it in this school by working hard to pass and try to make something of myself other than a bum? God! How I'd miss New Hamburgh. I can do better!" I stretched my hand out and grabbed Bill.

"Hold up guys. I'm not coming. I'm going back."

Charlie hissed at me:

"I always suspected you of being a sissy. We never should have befriended you. Come on Bill, Ev, let's get going."

Ev said: "No, I'm going back with Charlie."

At that we both turned and headed back to our dorm. It was more difficult to get in than out. We had to go through the basement furnace room and quietly sneak upstairs. We were back before 1:30. When I crawled in bed, I was more content than I had been in months.

Sunday morning after church we were all asked to go to the study hall for a meeting. Mr. Quaile announced that two boys had run away. He requested anyone who knew anything about the disappearance to come to his office. I didn't go, to snitch on Charlie and Bill seemed wrong. Ev didn't say anything either. We just waited. By Monday evening the truants hadn't been found. Tuesday morning another school meeting was held. We were told Charlie and Bill had been picked up by the police outside of Newark, N.J. hitch hiking on route 1. They were returned to their parents. We never saw either of them again.

By Thursday my conscience would not leave me alone. Just before study hall I got up enough nerve to knock on Mr. Quaile's office door. When I stood before his desk, I stammered:

"Sir, I would like to confess. I was in on it with Charlie and Bill. I climbed out the window with them and started to leave. I turned back once we got in the woods. I couldn't go through with it. I knew I was just being a coward and doing something very wrong. I didn't let you know I was involved when you asked all of us if anyone knew what and where the runaways were going. I didn't feel I could turn on them. I'm sorry, Sir."

"Son, thank you. We all know you have been having a difficult time. Perhaps this will turn things around for you. This is a good school. We have standards. They are there because we believe they will help boys mature and become good men with a foundation of the right principles. Christmas vacation is almost here. Go home and enjoy the holiday and then come back with a positive attitude. Thanks for coming to me. You are going to do just fine if you work hard. We are all here to help you succeed."

The lowest point in my career at Salisbury had come to an end. I have never been proud of what I did. It took me several years to tell my family about the episode. Over the Christmas holiday I did return the money I had borrowed from Aunt Nell and McVan Photo Company..

CHAPTER 13

CHRISTMAS VACATION WAS full of surprises but I did manage to do some studying. I was so far behind I realized it was either study or end up flunking out. It was difficult to discipline myself to accomplish something every day. There were so many other fun things to do. Twice I goofed off and went in to New York City with friends to see and hear the Big Bands. We would catch as many shows in a day that we could cram in before catching the train home.

A few days into the vacation, Mom surprised me once again. Apparently, Mrs. Huser had called her a few weeks before and asked if I would take Amy Lu, her daughter, to the Westchester Cotillion on December 29th. My mother felt obligated and said she was sure I would be delighted. When she told me this I felt trapped. I dreaded being stuck with that girl. She was fat, not attractive and had a condescending manner of speaking. I was annoyed my mother hadn't found some excuse to say "No".

On Christmas day, Mom gave me two tickets to the Broadway show "You Can't Take It With You" and said I could invite any girl whose parents would allow her to go. I think she was trying to make amends for Amy Lu and the Cotillion. I tried to take Nancy Nichols but the tickets were for after the Cotillion and she said she would be in Boston visiting her grandmother. I couldn't make up my mind who else to ask. By the time of the date with Amy Lu I still was unsure whom to ask.

On the eve of the Cotillion Amy Lu had invited five other couples to her home for dinner before the dance. It was a pleasant get together. Amy Lu had slimmed down. Had made herself look more desirable and talked more sensibly. My eyes, however, could only keep drifting to another: Peg Milton. She was petit, with dark lustrous hair, a mouth that seemed to continually smile between fetching dimples and eyes that beckoned. She was also a conversationalist who immediately put you at ease. For a girl so young she certainly knew how to handle herself. I was captivated and made the evening a campaign to persuade her to go to the theatre with me. By the end of the evening I still had no commitment. I remember little else of the Cotillion.

The next day I called Peg. She finally said she would love to go with me but first had to obtain her parent's permission. I told her I'd call later, around eight after dinner. When I did she told me "No". Her parents did not know me and would not let her go out with someone who was a stranger to them. I was devastated and in a quandary. When I told my Mom of my disappointment, she said she had purchased the tickets in the City when she was with Mrs. Ferguson and she had also bought two tickets to give to Gordon, her son. I called him to see what he was doing about a date. He said he was taking Louise Mitchell and perhaps if I called her friend Joan Spagnoli she would go with me. I knew Joan and her family but she was just someone who was around but not noticed much by me. Desperation makes for unusual measures. I called her. To my surprise she was thrilled to hear from me. When I asked if she could go to the theatre with me she said: "Yes" but had to ask her folks. She did so while I waited on the phone. The answer came back in the affirmative. We arranged for me to pick her up around 4:30PM on January 2nd so we would have time to walk to the station and catch the train to the City. On the scheduled day I arrived at her front door and knocked. Mrs. Spagnoli opened it and invited me in.

"Charlie, it is so nice that you asked Joan. She knew Louise was going with Gordon but had no idea you would ask her. She is thrilled."

Before I could respond, Joan appeared at the top of the stairs. She was dressed exquisitely, had her dark hair in the fashion of Katherine Hepburn in "Philadelphia Story", had make-up on discreetly, looked very tall and was quite mature. I could only stare while mumbling:

"Hello."

Down she glided, lightly reached for my hand and said"

"Oh, I'm so pleased you called. I knew you were home but never dreamed we would go out together. You look, wonderful. That school you go to must treat you well."

I didn't know how to respond. Her hint of perfume had me in a daze and, if truth were known, I hadn't thought of her once until Gordon mentioned her name. She was totally different than I remembered. Her mother handed me her coat, I helped Joan into it, said goodbye to Mrs. Spagnoli and we walked out of the house. On the way to the station our conversation was stilted. My tongue seemed too big for my mouth. We got on the train as soon as it got in the station. Gordon and Louise were located and we sat down across from them. Gordon and I had decided we would take them to dinner at Schraffts, which was on the opposite side of 42nd street to Grand Central Station. I can't remember what we had to eat, what Louise looked like, how we got to the theatre or even how we enjoyed the play. We did get back to her house before mid-night, as I had promised Mrs. Spagnoli. Joan unlocked her front door, turned quickly and threw her arms around me, softly saying:

"Charlie, I had a wonderful time. Thank You. The whole evening has been like a fairy tale. Please write and when you come home again call me. I'd love to see you".

I didn't know how to respond. I stammered something, which probably made no sense. Two days later I was back at school facing the uphill battle of my classes. One thing for sure, I didn't forget her!

Good intentions didn't translate easily into fine results. As hard as I struggled there was no lessening of my teachers despair. The Reverend Mulligan, who taught us Religion twice a week, must have been taking lessons from Mr. Keur. One day, in class, he became so frustrated with one of my answers, he turned his back, then whirled around and threw the chalk in his hand at me:

"Mr. V., you certainly must know better. Don't you ever study the assignments? If you do, you must read and dream at the same time. Now, think hard and give me a proper answer IN THE KING'S ENGLISH!!!"

As usual, I retreated in to my shell and could think of nothing relevant to the question. Once again, I was saved by the bell but not before witnessing the Reverend's look of dismay. It seemed I was destined to be withdrawn from the school.

That afternoon on my way to the gym, Mr. Quaile leaned out of his office window and called:

"Charlie, do you have a minute? I'd like to have a word with you".

Shaking, knowing I was in for it, I knocked on his door. When it opened, he clapped me on the shoulder and said:

"Charlie, Reverend Mulligan has told me about this morning's occurrence. It seems you are still having difficulty with the academic requirements. I personally believe you have just gotten off to a shaky start. The operation didn't help but that is not the main problem. I think you have lost confidence in yourself. That is foolish. I have watched many a boy in this school through the years. I believe you are one that can do well. I have told all the Masters it is our job to help you find yourself. In the relationships with other students and the way in which you handle yourself on the athletic field it clearly shows that you are not one to quit, have exceptional leadership ability and can and will be a credit to this school. Please give yourself a chance, relax a little and approach your studies with confidence. You have it within yourself. I'm counting on you. Now, go over to the gym and play hard."

I walked out of his office with a happier outlook than I had had for a very long time. He gave me back self-respect.

A few days later, just before study hall, I went to my mailbox and saw two envelopes sticking out. Removing both I saw the top one was from Joan but the other had no stamp or return address. It merely said: "Mr. V". Tucking Joan's letter in my pocket, I opened the other. Inside was a short note:

"Mr. V, please come to my quarters at 4:30PM tomorrow afternoon".

It was signed: Mr. Keur. I knew that deep trouble was coming. The next twenty-four hours were tortuous in anticipation. Arriving at his door on the second floor of North Dorm, I forced my hand to knock. It was quickly opened and there stood my executioner, his hand stretched out to shake mine, a smile on his face, politely saying:

"Welcome. Thanks for being so prompt. Take a seat, anywhere will do. How about a cup of tea? I usually have a cup this time of day. Do you take lemon, milk or nothing, Sugar?"

Answering, I looked around his austere accommodations, noticing cigarette ash everywhere, even on top of his grand piano. (Besides being the English teacher, he played the Chapel organ, was the music teacher and coached the junior varsity football team) He handed me the tea and continued:

"Charlie, it is time we talked. All of us who teach have watched your lack of academic progress. We believed we could terrorize or shame you into addressing your studies properly but now we realize your situation requires a different approach. I know Mr. Quaile has spoken with you and now it is my turn. You are not dumb. We all can see great potential in you. The manner in which you approach classes and homework is very wrong. It is not a confrontation. It is an exploration. None of us have ever heard you ask a question in class. I'm sure when you are studying you don't have your mind explore what you are reading but merely look at the words, sentences and paragraphs without consciously absorbing the picture being expressed. You must always question and investigate what is written to really understand. Please start asking questions in and out of class. Do you see what I'm trying to tell you? I know you must because I have seen you do these things instinctively when you are on the football field. You are one of the best students of the game on this campus. That's why we know you can do it in the classroom. Give yourself a break and approach your studies in the same manner."

"Well I don't like to ask questions in class. The other guys are so much smarter it makes me look stupid."

"They know you are not stupid. If you don't ask questions and just sit there that's when they probably wonder why you have no interest. Anyway, they are more concerned about themselves. You must become more involved in your studies. Don't you understand that?"

"I get confused. There always seems more to what I study than I am able to find."

"That's what I'm talking about. Ask the questions to yourself as you study. Dig for the meanings. Only you can channel your mind. We can only point the way. Try, please try. You are a fine young man, one of the more popular in school and very good in athletics but life is more than being nice and performing in sports. It is about gathering knowledge and using it to accomplish goals you set for yourself. Think about the goals you would like to reach. There, I've said enough. It is up to you. Just know that you can always ask for my help or from any of the other masters. You have to ask. We cannot deign your questions."

At that, he told me to report to study hall, shook my hand again and said goodbye. It was the beginning of a relationship that paid me tremendous dividends. A change was set in motion by both meetings with Mr. Quaile and Mr. Keur but it took years to straighten my study habits to where it became second nature. Even beyond college.

I finally got around to reading the letter from Joan. It was so flirtatious and good natured it made me feel happier than I had felt in days.

February of 1941 produced an abundance of snow. Skiing was considered one of Salisbury's major sports. A large hill in front of the school was always kept groomed. No trees or shrubs were allowed to grow so that snow would fall fairly evenly on the slope. Our ski instructor was Mr. Hamlin. He was also the French Master. I had been on skis before but never had the proper equipment or been given any instruction. That changed under Mr. Hamlin's watchful eye. He spent hours with the novices teaching us the basics. I came to love the sport. Downhill racing became my initial interest. I was not very good at slalom and thought cross-country skiing boring. One side of the hill was devoted to jumping. There was a high tower from which a fast run led to the jump lift where the skier would take off to travel through the air to the down grade landing. Distances of 55 to 70 feet could be made by the accomplished. Seeing them fly through space intrigued me. However, I couldn't envision ever doing it.

Four weeks later we had the term's final exams and then the Easter break. I thought I had done fairly well on the exams but knew the grades would not be posted until we returned from the break. I spent those ten days worrying. No particular plans had been made but one day Steve Davies asked me to go in to the City with him. We went to Bannermans — an outlet for old military equipment. They sold antique guns, swords, bayonets, helmets, uniforms, etc. Steve purchased an old German rifle and I bought a French bayonet engraved on its' shaft with a soldiers name, rank and year obtained — 1876. As soon as I returned home I hung it on my upstairs room wall at the top of the stairs. From that day on, when I got home late at night and went up to my room, I'd grab the bayonet off the wall, unsheathe it and shout"

"En Garde', I've got you covered. Defend yourself!"

I never found an adversary!

The rest of that vacation was spent going back and forth to New Hamburgh to help my Uncle on the hill. It was preparation work for the new growing season. Bill and I were assigned the nasty jobs while my Uncle and sometimes Dad did the important work, which tended to be more prosaic. When Dad was working in New York I stayed with Aunt Nell. As always she spoiled me.

When the Easter break was over, I was nervous about the grades I would find posted. They were always tacked up in the

Common Room for all to see. I tried to time my visit to that room when others would probably not be there. Sideling into the room, I noticed only one other. I forced myself to the bulletin board and looked for my name. Finding it, I scanned across the sheet noticing all the marks. I passed all subjects with the exception of Latin. I was relieved and upset. On my way back to my room, I decided to go directly to Mr. Tappert's apartment and ask him what portion of the course caused my failing grade. I thought it better to question him now rather than in class. Fortunately, when he opened the door, he was alone.

"Sir, I just saw my grade for last term. What are my weakest areas? I am determined to pass this class and I'd appreciate your telling me where I have to concentrate more."

"Charlie, you are unbelievable. You have no strong area, just week areas. This is comical! You don't like Latin and you make no real effort to learn. I don't know what to say, other than, STUDY!" It's a bit late in the year to come to me for help, which I guess you mean by this visit. I could really laugh. This is absurd."

"Sir, I want to pass."

"Pass? The point of this course is not to pass. It is to learn. You must want to learn, not just pass. You are a nice young man but you really don't understand why you are here. It is not just to pass. It is to learn, understand, find relationships between your courses and have an interest in discovery. That's what learning is, a voyage of discovery. Enjoy the challenge. Don't fight it. Oh, what's the use? One day, maybe, you'll wake up."

"Sir, I would like your help."

A long silence followed. I thought perhaps I should just leave but I really didn't know what the right thing to do was. He finally said:

"This really is comical. Oh well, I'll give you some help. I guess that's what I'm here for. But, understand, you are going to show me you really want to learn. Come back Wednesday afternoon before study hall. I'll get you excused so we can start trying to make you see the light. Now leave and think over all I have said."

"Thanks, Sir. I'll be here Wednesday."

And so started my real introduction into the meaning of learn.

The next seven weeks found me studying harder than ever. Besides receiving extra help from Mr. Tappert, I was also being helped by Mr. Keur in English. They were not easy on me but I came to appreciate their dedication to their profession. It turned out that each of them was helping other students as well.

121

The ordeal of studying was relieved by baseball, tennis and then track. I made the second team in baseball. We had five games against other schools and won four. My position was centerfield. Hitting the long ball was not my forte' but getting on base and stealing bases was. Often I could beat out a slow grounder and once on base steal my way around to third. I loved the game. Tennis proved a real challenge. Seniors to second formers competed against one another. I held my own and learned much from the coach, our Head Master Mr. Quaile. I really admired that man. He had been an All-American tackle at Yale, was a very thoughtful gentleman and treated everyone even handedly. He was a tough disciplinarian but always fair.

Final exams came all too soon. I studied and studied and walked out of each exam believing I had probably failed. Exams over, we had the big end of year track meet. I had entered the 100 yard and 220 yard dashes, the high jump and broad jump. Again, there was no separation between the upper and lower forms. Luck was with me. I placed second in the 100 and 220 yard races, sixth in the broad jump and seventh in high. I was beside myself with joy and probably conceit.

The day after the meet our final grades were posted. I Passed! Not by much but I survived each course, even Latin. My highest grade was History, followed by Religion, English, Science and Latin. The extra work done with Mr. Tappert and Mr. Keur had paid off. Both Masters were pleased and told me they thought I had begun to approach my studies properly. At the time of the Easter vacation, Mr. Hamlin head of the student advisory panel had indicated they were seriously considering recommending my repeating the Second form. After seeing the results of my finals, Mr. Quaile turned that idea down. He called me in to his office on the last day and told me:

"Charlie, it would be a lot easier for you to repeat but I think you have proven you can buckle down. I've watched you fight adversity all year. You came back from a long illness that put you far behind your class, you realized your mistakes in choosing some bad friends and changed your approach to your studies. You deserve to continue on and it's my hunch you'll be a credit to this school. I like the way you don't give up. Go home and have a great summer and come back in the fall with renewed determination."

With those words, he made the year seem more than worthwhile. Driving home, Dad said:

"Boy, you're lucky they didn't make you repeat. If they had we would have sent you to a military school. At times, we wonder what's to become of you. This summer, I expect a lot of hard work out of you and no troubling behavior."

So began the summer of 1941.

Chapter 14

It was a summer that couldn't make up its' mind whether to be hot or cool. It made no difference. Planting, weeding, hoeing, fertilizing, watering and picking produce had to go on.

That year we had planted the largest vegetable garden we had ever planned. Our orchard had also expanded. We had apple trees, peach trees, pear trees and six beehives. We grew enough to feed the whole darn town. Why? Because my Dad wanted to make certain I had enough work to keep me busy! It seemed no sooner had I finished weeding several rows than weeds would be sprouting where I had started. I'm sure it was a scheme to keep me out of trouble. By the third week in July, we had more than we could possibly eat. Uncle Le and Aunt Gertie were given far more than they could consume. Aunt Nell was given so much she joked she was going to open a vegetable market in the Post Office. I think this gave Dad the idea of my peddling the vegetables through town. I was horrified when he broached the subject. My reaction was:

"We can't sell these vegetables or fruit to our friends. Anyway, most of them don't have the money to spend for food they really don't need."

He was adamant. Generously, I was to keep 20% of what I sold.

He won. The next day a large wheelbarrow was loaded with produce and I started hawking my goodies in town. Little kids soon started dogging my steps, darting in and out snatching stuff from the barrow. When I stopped in front of a house to call out my wares and to ask the lady of the house if she would like to buy some fresh vegetables, the kids would try to grab what they could. It seemed to be turning in to a game. The next day, I commandeered a large wagon from my uncle, loaded it with produce, displayed them the best I could, and covered it with a tarp. It was heavy and very awkward to push. Crossing Bridge street, the rumble of the cart alerted the kids to come running. The tarp kept their hands away but the entourage still grew. It became fun teasing them and developing my pitch to the unsuspecting purchasers. I sold more than anticipated. All the ladies seemed to get a kick out of my being the Pied Piper. At stops where I knew people were struggling to make ends meet, I often just gave them what they wanted at no charge. This turned out to be a mistake. If I ran out of things and passed their homes, some would come out and grumble:

"What? None for us today?"

I learned that once people get something for nothing, they grumble if those gifts stop coming. A number of people wanted to know why I wouldn't deliver some of my uncle's flowers to them. When I explained that all were under contract for wholesale florists in New York City, they didn't seem to believe me. I was glad when the summer had ended and I no longer had to make my rounds with my wagon. All other aspects of the summer I never wanted to end.

Several days after my start of selling our produce, the wind shifted to the northwest. Its' force was at least 25 knots. The puffy clouds raced across the azure blue sky. It was too tempting to ignore. I quit the hill early that afternoon. Hoisting the sails on SiSu, the boat bucked in the waves eager to free itself of the mooring. Dropping that line, I checked my watch and headed down river to see how fast a run I could make to Newburgh, nine miles away. Tide and wind were with me and I picked up a mooring at the Newburgh Yacht Club just forty-four minutes later. This was a fantastic run for my nineteen foot sailboat. It was an exhilarating experience. At 5:30 PM I started the trip back. I was exhausted on my return. It was 10:23PM. I can't remember how many tacks it took to achieve my destination. It was one of the most thrilling sails I had in my young life.

Securing the boat, I noticed another larger boat moored in our harbor. It was a sloop of about 36 feet in length, with beautiful lines and a name across her stern; "EDWA". When I returned to the island, I asked Mom if she knew who owned her. She hadn't even noticed it had come in. The next day I went over to the Post Office. If anyone knew it would be my Aunt because all news reached there first. Sure enough she knew. It belonged to Captain Frank Drake. He had just bought her and had her named after his two children — Edna and Walter. I was also informed that he planned on keeping her in our bay. I was excited to have another boat near.

The next evening I ran into John Scardefield. He had a big smile on his face and acted as if he had found hidden treasure. He shouted to me:

"Guess what? Captain Drake has hired me to help him with his new boat. I'm to keep her shipshape and crew for him. I'm quitting my job at the estate and working on the boat full time. I'm even getting more money."

Having John on the bay resulted in an interesting side show. From the "EDWA" he had a good view of the island and as he gazed in our direction he would often see my sister on the front lawn. Most young men considered Nancy a very attractive girl. John became enamored. Soon, many evenings would find he and Don Croke rowing a dinghy around the island loudly singing: "You are my sunshine, my only sunshine, you make me happy when skies are grey, etc., etc.". (Always off key) It was hilarious but my sister was not impressed. Even though John was one of my best friends, she viewed him as uncouth and below her social standing. Her attitude never discouraged John.

Another event of that summer should be noted. Nancy Jane invited her best friend from Scarsdale to visit us for a week. She was Dana Davies, Steve's sister. We all looked forward to her stay. She was always fun, laughed at most everything and was a good sport. The third night of her visit, we were all woken by Dana's scream and laughter. She had needed to go to the bathroom, picked up her flashlight, walked to the outhouse and sat to relieve herself. Doing so, she reached out and put the flashlight down. It dropped right through the other hole. Her scream and laughter was the result. You guessed it. My job was to retrieve the light. From that day on, every time we met she would remind me of the incident.

Returning to Scarsdale after Labor Day, it was the usual rush to prepare for my return to Salisbury. No happy flirtations or troubling events occurred. I guess I was too worried about the new classes and unhappy over leaving my town and life on the river.

CHAPTER 15

BACK AT SALISBURY my attitude was more positive. I had come to realize it was a great school. As difficult as the studies were it was obvious that the first year learning experience had done me a lot of good. The Masters had shown a real interest in me as an individual and had changed my outlook. The beauty of the surroundings made every day fresh and stimulating. When comparing all the positives to the negatives of my schooling in Scarsdale I knew fortune had shined on my life.

Some changes were noticed at once. Several students had not returned and many more had enrolled for the first time. Our third form was twice as large as our second had been. Ev. Yeaw had not returned because of his poor marks. His absence was a real disappointment. We had hoped to be roommates again. Instead I was assigned a single room on the North Dorm which was supervised by Mr. Keur. I was not happy having to room alone but was told it would afford greater privacy with fewer interruptions of my study time. While unpacking, there was a knock on my door. When opened who should be there but Ron Erskine, the opposing tackle from The Harvey School and my drop kick friend. He had enrolled as a fourth former and was also living on the North Dorm in a single room. We caught each other up on all we had been doing since those days. He asked if I had met his friend Jack Zimmerman who had also enrolled as a fourth former. He, like Ron, was from Scarsdale. When I said no, he insisted we go find him. It turned out Jack was on the third floor of Payson Dorm. When we found him, it was quickly obvious our friendship would grow. Ron was thin with sandy straight hair on top of a ruddy face containing smiling, questioning eyes and a narrow, pointed nose over a mouth outlined by rather thick laughing lips. He was nearly five foot ten inches tall but all was over-shadowed by a rich, deep voice that gained attention when it was used. Jack was stocky, about five foot seven, light brown hair, also of ruddy complexion, with serious eyes, a thick nose and rough looking lips over a strong chin. When he spoke, it was with measured thought, very erudite and with great kindness. Our first get together was the beginning of a solid friendship. Our personalities meshed well.

Of my other classmates, Jack Vigneron became one of my closest friends. He had started in second form with me but lived at home in town during that first year. He and his roommate, Art Gossner, lived in the room next to me. Jack was a good student, very methodical and avoided controversy. He was about my height, on the pale side with very dark, straight, black hair. I liked him. He was dependable. Art was unusual looking. He had also been in the second form with me. He was a good guy and became the character of our form. He was called "Zombie" and good-naturedly accepted that moniker.

The second week back I went to Mr. Quaile and asked permission to build a log cabin in the woods. He was presented with a list of the students who had agreed to build it with me. After a long discussion involving the requirements to be met and a detailed list of specifications that had to be followed, he gave his assent. Any deviations from the specs had to receive authorization from Mr. Stern, the Master who was assigned to oversee our efforts. Ten of us formed the group to undertake the project. The following Sunday afternoon we cleared the land, dug trenches for the rock foundation and started felling trees for long straight logs. On the fifth Sunday we began to notch the logs so that they fit securely together. Mr. Quaile and Mr. Stern visited the site that day and commended us on our progress. We were thrilled. Our confidence grew that the cabin could be completed by the school year's end.

A week later it was announced that Mr. Quaile was entering the Columbia Presbyterian Hospital in New York City. He had developed severe bursitis in his right shoulder. Being an avid tennis player he was determined to have the problem repaired. Three days after he had gone into the hospital will live in my mind forever. Sitting at my desk in Study Hall I heard the squeaky shoes of Mr. Myers, walking softly from behind me, passing and stopping three rows up at Pug Quaile's desk. He tapped Pug, the Head Master's son, on the shoulder and motioned for him to follow out of the room. Thinking it strange, it was difficult to get back to my studies. Ten minutes later a number of the other Masters started entering the room. Then those students allowed to study in their rooms began to enter and stand at the back. Mr. Myers returned and went to the front of the Hall. Clearing his throat he said:

"Gentlemen, I have some very sad news to report. Mr. Quaile died on the operating table this afternoon. There will be classes tomorrow as he would have wished. The funeral service is being arranged and further announcements will be made outlining our schedule changes. Please join me in a few moments of prayer for our beloved Head Master."

We were all stunned. Many tears were shed, including mine. None of us could believe what had happened. The next few days passed in a fog. Of all the Masters, I revered Mr. Quaile the most. All of us had been in awe of him. At the same time, we knew he was a man we could trust and rely upon. He always said things straight out with no attempt to placate. To me he was the epitome of what a man should be. His demeanor was my model of a true leader and remains so to this day.

The funeral was overwhelming. Many hundreds attended. It had to be held at the big church in town rather than in our school chapel. The void created took many years to supplant. Mr. Myers was made the interim Head as the Board of Directors searched for a replacement. He did his very best under trying circumstances. He deserved far more credit than he received.

The football season ended under this emotional cloud. The season had been good to me. I had advanced to the second squad, was the starting halfback and scored more points than any school player in history. This was not due to my outstanding performance but largely because we had a terrific line and my point total was increased by being the extra point and field goal kicker in addition to scoring touchdowns. The team was undefeated. Coach Myers informed me that in the next year he intended to use me on the varsity. My happiness was more than a little obnoxious.

Thanksgiving weekend soon arrived. From Caanan, Ct. I caught a train to Poughkeepsie and then changed to another for New Hamburgh. Dad, Mom and Nancy Jane drove up from Scarsdale. We had the turkey dinner at Uncle Le's and Aunt Gertie's. It was as delicious as ever but it felt awkward not having Aunt Nell with us. Before going to the Yacht Club I ran over to her house. She enveloped me in her arms and started to cry. She felt so alone and couldn't hide the fact. I stayed until she forced me out her door, telling me to go see my friends. A smaller group than usual had gathered for the shooting. Their welcome was boisterous but somehow the thrill of the competition was not the same.

Returning to Uncle Le's it was time to take the stuff over to the Island. We were spending the next two nights there. During the night It turned cold. I was up several times stoking the fire. In the morning I awoke to heavily falling snow. Getting up, Dad said:

"Boy, keep that fire going and put the kettle over the fire. We'll need something warm to drink. With no insulation and no heat but the fire this cabin is too cold to stay for another night. I think we had better go back to Scarsdale."

"My return ticket to school is from here. I'll stay up and you may even have trouble driving back because it has snowed at least six inches. If it doesn't stop soon I doubt the roads will be clear."

"You're kidding? Is there really snow?"

"Yup. As soon as it gets lighter, you'll see."

"Wow. We can't stay here. Let's hope it stops."

It did but not before ten or so. The roaring fire had helped warm the place but it was still pretty cold. Much discussion followed and around one o'clock it had warmed sufficiently for Dad to drive back to Scarsdale. I decided to stay with Aunt Nell before catching the train back to school in the morning. It was important to be back then to spend the day working on the cabin which we were building.

Aunt Nell was thrilled to have me stay. She prepared a big dinner and we had a nice evening to ourselves. It was like old times. Obviously, she was extremely lonely. For the first time I realized that an adult living alone had a life truly different than what was normal. It saddened me so that I promised myself I'd keep more closely in touch. I was then off to Salisbury.

Two Sundays later a group of us were sitting in the Common room shortly before lunch. The radio was on as we listened to music of the day. Suddenly the program was interrupted. An announcement came on:

"We have just received a news bulletin. Pearl Harbor is under attack by the Japanese. Much destruction has been reported. Stay tuned. We will bring you more as it is received."

In shock, we spent the rest of the day glued to the radio following the increasing terrible news. We all knew that war had arrived for the United States. Older students talked of enlisting immediately. Mr. Myers called a meeting of all students at 5:00PM in the Study Hall. Before the meeting we all knew the Japanese had bombed our fleet in a surprise attack and that much destruction had occurred. At the meeting we were told the school would be blacked out every night. No lights would be allowed outside, all shades pulled down and no cars allowed to be driven near the school with their lights on. Authorities were fearful more attacks would come and most from the Germans. It was seriously thought our school, perched on a mountain top, might be targeted by incendiary bombs and used as a beacon for incoming planes flying to raid New York City. As far-fetched as that theory seems today, it was believed within the stunned reaction of the time. Life had changed for all of us!

Each day the news became further bleak. On December 8th, Germany and Italy formally declared war on the U.S. The Japanese bombed Clark Field in the Philippines, our Air Force proved incapable of withstanding the attacks. They were decimated and actually withdrew their remaining planes to Australia. The world seemed upside down and places we had never imagined existed became common ground for fierce and inhumane battles. It seemed our country was reeling. Amidst all this news the end of term exams took place.

Eleven days after Pearl Harbor our Christmas break began. The first news received on returning to Scarsdale was that Lt. Commander Register had been killed in the initial attack. He was one of the many fatalities suffered in the sinking of the "Arizona". The war became even more real. His death was hard to accept. We all grieved for his family. I couldn't stop thinking about how nice and supportive he had always been to me.

The war had now become personal. As a teenager, our lives went on with some normalcy. The war was always there but my friends and I were still too young to enlist so we concentrated on those things teenagers do. Shortly after we got home, Ron Erskine, Jack Zimmerman and I went to New York City to catch the big bands playing at the various theatres. We spent the day going from one theatre to another. We saw three bands, four movies and the same newsreel again and again. By the time we got home we were bleary eyed. I don't think I ever saw as many shows before or since. It was fun but once is enough!

One day I asked my Grandmother for a date. She thought I was kidding but I wasn't. We agreed I would take her into the City, have dinner and then go to Radio City Music Hall to see the Christmas show and the Rocketts. The treat was to be on me. Some of the money I had earned over the summer was to fund the outing. It turned out to be a wonderful evening. We really had a good time together. She had always been "someone special" but when she stayed with us in the Fall and Winter months she was more neglected than included. Her life story had always been a mystery,

I had never been told anything of my Grandfather, her husband. I knew she had been born in New Zealand, had married my grandfather when she was in her twenties, moved to Australia and Tasmania where my mother was born. Moved back to Melbourne, Australia where her three other children were born, had been shipwrecked with her children on her voyage to America, settled in New York City for a short time and then moved with her husband to New Hamburgh when my Mom was sixteen. Strangely, never were any of the particulars discussed. I did know that my Grandfather died in 1917. It was to be another forty years, long after her death, before I began to uncover both of their amazing stories. Those are the real histories to be written before they become lost!

The night of the "date" when we returned home, MeMa hugged me so close and said it had been the nicest evening she had experienced since leaving Australia. I was happy we had the date but wish I had taken the opportunity to learn more of her life. Perhaps she would have told me what had been cooped up for so long.

At Christmas I was given a Mido self-winding watch from Mom and Dad. I was ecstatic over receiving it and to this day it still works. I don't believe it has ever been cleaned or serviced. The day was also memorable because it was the first time my sister was visited, on such a day, by a young man-Talbot Goodwin. He came laden with gifts for her. To see my family's reaction was a panic. All my Mother could say was:

"This is not appropriate. No young man should come calling uninvited on Christmas day."

Fortunately, I don't believe Talbot caught on to her dismay. Nancy Jane was delighted and MeMa was overwhelmed with the romance of it all. My sister was very popular and had many dates but to have a suitor invade the sanctity of our home on such a day was almost too much for our parents to handle. As the day lengthened, tensions eased and Talbot stayed until late in the day when it was time for our Christmas dinner. From that day on, it seemed our home was always crammed with eager young men.

The following day we learned from the "Powers that be" that the Cotillion would proceed in spite of the war because: "Too many of our brave young men would all too soon be in the Armed Services and they deserved a cheer-up fling." Still too young to be categorized as a "brave young man" I was nonetheless expected to attend the affair. As usual, Amy Lu had maneuvered to be escorted by me. We survived the dinner and dance. It turned out to be an interesting evening. Another girl caught my eye. Her name was Sally Marshall. We danced many numbers, ate together during the "repast" and by the end of the evening she had agreed to go in to the City with me to see a show if her parents gave their consent. Amy Lu was a little upset but it was obvious we were not on the same wavelength. We were friends but at arms' length.

Calling Sally the next day I was told her parents would not give their permission. I was devastated. Christmas vacation turned into a bummer.

New Years' Eve was spent with a group of guys playing ping-pong and other games at Gordon Ferguson's. None of us had any dates. All admitted we wished otherwise. The big drawback of being away for most of the year at an all boys' school was the small number of the opposite sex we came to know.

1942 opened on a grim note presaging the months ahead. Changes could be seen everywhere. The Country was on a full wartime basis. The continued shock of Pearl Harbor was fortified by the disasters being experienced by our forces in the Pacific. The Japanese were pushing us over. All were stunned by the brutality of their onslaught. It became obvious that many, many men would be needed in our armed forces. Mr. Myers and his staff had spent part of the holidays making a "Ranger Course" of approximately three miles through the woods. Every day we were required to run the course to get ourselves in top physical condition. Our normal athletic teams were continued. The "Ranger Course" was an additional requirement. We all took it seriously, particularly the older students. Mr. Myers also told me we could no longer build our log cabin. As he put it:

"More important things required our attention".

Last terms marks had been posted on our return. Amazingly, I had passed all subjects with a "Gentlemanly average". Class work still remained a challenge but I was making progress. The struggle to keep up never seemed to abate. Having no room-mate did not lessen the distractions from my studies. Instead my room seemed to be a magnate for my friends to congregate and indulge in Bull Sessions. Admittedly, these masterful discussions were enjoyed and stimulated my mind. Many an hour was spent discussing the war, both in the Far East and in Europe. My maps were resurrected for both theatres of operation and hung on my wall. I was learning geography to a greater extent than ever. Our "Gab Fests" became so frequent and vocal it induced Mr. Keur to pay a visit. He demanded an end of the sessions. We were all crushed but it did result in an improvement of my studies. He followed that visit with an invitation for tea. I was certain another lecture was in the offing. On arrival, he greeted me as before. Once tea was in hand he launched into the expected summary of my situation:

"Chuck, the Masters have just held the review of the school year to date. Much has happened to take our eye away from the purpose of this school. All agree it is time we returned to what we are all here to accomplish. We have reviewed the progress of each student. Your evaluation underlines several facts. First, you are still having difficulty keeping up. Second, too much of your time is spent on unnecessary sessions that I terminated yesterday. Third, your development of a questioning mind is improving but needs more attention to reach its' full potential. Fourth, the enthusiasm for sports should be tempered by an equal enthusiasm for study. Fifth, you have become a leader in this school at an unusually early age. Sixth, it was agreed by every Master that you have great promise but you need to build a better relationship with your instructors. We care for all students and want them to reach out for help. You still fail to do that enough. Please think on what I am telling you and act accordingly."

On that note the tea time discussion ended. I took it as a pep talk and left committed to do better.

It was a good winter for snow. Skiing consumed most afternoons. My expertise improved and I was put on the ski team as a downhill racer. We had one meet, which was at Berkshire School. I came in next to last in my event. I still had much to learn. For me the ski jump generated the most excitement. I watched in awe as a jumper from Hotchkiss jumped 86 feet. I was tempted to try to learn the event but quickly discarded the idea when I saw a jumper from Millbrook fall and break his leg.

The Easter break seemed to rush upon us. I caught the train with Gordon Ferguson. During the trip he told me of his new girl-friend. Over Christmas he had met a girl from Larchmont. He thought her a real looker and planned to see her as much as he could over the break. I thought nothing more of this conversation until a few days later when he called asking if I'd bike the eight miles over to Larchmont with him. Having nothing better to do, I agreed. We rode over to Mamaroneck High School and met his latest. Her name was Susan Waterman. After introductions, a cute girl standing by looked rather embarrassed. Gordon soon realized there was awkwardness and asked to be introduced. That is how I met Natalie Hugh. Cute, she certainly was. Her blondish hair was cut short, was curly and framed a face containing sparkling blue eyes, a pert nose and a smiling mouth. She was five feet one inch tall, with a body that emanated vibrancy. The joy in the sound of her voice somehow reflected her demeanor. Her clothes expressed inner comfort. I liked her at once. We became good friends and remained so for years. It was a relationship that saw us together a lot and encompassed many good times. Strangely, I never asked her to come to a school dance weekend. One time she even teased me about it. Over that Easter holiday we went to the City often, attended several local dances and parties, saw a number of movies together and had dinner at our respective homes. Very little time was spent with Gordon and Sue, although he and I would ride to Larchmont together.

Several days were also spent in my river town. It was that time of year when Uncle Le needed help in preparing for the new growing season. I spent one night at the island. I was alone and found it almost as cold as when we had been there at Thanksgiving. Still, it was great to be on the river to indulge my senses with all the familiar joys. The town had many in the Army, Navy or Marines. All were concerned in particular for John Petrapole. He had been in the Phillipines when the Japanese invaded. Subsequently, he had gone to Corregidor and now was assumed to be on the Bataan death march. Reports of this terrible event were starting to be revealed and our anger over the Japanese increased. A number of my friends were starting to enlist. John Scarderfield was determined to join the Navy as soon as he turned seventeen. He had a year and a half to wait. When I returned to Scarsdale there was more bad news. An old flame of my sister had been shot down over New Guinea on a flying mission from his base in Australia. Sadness seemed to be everywhere.

Easter behind us, it was back to school. It was the home stretch to summer. Studies were difficult but manageable. Each afternoon, after the Ranger Course run, was baseball practice. I had been elected Captain of the Junior Varsity team and alternated between centerfield and second base. My batting average was a low 235 but base running kept me valuable to the team. I tried batting lefty as well as righty with equal results. The Coach soon told me when to go to the plate as either one or the other. He figured I could get more walks by changing sides according to the pitchers' weakness. Our pitchers were so good we were undefeated for the season.

The end of the year track meet was good to me. I won the 100yd dash, was second in the 220yd, second in broad jump and fourth in high jump. My head was getting too big. Coach Myers took me down a peg. After the meet he said:

Chuck (somehow everybody had started calling me that) you may think you are good but let me tell you, at a real competition you wouldn't even be noticed. Serious track stars train all year, not two weeks. In running all you would see is the rear ends of those in front." Ouch!

When the final grades for the year were posted I had passed all subjects but again failed the Honor Roll.

CHAPTER 16

THE DAY AFTER returning home found me on the train from Tarrytown to New Hamburgh. Uncle Le needed help. Water for his garden and our vegetable acreage had to be pumped from Wappingers Creek, one hundred and eighty feet up the hill to a large storage tank. The pumping system had broken a few days earlier so a new one had to be installed before he lost all his seedlings. He'd called Dad and asked if I were home from school yet. He needed my help. It was a quick turn-around for me but I really didn't mind. We estimated the job would take the better part of three days. It took over a week. We prayed it would rain some to keep the seedlings moist. It stayed dry. The third day it became necessary to spend the evenings lugging large milk pails of water from Charlie Wick's farm to the hill. The only truck or car we had was my uncle's 1930 Ford. He had already taken the back seats out and trunk off so he could use it as a truck. Bill and I were to fetch the water while Uncle Le watered his plants. Neither of us had ever driven but we both learned that week. Why we didn't strip the gears on that old car, I'll never know. It was a circus doing this water caravan. It kept Bill and me in continual laughter. At the end of the repair work, our water supply was better and more reliable. The old car convinced Bill he should never drive again and he never did.

That whole week I lived on the island by myself. My cooking was not the best so most dinners were spent with Aunt Nell. We both enjoyed being together again. One night we were joined by her boyfriend, Uncle Edgar. I hadn't seen him for years. I soon gathered he was a frequent visitor when his job brought him to the area. He actually had some sort of home in the next town but hardly ever stayed there. He said his sister had moved in. It was all very confusing. A stranger man would have been hard to find. Why my aunt was so stuck on him, I couldn't figure. Sitting there that evening, it was hard not to notice what an unusual couple they made. He was tall and gaunt with the largest nose I had ever seen on a man. His voice was very deep and when he spoke the conversation was always boring. My Aunt was thickly square, supported by rather heavy legs. Her hair was dyed dark brown, hiding what would have been luxurious and almost snow white. It was cut rather short. She wore thick eyeglasses, talked with a slight lisp through thin lips that were surrounded by streaky lined skin. Her forehead indicated intelligence. But her greatest attribute was a warm, loving and sincere personality. For some reason, they just didn't seem suited for one another.

That evening, I learned that his passionate hobby was photography. On his vacations, he traveled to scenic locations all over the eastern section of the country to take pictures. In later years, I became the recipient of his photo equipment. It was of the very finest. He sent many of his pictures to photographic shows and contests but sadly, only won one prize. However, that night, he convinced me he was an unusually gifted photographer.

Regardless of those thoughts on that evening, it was a wonderful time spent with the woman who had always meant so much to me.

The summer started in earnest when my Mom and sister joined me at the island the following weekend. The normal routine returned. The work on the hill was never ending. I had tried to talk Dad into raising my pay from ten cents an hour to fifteen. He wouldn't hear of it. This year the garden was bigger than ever.

By the end of July, we all learned why the garden had become so large. Dad had come up for a week's vacation and enthusiastically joined me on the hill tending the vegetables. While we were pulling the fastest growing weeds in the USA, he told me:

"Boy, I have had a cold cellar built in Scarsdale to store vegetables for the winter. The area under the maid's room, leading from the cellar to the garage has been dug out and a cement room made with proper ventilation. It is large enough to store vegetables without their rotting."

I thought to myself, it would have been better and cheaper to buy all the vegetables and save me a lot of work, but I didn't have the nerve to express my opinion out loud.

A day later in the week we were at the weeds again. It was early afternoon and my uncle showed up earlier than usual from his lunch. He jumped out of his old car and walked towards us.

"Reg", (most people called my Dad that) we just had a telephone call from Walter Krahl. I'm afraid there is some bad news. Roxie's mom passed away this morning."

We were shocked. My grandmother, MeMa, couldn't have died. But it was true. We dropped everything and went back to the island to tell my Mom. Crossing the bridge, I could see my Dad didn't know how to break the news. As we walked into the cabin, Mother said:

"What's wrong? Why are you back so soon?"

Dad didn't say a word. He just looked at her and then at me. He nodded and Mom said:

"Tell me. What's wrong?"

Still no words came from Dad. She then looked at me and I said:

"Mom, it's MeMa. Uncle Le just had a call from Uncle Walter. MeMa passed away this morning."

I'll never forget the look on Mom's face. It just fell apart. Then the tears came with racking sobs. She reached out to me and held on tight. I was afraid she was going to collapse. Dad still couldn't say anything. He was too tongue tied with worry for his girl. In a minute, Mom loosened her arms and turned to Dad. I left. It was the first time I had ever witnessed my mother's reserve and constraints leave her.

My sister had taken our car, a 1938 LaSalle, shopping. When she returned, I broke the news to her. All of us were soon adjusting to the realities. She drove Mom over to Uncle Le's to use their telephone to call Aunt Eva and Uncle Walter to learn all the facts and to help make the necessary arrangements. Dad and I just stayed at the island. In a little while, he said:

"Boy, I couldn't get the words out. I knew how hard she would take it. Thank you for speaking up. I think, it was better coming from you."

That is all we said to each other until that evening when we all discussed how we would get to the funeral and when.

It was decided that Mom and Dad would drive to Emporium, Pennsylvania, where Aunt Eva and Uncle Walter now lived. Nancy Jane and I would take the train to Altoona, where we would be met by someone and driven the rest of the way to Emporium. They left early the next morning. We caught our train two days later. The trip was interesting because it was the furthest west I had ever been. By the time we arrived, both of us were covered in soot. I had the train window open the whole way because of the heat. The coal fires for the steam engines threw black soot everywhere. With no air conditioning and a heavy sweat, the coal dust ground into our skins. We looked like "darkies" when we arrived.

The rest of the family was already there. Uncle "Glad", Aunt Vietta and their two children — Gaye and Broth, Uncle Roy and Aunt Leona, Aunt Eva and Uncle Walter and of course, Mom and Dad. The fourteen of us were the family. I doubt a group of names of such peculiarity seldom occur. Roxie, Eva, Vietta, Gaye, Glad, Broth, Walter, Roy, Leona and Reg. All we needed was Gertie, Nellie and Edgar. My sister and I often found hilarity in our relatives. Their names undoubtedly must have influenced their personalities..

The funeral was small. It was held at the funeral parlor. Only the family and a few local friends attended. In accordance with my grandmother's wishes, she was cremated and the ashes were eventually spread at sea. I was deeply touched by her passing. I had loved her thoroughly. My wish had always been to learn the details of her life. She was a romantic who exuded love. Pictures of her as a younger woman showed a very attractive and striking woman. To this day, I keep a picture, as I knew her, on or near my desk. I often smile over the memory of her as my roommate.

After the "Goodbye ceremony", we all returned to Aunt Eva's for the usual party. Uncle Glad was a great drinker and showed his talents with fervor. The rest made an effort to keep pace but he was the undisputed winner. Mom and Dad rarely drank and lagged far behind. With the affair in full swing, my cousin Broth and I took off to explore the stream behind the property. We jumped from rock to rock. Fell in as often as landing on our targets and had a great time until the sound of a rattle snake was heard. We froze. Then Broth shouted:

"Look behind you. I think I saw him!"

I froze again. The rattle finally stopped. We waited. No more noise than the rippling water. Slowly, we inched our way back up the stream. Reaching the field, we broke in to a fast run for the house. We made it. No one believed our story. All were more interested in their glasses. Aunt Eva jumped up and said:

"Come on kids, I'll take you for a drive."

Out to the garage we trooped. Sliding in to the back seat, my sister said:

"I think she is drunk."

Off we went. The scenery seemed to fly by. Swerving on to a lonely street, my Aunt raced down the road. Broth, was in the front seat, he yelled:

"Watch out for the chickens!"

We all looked. Ahead were fifteen or twenty chickens crossing the road. My Aunt laughed and plowed through the lot. Feathers went everywhere. She never slowed. Her laughter was almost maniacal. We all begged her to slow down and take us home. No such luck. Her foot clamped on the pedal and we sped from road to road accompanied by screeching tires. Gaye started crying and the rest of us hung on for dear life. Sanity, of sorts, crept slowly back into our aunt. We arrived at her house frightened and probably with a few wet pants. I don't think we ate that night. The adults were in a mopping up operation until very late. Each family had been assigned their own rooms. It was tight sleeping but we did. Aunt Leona and Uncle Roy were staying at a guesthouse down the road. How they got there is a mystery. It had been quite a day.

When we returned to our island after the funeral, things quickly returned to normal. Work continued on the hill. The weeds had grown to a stage where they were starting to smother the produce. The amount of vegetables, melons and raspberries was so plentiful it was decided I should offer a discount to my customers. It also meant that I gave away a lot of stuff to people who couldn't afford to buy on a regular basis. This was good and bad but it did consume much of our over production. The amount of work necessary to catch up required me to spend even longer hours working. This prevented me from seeing my pals as much as I would have liked. Most evenings, after a late supper, I would launch the canoe and paddle out to the middle of the river. It would be dark. I'd stop paddling, stretch out and gaze at the stars while drifting with the tide. It was very peaceful and the heavens seemed close enough to touch. In August there always seemed to be more shooting stars and toward the end of the month the lights of the aureole borealis could be seen flashing from the North Pole. The wonder of it all made my existence seem insignificant but instilled in me a sense of joy and contentment in being part of the universe. Similar feeling have often returned in later years while sailing or anchored at night staring into the canopy above.

One evening I was hailed by men tending the Draw Bridge spanning Wappingers Creek as I paddled bye. A large powerboat had tied up to the pier alongside the bridge. The skipper wanted to take the boat up the creek to the Bleachery dock but was unfamiliar with the channel and in darkness was afraid he'd run aground. The men at the Draw Bridge suggested he ask me to guide them. When I got alongside the boat the Captain asked. I agreed with enthusiasm. The two- mile trip in the dark was the first for me as a guide. I hoped and prayed I didn't make any mistake. I didn't and after they tied up to the dock the captain insisted on giving me a tip. I was floored when I saw what he had given me — a five -dollar bill! That was the equivalent of working on the hill for ten days. On my return, the men at the bridge asked me to stop. The boss said:

"Son, we thought you'd like to do that. We often get bigger powerboats here that want to go up but are leery because they don't know the channel and it's not marked. What do you say if we give you three blasts on our horn when someone needs a guide? If you are on the island and hear the signal you could probably pick up some tips. Are you willing?"

"Gee, Great! I'd sure like to do it."

So began my career as a guide. I never had anyone run aground, thank goodness. Over the years, I made close to two hundred dollars.

As the summer was ending, Steve Davies came up for a long weekend. I shortened my hours on the hill so we could spend more time around the river. He still was not interested in sailing so SiSu remained tethered to her mooring. We canoed, swam, explored the woods, crabbed and fished. The crabbing was exceptionally good that year. One day we caught a bushel basket of hard shell crabs in a little over an hour and a half. Steve was one of my Scarsdale friends who enjoyed my New Hamburgh friends. He and John Scardefield got along particularly well. We spent several evenings with John and Don Croke. On one of those outings we went to the new community center (the old abandoned Presbyterian Church had been obtained by the town for a community center where the young crowd could gather). The main floor had a large hall, free of pews and chairs, with a stage where a Victrola had been installed. On most Fridays and Saturdays evenings, kids would gather to dance. I had only been one time but John and Don convinced Steve and me we should join them there on Saturday. Steve fit right in with everyone. Rose Cameli soon came over and I asked her to dance. She was about four years older than me, was a very nice girl and very good looking with her dark eyes, dark hair and rather dark complexion. I used to tease her that she looked more like a gypsy than a gypsy did. Her laughter was infectious. Dancing with her was like holding a light feather while it drifted across the floor. As we were gliding around, I looked for Steve. He was with Edith Newman. They seemed to be having much to laugh about. I knew Steve fancied himself a lady's man but this was the first time I had been able to watch him with a girl. I then danced with Joy Hamilton . She'd asked me and I couldn't refuse. She too was older but one of the nicest and most thoughtful girls in town. I don't think she ever had a bad thing to say about anyone.

I kept looking for Steve. He was nowhere to be found. At ten thirty, the evening was beginning to close down but Steve was still "among the missing". So was Edith. John and Don said they had to leave. I hung around until eleven, helped lock up and went back to the island alone. As was the case when any of my friends came for a visit, I had pitched a tent down by the shore to have more privacy. I went to bed but had to stay awake for Steve because I had to lock the gate after him. Shortly after twelve thirty he appeared. I loudly whispered:

"Where in the devil have you been? I stayed until the end and even locked up but I had no idea where to look for you. What happened?"

"Sorry. It was a great evening. I didn't have a chance to tell you we were leaving."

"You still haven't answered my questions."

"I walked Edith home. It was a nice evening."

"Edith has a pretty wild reputation. I hope you didn't contribute to it and that you're okay."

"Let's not talk about it. We had fun and that's all you need to know. Now let's get to sleep."

It took a while for me to get to sleep. I had always known Steve to be a dare devil but hadn't realized he was overly fixated on the opposite sex.

The next morning I was up at my usual time. Steve soon dragged himself out of bed. When he looked at me, he broke out into a big grin. Neither of us discussed the night's happenings. We decided to take the canoe out to the reef and cast for stripe bass.

145

The tide was perfect so we caught many but had to throw them all back because they didn't meet the legal size of sixteen inches.

Steve kept looking at the western shore with its high hill that had been cut off to allow for the railroad bed along the river. It was a perpendicular angle to the top. The precipice was at least two hundred feet high. When we had finished fishing he said:

"Chuck, let's scale the face of that rock. I've always wanted to rock climb and that looks perfect."

"Are you kidding? It goes straight up! We'd kill ourselves trying to climb that."

"Come on. Don't be chicken. I can see all sorts of toe and hand holds. It will be a lot easier than you think. Come on, it won't take long."

I was nervous about it and probably chicken but as he kept on I finally agreed to give it a shot. We beached the canoe in a small cove behind a small underpass of the railroad. We started off easily enough. Thirty feet up it became more difficult. We had to move from toe- hold to toe- hold and finger hold to finger hold, in smaller and smaller depressions. As we reached sixty- five feet up, a long freight train rumbled around the corner. As it passed below, everything seemed to vibrate. Sweat was pouring off me which made it more difficult to hang on. I desperately wanted to go back down but that seemed more impossible than going up. Hours seemed to crawl by and certainty grew that this was my last day. I had never been so frightened. Steve started grunting and whistling. I could tell he was also nervous. We had to keep going. Finally we reached the top but how to throw ourselves over to the firm ground became another challenge. We agreed to count to ten and then make the move. At ten, we heaved ourselves up, grabbed for branches, roots or anything to hold us from slipping back to our deaths. Somehow we both made it. Steve began to laugh uncontrollably, admitting, between breaths, that he had been more scared than at any time in his life. We were two very lucky boys. It cured me of ever becoming desirous of rock climbing.

Steve left the following day. I thought him a wonderful guy and friend but feared he would push himself through too many crazy things and be lucky surviving to a ripe old age.

A week more remained before returning to Scarsdale. The last night, John Scardefield said he doubted we would see one another until after the war. He was going to enlist in the Navy on his seventeenth birthday in March. I thought we'd probably see each other at Thanksgiving or Christmas but we didn't.

Back in Scarsdale things seemed as chaotic as they were in New Hamburgh because so many of my friends and acquaintances were leaving for military service. Most of my sister's boyfriends were already in. I wondered if the war would still be on by the time my turn came. The Germans and Japanese seemed invincible. With all of that, confidence was high that we would eventually prevail. It was just a question of how long it would take. Excitement reached a new level in our neighborhood when a home on Roxbury Road was raided. The owners were arrested for subversive activities. They had been discovered to be German agents and members of a Bund cell. How they were discovered no one knew. They had always seemed like nice people. Johnny McCullough used to deliver them the Saturday Evening Post when he had his route. They had always tipped him substantially at Christmas. He was floored when their activities were made public. Two days after this episode I was on my way back to school.

CHAPTER 17

SALISBURY SCHOOL WAS different. A new Head Master had been appointed. The Reverend George D. Langdon came from the Pomfret School, which was also in Connecticut but not in our league. His background was entirely different from that of Mr. Quaile or Mr. Myers. He was an ordained Episcopal minister.

I will never forget the first time I met the new Head and his wife. The first day back, I was walking across campus when Mr. Myers, who was with another couple, called out:

"Chuck, please come and say hello to our new Head Master and his wife."

Going up to them, I reached out my hand to the new Headmaster. He gripped it gingerly.

"How do you do, Sir? I'm Chuck Van Anden starting my fourth form year. I'm very pleased to meet you."

Turning to Mrs. Langdon, I held my hand out and said:

"Hello. Welcome. It's a pleasure meeting you."

She was fumbling in her pocketbook for a pack of cigarettes, finally found them and said:

"Have a cig."

I could have dropped through the ground to China. Instead, I looked into her confused face and politely refused, saying:

"No thanks. Students are not permitted to smoke while in school."

"Oh, I'm so sorry. I forgot."

At that, Mr. Myers took hold of my arm and said:

"George, Chuck is one of our better young athletes. We have great hopes for his future contributions to our teams."

Rev. Langdon grunted and said:

"Is that so".

On that high note, my introduction was over. Walking away, I couldn't help but think I had started off on the wrong foot with the new Head Master.

The next morning, after chapel, a school meeting was held. Our new Head Master welcomed us all, said he looked forward to the new school year and outlined a few changes he believed were overdue if Salisbury was to stay in step with the new academic culture. Students were to be given more freedom in an effort to broaden their pursuits. Increased attention would be placed on the arts, a lesser emphasis would be placed on sports and the overemphasis of competition. He emphasized, we should all be cognizant of the diversity of individuals and therefore, students not wishing to join in sports could spend that time at leisure, walking or delving in to hobbies of their choice. The Prefects would still be responsible for maintaining discipline but any punishment would have to be approved by him or the appointed nucleus of Masters. The no smoking rule would still apply but students would no longer be required to meet with him and promise with their honor to obey the rules. (He later explained the requirement to meet with the Head Master on a one to one basis and be required to promise on your honor to obey school rules while shaking his hand and looking him squarely in the eyes put too much pressure on a student.) He would also take under consideration the establishment of a smoking room for seniors. Other changes would be announced once they had been discussed with the faculty. On that note, the meeting ended. Students were dismayed. Some liked what they had heard but others had grave misgivings. I was in the latter category. Our school song started with:

"Loyalty and honor, Sarum
We, thy sons, now pledge thee"

It seemed our new Head Master thought that too harsh.

Besides the new Head, there were many masters who had left and new ones appointed in their places. Perhaps it was my imagination but the new were very different, more lenient, very casual and determined to act as "one of the boys". To me, they seemed false and not dedicated to teaching. Our new French Master spent more time telling dirty jokes than teaching. Our English teacher, though recently married, regaled our class with stories of alleged past sexual conquests. It was so different than the past two years, it was difficult to accept the change. At first it was fun to listen and laugh but a nagging doubt began to seep in to many of us who had lived under the Quaile educational environment.

The school year saw an influx of foreign students. We gained two from England, one from Brazil, one from Greece and two brothers from Russia. The latter were White Russians. They had fled Russia with their parents in the mid1930s, lived in Belgium and fled that country when the Germans invaded. Actually, they were part of the Royal family, cousins of the murdered Czar. Before escaping from the Nazis, the older brother had lost most of one hand when he picked up a hand grenade. They were good guys, fitted in with the other students well and were admired for the determination they showed in mastering the English language. Even with their handicaps, they became good students and entered in to all of our activities. The younger one, Dimitri, became a close friend. He, Ozzi Prioulx from England and I would spend hours discussing the war's progress, politics and world affairs. We'd kid one another that when Ozzi became Prime Minister, Dimitri elected Ruler of Russia and I became President, we would solve all the problems of the world. Such are the musings of the naïve. Nevertheless, it was fun, educational and harmless.

Football became an obsession for me. I loved the game. Once again, I was on the junior varsity and had been elected captain. We played from a single wing formation and I was the halfback. We were undefeated for the year. During our fourth game, the varsity coach, Mr. Myers, was watching us play and saw me punt a ball forty five yards into the coffin corner. After the game, he approached me and said he wanted me to suit up for the rest of the varsity games, as well as to finish out the year with the junior varsity. There were three more scheduled games for the varsity. On the first, I was put in to punt whenever it was required. In the second game, I did the punting and when we scored to tie the game at nineteen all, he asked me to try to kick the extra point. The normal kicker had missed two of his three attempts. I asked if I could do a drop kick. He said okay. In I went. The ball was hiked and my drop kick went right through the uprights. It became the last drop kick in the school's history. All those practices years ago, with Ronnie and Shirley Erskine, paid off.

The last game of the year was at Pomfret. I sat on the bench until the last quarter. The game was tied at 14 to 14. Pomfret had been held inside their own forty eight yard marker and had to punt. Coach Myers told me to go in and play safety and when I caught the ball to run as hard as I could up the field. When the punt was made, it was high and coming right to me. I watched it descend, reached out to catch it and at the last second took my eye off the ball. It bounced right through my legs, touching me and rolled into the end zone. Pomfret fell on the ball and took the lead. I was shattered! On that note, my season ended. It took days for me to get over my embarrassment.

Thanksgiving soon arrived. This year there was no going to New Hamburgh. School remained open and classes continued with the exception of Thursday, which we had off. The Saturday of that weekend was the Army/Navy game. Glenn Davis and "Doc" Blanchard were the stars for Army. I was an avid fan. Miss Harris, our dietitian, was going away for the weekend and I prevailed upon her, before she left, to let me listen to the game on the radio in her apartment. A classmate- Bill Thompson- heard me making the arrangements and asked if he could join me in listening. He had never been one of my close friends but he was an Army fan, so it was agreed he could listen with me. Army slaughtered Navy. When the game ended, Bill spoke:

"Chuck, I have wanted to talk to you since the beginning of the year. Why can't we become better friends?"

I didn't know quite how to respond but made an effort:

"Bill, you are a friend. It's just that we have different interests and therefore are not close friends. That doesn't mean I don't like you. You have different friends and we are involved in totally different aspects of the school. So, it's normal not to be close."

"Well, I think we should work together. We both love the school and it would be good for us to join forces in keeping morale up. Everybody knows you are going to be the Head Prefect in two years and I'd like to be part of your circle of friends."

"Bill, are you crazy? I don't think for a minute I'll be Head Prefect. There are plenty of guys who would be great, who are far better students, are involved in a myriad of things and anyway, who knows what new students will enroll that may be far more deserving. Look, we can certainly be friendly but let's not sit here and scheme how the prefect group will be structured when we become sixth formers. I have to keep my efforts on studies. It doesn't come that easy for me. You are the much better student."

"Oh, come on Chuck, you're popular with everyone. You are always elected captain of any team you are on, have a smile and good word for everybody and most see you as the coming Head Prefect."

"Look, let's end this discussion. Who knows what two years will bring."

Shortly after this uncomfortable discussion the school term ended and Christmas vacation started.

Three days after returning from school, the temperature dropped, clouds moved in and a white, fluffy snow piled up. It covered the land with a blanket of nineteen inches. The only way traffic moved was by tire chains. By the time three or four miles had been traversed, some links would be broken and you would hear the clack, clack, clack of the dangling pieces hitting the car fenders. It always seemed a hassle to put the chains on and to repair the links. In our family, this was always my job.

The day after the storm, my sister drove us to White Plains to go Christmas shopping. The drive was a harrowing experience. She skidded into snow drifts, spun the car once and nearly ran an old man down because the brakes wouldn't stop the car. Besides these minor mishaps, I remember the day as being one of the most festive. Everybody seemed happy and full of smiles. The Salvation Army's Santas all rang their bells with extra vigor, probably to stay warm. People in the stores were friendly and more polite than usual. The Christmas carols being played in stores thrilled my ears and I was proud and happy to be with Nancy Jane. We were trying to find something to put under the tree for Mom and Dad. When shopping was finished, we started home. Part way, the familiar clack, clack, clack started. Nancy pulled to the side of the road where snow had been plowed high. Out I jumped. The left rear chain links had broken in several places. Kneeling, in an attempt to fix them, a car tried to pass. It started to skid. The front moved out and the rear swiped our car, missing me by inches. I actually felt air movement on the back of my neck. The other car straightened and drove off. My sister pushed open her damaged door, jumped out and started shouting at the departing vehicle. It was the first time I ever heard foul language come from my sister's mouth. It somehow made me laugh. She turned around and grabbed me and began to cry. Between her tears, I heard her say:

"I thought you had been hit. I was so scared. Are you all right? Get in the car. I want to get home."

Off we drove with the links still broken and the accompanying clack, clack, clack being tolerated. From her reaction, I knew for a certainty she cared for her little brother. To this day, I have never again heard bad language from her lips.

The day after Christmas, Steve Davies called and asked me to meet him at the Scarsdale Golf Club to go skiing. He had been given new ski equipment and was anxious to try them all out. My good skis were at school but Dad had an old pair from when he was a boy. He said I could use them. It was a four-mile cross-country ski jaunt through the woods to get to the club. On the way, I could tell that the old leather harness was about to give out. On arrival, I could see Steve was having a blast roaring down the hill, taking moguls with ease and turning in and out of the other skiers. My first run was good but I didn't dare put much pressure on the harness. On the second run, I tried to keep pace with Steve and was going faster then I should have and approaching the last mogul I could feel the harness give. My control was limited and as I shot wide over the mogul I knew I couldn't make the proper turn. Instead, I plowed into a photographer, standing on the side of the hill, taking pictures of all the skiers. I knocked him flat. Fortunately, he was not hurt nor was his camera equipment damaged. He was a good sport and helped me get up, saying:

"I've been watching you and wondering when your skis would break. They have got to be the oldest on the hill. Where did you get them?"

"They were my Dad's when he was a kid."

"I'd like to get a picture of you on them. Call your friend over and let's go further down the hill to where it is not as steep. I'll take a picture of the two of you and have it put in the paper. I'm the photographer from the Scarsdale Enquirer."

We went down. He took several shots of us on our skis, asked us our names and then departed.. The following Thursday the next edition was published. On the front page was the picture of Steve and me with the following caption: "Steve Davies and Chuck Van Anden skiing at the golf club. Note Chuck's ancient skis." Our phones rang for a week. Celebrity status is fleeting.

It was then time for the Westchester Cotillion. This year it was to be held at the Siwanoy Country Club in Bronxville. As usual, Mrs. Huser and my Mom had conspired for me to escort Amy Lu. My complaints were so forceful, Mom finally promised to never make the arrangements again. But I still had to take her this time. Prior to the dance we went to a dinner party at one of Amy Lu's close friends. It was a very large home and the dining room was easily twice the size of ours. Ten couples were in attendance. Her friend, Audrey, was the hostess. The dinner was ever so proper but I managed to show how gauche I could be. After being served the main course, I turned to talk to Amy Lu and in doing so put my elbow into my meal, tipped the plate and spilled all on my lap. My face turned the color of Christmas ribbons adorning the wreaths hanging over the fireplace. I was a mess, the floor was a mess, the tablecloth was a mess and all eyes were on me. Excusing myself, I went to the powder room and attempted to clean up while the maids and butler cleaned the mess I had left behind. The dinner party ended shortly thereafter and we all departed for the dance. The Husers let me drive their car.

[An interesting follow up to that dinner party occurred fifty years later. My wife and I had just moved to Essex, Connecticut after my retirement from business. Several weeks after moving in, I had a call from Audrey Watson, who lived up the street, inviting us for cocktails. We were happy to accept. When we arrived and introduced ourselves, Audrey said: "Chuck, are you the same Chuck Van Anden from Scarsdale in the 1940's?"

When I said:

"Yes"

She laughed and said:

"You came to my home with Amy Lu Huser before the Westchester Cotillion dance at Bronxville in 1942. You spilled your food all over yourself and the table."

I blushed again a deep red:

"I'm the same guy."

We had a good laugh.

She and John, her husband, became very close friends to us and we had many a good time together. Unfortunately, she died three years later of cancer and John died nine months afterwards of the same disease. On John's last day of life, my wife and I were flying to Turkey to go sailing for two weeks. John had his daughter call me at ten in the morning. When I picked up the phone she said:

"Chuck, do you have a bottle of Vodka in the house? If you do, Dad would like you to bring it over."

I told her I did and would be right over. When I arrived, she was waiting:

"Dad would like you to make two Vodka and tonics and take them up to him in his bedroom."

The drinks were quickly made and upstairs I went. John was trying to lift himself up, so the drinks were put down and we worked together to get him in a sitting position. He looked at me and said:

"Chuck, I know you are going to Turkey tonight. I won't see you again. I want one last drink with you. You have been a great friend, we have had a lot of fun, let's drink to the future. I'm sure we'll meet again."

At that, we touched glasses and had our drink. (My first and last at that time of day.) He eased back down, reached out, shook my hand and I left. He died fourteen hours later while we were flying over the Atlantic. He was a marvelous man!]

The Cotillion was the usual affair. All the girls were stunningly dressed in long gowns, all the young men were in tux and the music was provided by a Big Band playing all the wonderful music of the day. No girl caught my fancy and Amy Lu and I managed to avoid each other's feet while dancing. It was hard to believe such gaiety could exist in the midst of a raging, tragic war. On the way home, it started to snow again.

CHAPTER 18

THE FIRST MONTHS of 1943 saw signs that the war might be stabilizing. The Germans were no longer pushing our troops around and the Japanese onslaught in the Pacific seemed to be slowing. So many guys I knew were in the service. More than half of last year's graduating class were in uniform. All, in our class, felt certain our time would come and that belief instilled a different dimension to our lives. We took things more seriously but certainly extracted all the joy we could out of each day. My grades continued to improve. They remained at a safe passing level but the honor roll still failed to record my name. Over the Christmas break, when kids from the Public schools asked what my scholastic average was, they always laughed when I said 72. Most of them would tell me they were maintaining an average of 87 or higher. They couldn't believe it when I told them nobody received grades like that at our school and that the best students were lucky to receive an 83. In fact, top honors were won with that average.

Morale in our school was deteriorating. The prefects were doing a good job but the lack of support they received from Rev. Langdon was noticed by most and helped undermine their efforts. His, "Boys will be Boys" attitude only encouraged more students to flaunt the rules. Incidents of smoking became so common Mr. Myers, was openly fearful that the main building, an old wooden structure, would go up in flames. It became noticeable that the faculty was beginning to split along the older and newer masters. This led to a growing divergence within the student body, between the newer and older students. A number of us began to wonder if it wasn't time to start looking to transfer to other schools. Perhaps, it was just reflective of the winter doldrums but the feeling was too widespread to use that as an excuse.

At the beginning of the term, my ski interest changed. One afternoon, Bob Clausen coaxed me into climbing to the top of the ski jump tower. Looking down the track to the lift-off I was very nervous but somehow he inveigled me to slip my boots into the harness of a pair of jumping skis. He told me to slide the skis back and forth and crouch into a take- off position. I did but held on to the railing to make sure I wouldn't slip and go down the track. When I stopped and relaxed, I bent to take my boots out of the harness but before I could release them I felt a big push on my butt and off I went. It was impossible to stop going down without hurting myself. The jump was under me and I was propelled into the air. Forty-six feet later the skis touched down and I sat, sliding to the base of the hill. No bones broken and exhilaration pounding in my chest. The skis quickly came off and up to the tower I went. Down I came again. My jump was about the same distance and I fell once more. Determined, I tried again and again until I finally learned to spring into my jump, angle my body forward while in the air and land correctly.

My distance became better and jumping became my winter sport. I continued jumping for about five years and entered many a competition through- out the Northeast, never winning a contest. In fact, I don't think I ever placed higher than fifth. It didn't matter to me. It was just tremendous fun.

By March, the war news became better. General Patton had taken command of the North African campaign. The U.S. Army responded to his leadership in spite of some journalistic dislike of his flamboyant personality and the jealousies of more timid commanders. The victories being won built confidence in the troops and brought a new sense of optimism among the general public. The pins on the maps hanging on my wall began to move forward rather than back. Being naïve young boys, we were fearful it might end before we were old enough to participate.

Spring arrived, the Easter holiday came and the snow still lingered. Regardless of the remaining icy streets, Gordon Ferguson prevailed upon me to join him on his bike rides to Larchmont to woo Sue. He had got it into his mind that I should pursue Natalie. However, I had no illusions about my relationship with her. Good friends we were but there was no real romantic feeling. The rides became so frequent I started spending\ nights at his home because it shortened the roundtrip ride by six miles. Gordon liked to sleep late so I found I was up two or three hours before him. I couldn't understand why his mom let him get away with such laziness. She soon saw my boredom and put me to work tidying her yard of the winter debris, cleaning the garage and washing windows. I felt like a hired man. The answer should have been to get Gordon up at a decent hour but that was never considered. As much as I liked him, I knew he was lazy. I just couldn't believe how much he was indulged.

One day, everything changed. Mr. Ferguson came home. He was the CEO of a large paper company and spent more of his time away than at home. He had no patience with laziness and soon had Gordon hustling and toeing the line. Just how strict he was I soon learned. On the Thursday before Easter, we were off again to Larchmont to take out our dates. Mr. Ferguson told us we had to be back by eleven o'clock. We spent the late afternoon with our girls, cooked out at Sue's, even though it was cold, and then went to the movies. The movie was out at nine. We treated ourselves to sodas and then took our girls home. As he was leaving with Sue, Gordon said:

"Chuck, I'll see you at my house at eleven. Don't linger at Natalie's. It takes about forty-five minutes for us to get home. Dad's a stickler for promptness."

"Okay, let's meet on Palmer Avenue or I'll see you at your house."

I walked Natalie home where I had left my bike. As I was saying goodbye, the thought entered my mind that I should kiss her since I wouldn't be seeing her until summer. She looked at me. I looked into her eyes and could see she knew what I was thinking. We both smiled. I reached out and pulled her to me. The kiss was fun. We tried it again. It was more fun. We both started laughing. She slipped away and looked hard at me and spoke:

"Chuck, that was nice. Kiss me again and then you had better leave. I like you and we are good friends. Let's not get carried away."

I reached for her again and stole another kiss, then got on my bike and rode off. It was already eleven o'clock. To this day, I don't know if that was a clever brush off or a very sensible girl. In any event, we remained good friends for years. It was only after she married and moved with her husband to California that we lost touch.

Riding my bike, I was soon on Palmer Avenue but there was no sign of Gordon. I peddled as fast as I could to his house. It was twenty to twelve when I got there. Quietly opening the backdoor, I crept towards the front staircase. As I raised my foot to ascend, a voice called from the darkened living room:

"Chuck, would you please come in here?"

Nervously, I entered. Mr. Ferguson was sitting in his chair by the fireplace. He switched on a lamplight and said"

"Chuck, it is almost midnight. When I say eleven o'clock, I mean eleven o'clock. Gordon is home and already in bed. As our guest, you are expected to adhere to our rules. You cannot do as you like. I am very disappointed."

He continued to lecture me. I can't remember his exact words but they did hit me hard and my embarrassment was great. It was the most severe reprimand I had ever experienced. It lasted for nearly twenty minutes. He never took his eyes from mine. When I was dismissed and went to bed, I dreaded having to face him in the morning.

I shouldn't have worried. When I came down for breakfast, he was already there. Being the first up, we were alone. He was very friendly and we spent an hour or more discussing many different topics in a good give and take manner. I realized he was tough, said what was on his mind succinctly and I then decided he was an extremely interesting man. My admiration grew for him over the years. I'm sure, that worthwhile experience would never have happened if it weren't for my dalliance with Natalie. When I became older, Mr. Ferguson turned out to be one of my biggest supporters and we had many more interesting discussions. I was privileged to have him as an advisor of sorts.

Saturday turned out to be a surprise. Arriving home from the Fergusons, I found my sister entertaining a young man — Bob Clausen — the Head Prefect at Salisbury. Un-be-known to me, they had started dating over the Christmas holiday. They made a good couple and seemed to really enjoy being together. However, it seemed strange to have him as a suitor of my sister. We soon got over the awkwardness. He had already invited her to the spring dance weekend at school. They wanted to know whom I was planning on asking. My first thought was Natalie but then realized she had told me her cousin's wedding was on that Saturday. Bob said he'd be glad to fix me up with one of his sisters but I turned the offer down. Instead I started thinking I might ask Betty Bigelow. Johnny McCullough and I had taken many portraits of her and in so doing found her to be not only good looking but very funny. I was returning to school on Monday, so called her that evening. She accepted. On that promising note, Easter vacation ended.

I played on the varsity baseball team. It was the best the school had ever fielded. My specialty became bench warming. As the season progressed, it became obvious our game run totals were embarrassingly high. This eventually allowed for greater substitution. Playing in more games was the best training. By the end of the season, I had become a regular on the first nine, playing second base. That achievement was only reached because the normal second baseman had been injured. Luck always plays its' part.

CHAPTER 19

THE SPRING DANCE was soon upon us. Betty Bigelow arrived with a whole group of other girls from the Westchester area. My sister was also with that group. I noticed she tried to get my attention. After making sure Betty was shown to her quarters, I went in search of Nancy to see what was on her mind. I caught up with her on the front knoll of the main building.

"Charles, you have a problem with Betty."

"What do you mean?"

"She is acting awfully funny. Keep an eye on her and I will too."

"Okay. What should I be looking for? She looks ravishing. Are the other girls giving her a hard time?"

"I don't know what to say but something is not right."

"Gee. Thanks. I thought this was going to be a fun weekend. Are you sure you are not misreading her?"

"No. I'm sure something is not right."

On that note we parted and I went to find Betty. There was a baseball game that afternoon in which I was to play. I found her before dressing for the game and made arrangements for Jack Vigneron's date to accompany her to the game. It turned out to be a pretty dull game. We won 9 to 0. Afterwards there was a tea, then we all went to dress for dinner and the dance.

Dressed to the "nines", all of us with dates, assembled at the foot of the stairs to the girl's accommodations. We wondered what our dates would be wearing. As they started to appear, they all looked fabulous in their long gowns. A variety of spring colors seemed to enlighten the stairways. They were really a fascinating group of young ladies. Betty was one of the last to show. She appeared in a rose colored dress, cut daringly low. Her dark hair was swept up. A rose had been pinned amongst her locks that complimented her gown. She looked gorgeous! I quickly forgot my sister's warning, reached for Betty's arm and proudly escorted her into the dining room. Mrs. Myers looked at us as we passed her table and I heard her whisper to the Coach:

"Chuck's date is too exposed."

Embarrassed, I held Betty's arm tighter and prayed she hadn't overheard. I, for one, didn't think she was too exposed. From what I could see there wasn't that much to expose. It was not a comment that helped to make the evening begin with confidence. It was so unlike Mrs. Myers. I couldn't believe she was the one to dampen the evening's prospects.

The dinner and evening went off far better than that unfortunate affront. Betty dazzled all the boys. She danced with more partners than I could count. We laughed, kidded one another and even tried to tame a polka. She seemed to be having a wonderful time and I certainly did. The dance over, we escorted them to their stairway, sang, "Goodnight Ladies" as they ascended the stairs and grinned like silly fools. All evening, I had not seen my sister and her date except in the distance. They seemed in another world. I never had a chance to tell her that all had gone well.

The next morning, we met the girls for breakfast. My date failed to appear. Nancy Jane finally came down and grabbed my arm and walked me outside.

"Betty cried and carried on all night. We couldn't make her stop. She just sobbed and sobbed. Something is really wrong with that girl!"

"I can't believe it. We had a great time last night and she was beautiful and full of laughs. It just doesn't make sense. What could be the problem? We got on just great."

"Somehow, we have to get her to stop crying and come down. Why don't you write her a note for me to take to her?"

Not knowing what to say, I scribbled something like, I was waiting for her, had had a wonderful evening, was overwhelmed with her beauty and hoped I had done nothing too offensive. I then asked her to please come down. Nancy took the note up and finally Betty appeared. I could see she had been crying but said nothing other than she looked gorgeous. I then told her we could skip breakfast if she liked and instead go for a walk. She nodded yes, so off we went. Outside she started to cry again. I didn't know what to do. I looked at her and said:

"Betty, what's the problem? I'm so proud to have you here and I thought we were having a lovely time together. What would you like to do?"

She blubbered:

"I had a great time yesterday and particularly at the dance. It has been special. It's just, I can't stop crying and I don't know why. I feel so down. I'm frightened and don't understand why. This happens to me so many times but there is never any reason. Don't be mad at me. I want to be happy. I'm just not."

The crying continued and I kept holding her hand and had no idea what to do. She finally calmed down. We made Chapel in the nick of time. We sat in the back pew so we could leave if she started to cry. We made it through the service and left right behind the outgoing procession. Other people could see there was a problem and left us alone. We went for a walk in the woods so I could show her the cabins. She cried on and off but seemed calmer within herself. I was getting hungry, so asked if she thought she could handle lunch. She mumbled she would try. Entering the dining room, Jack Vigneron and his date called for us to join them. We did. In a few minutes, Betty was smiling and laughing as if nothing was disturbing her. She was that way the rest of the day until all the girls had to leave. She gave me a big hug when she left and said it had been a wonderful time and one she would always treasure. I was relieved to see the back of the bus. It was a most strange weekend. In four or five days, I received a thank you note asking me to be sure to see her as soon as I got home again. It turned out we never did get together.

The disastrous weekend over, school routine returned. Studies were hard but I was doing well with the exception of French. My tongue would not produce the strange sounds required. Comprehending the written word was easy. Verbalization and perfecting proper enunciation never seemed achievable. I became fearful of failing the course. Increased study didn't seem to help. When the final grades were posted, I passed all subjects, even French, but that barely. It was suggested I be tutored in that language over the summer. I dreaded informing my folks. Ron Erskine had asked Jack Zimmerman and me to visit him at his uncle's estate in St. Bruno, Canada, the third week in June. It was a great opportunity that I was now certain Dad would not allow because of the tutoring. Fortunately, the tutor selected was not available until after the fourth of July. After much discussion, it was decided I could go. My suspicion has always been, Dad decided it better for me to be in Canada rather than hanging around Scarsdale with time on my hands. He still was convinced trouble gravitated my way.

Before school ended, the yearly track meet was held. I came in first in the 100 hundred and 220 yard dashes, second in broad jump and third in high jump. The coach was particularly pleased with my time in the 100 yard dash. I ran it in 10 seconds. The fastest recorded in our league. I became determined to break my 10 second time.

The visit to Canada was the most adventurous traveling I had ever done. Jack had gone up a few days earlier with Ron. I caught the train to Montreal and then to St. Bruno by myself. At the station I jumped off the train and frantically looked for Ron. When I spied him and Jack, I was relieved. The next seven days were like a fairytale.

A chauffeur drove us to the estate. And, an Estate it was! We drove through a large entranceway, built of beautiful stone formed into pillars with a magnificent wooden gate that swung between. The manicured gravel driveway meandered through pristine landscaped gardens and past a picturesque chapel overlooking paddocks on one side and a golf course on the other. The drive separated and we took the right branch to the carriage house. It was here the three of us were to stay. After being shown to the room I was to share with Jack, I unpacked and cleaned up. I had arrived in time for the afternoon Tea. This was being served at the main house at 4:00PM. It was here that I was to meet our hosts, Mr. & Mrs. Birks. At the scheduled hour we walked to the house which sat on a knoll and was huge. Entering we were greeted by the butler. Gazing at the hallway, I couldn't help but notice the large dark oak staircase that circled up to the second floor. We were shown to the living room with an immense stone fireplace with the Scottish Arms of the family displayed above. I was then introduced to Mr. Birks. He was tall, with dark reddish hair, well-built and exceptionally strong looking. He was of middle age and looked every bit the part of a squire. As he surveyed me, I noticed he held a pipe in his right hand that he placed in his mouth as he reached to shake my hand. His greeting was openly kind which put me at ease. I then met Mrs. Birks. She was slim, on the small side with dark hair touched with gray. Her eyes were blue/gray and sparkled as she smiled. There could be no doubt that she was a shrewd, content lady. Her welcome relaxed my nervousness. I couldn't help but warm to her. Next introduced was Walter, Jr.

He was about my age, taller, wiry, wore glasses on a rather long face devoid of humor and emanated a barely restrained temper. We sized each other up and shook hands cordially. I then turned to join Jack and Ron at the window overlooking the large lake below. Suddenly, all seemed suspended, running feet could be heard in the hall, followed by a girls laughing voice. A vibrant fourteen year old girl burst in to the room. We were introduced and I immediately knew I liked her. She radiated happiness and intimated mischief. Her Name was Dianne Southerland, the niece of the Birk's. I could see that Jack was already under her spell but the most obviously smitten was her cousin, Walter. His whole appearance changed as he watched her. I could see it was going to be an interesting week.

Dinner was a grand affair. The long table seated twenty or more but this evening there was only the ten of us: Mr. & Mrs. Henry Birk's, Walter, Jr.(I can't remember whose son he was), Ron, Jack, Dianne, Sheila (Dianne's older sister, age 18), Donald (Dianne's younger brother), Mrs. Southerland and myself. Two maids served us and I couldn't help but notice the beauty of the china service, silver, crystal and linen. Discussion was light and easy to suit the different age levels. I did learn that the Birk's owned large tracts of land for lumbering and also owned a jewelry store in Montreal. Mr. Birks had been an ambassador for Canada to various European countries. He had served in World War 1 as an officer in the famed Scottish Black Watch Regiment. To say that I was awed is an understatement.

After dinner, I was given a tour of the Estate. Ron wanted to show me everything. The lake boathouse was larger than our home in New Hamburgh. There was a smaller building, further along the lake, with a living room, kitchen with fireplace and game room. Inside were ping- pong tables, other game tables, sofas and chairs, a Victrola, and bookcases jammed with records to play as well as a large upright piano and standing radio. This was the hangout for the young. From there we walked to the canoe shed, a dock with many rowboats tied alongside and a diving raft. Leaving that, we went to the tennis courts and then to the private golf course with its' own clubhouse. I think the course only had nine holes. When Ron had invited me, I had no idea what was in store. I began fretting that I might not have brought the proper attire.

It was getting late so the three of us went back to the carriage house and to bed.

When I awoke, the morning sun was streaming in our window. It was not yet six but Jack was already up. I quickly tumbled out of bed and suggested we go to the lake for an early morning swim. Slipping on our suits, we went out and ran to the shore. The scenery was breathtaking but not as much as the water when we dove in. I was out like a shot. Rugged Jack swam off to the diving raft. How he stood the freezing water I'll never understand. He tried to coax me to join him but I had more sense. Sitting on the pier, I watched him dive several times before swimming to the pier and raft. He asked me to give him a hand to help him out. Like a dumb idiot, I reached down and was promptly in. The second submersion didn't seem so bad but I didn't linger. We then decided to take one of the canoes for an exploration of the lake. Paddling along the shore, we passed beautiful birds chirping greetings and on the far shore saw deer drinking. They ran back into the woods as we approached. Turning around, we had a perfect view of the Birks' compound. The sight was beyond anything I could have dreamed. A more idyllic setting could not have been imagined. We returned to the carriage house and found Ron still asleep. We showered, shaved, cleaned up and dressed. Jack made breakfast with what he found in the refrigerator. It was one of the largest I had ever consumed and certainly one of the most delicious. Ron was still asleep when we finished, so we washed our dishes and put things away before leaving for a walk around the grounds. Returning, we agreed we would both make excellent squires.

Shirley and her mom weren't expected until early afternoon so Ron suggested we warm up on the tennis court. They provided a slew of racquets for guests to choose from. After selecting our preferences, we started. We completed three or four volleys and then Walter, Jr., Dianne and Sheila showed up. They all wanted to play. We drew lots to see who would be partners. I drew Sheila We then drew to see which partners would face off. Sheila and I were not part of the doubles so we played singles. She beat me 6 to 3. That disaster over, we all stopped and went to the cabin by the lake. We spent an hour or so playing games. It was then time for lunch, which was to be served in the cabin. While eating, Shirley came. She immediately took charge. Lunch finished, it was back to the courts. Shirley and I were to play Dianne and Walter. We beat them handily. Next we took on Jack and Sheila. We won. Walking off the court we noticed Walter in a foul mood. He claimed all my serves were done with a foot fault and I should have been disqualified in our last match. In the re-match he was going to call all my foot faults. Shirley came to my defense, which only made him scream at me more. I told Shirley to have Jack as her partner and I'd sit the set out. Walter would have none of that. He insisted I play. We did and Ron and Sheila acted as umpires. Every time I served, Walter called: "Foot fault!" Ron and Sheila would overrule him which only made him surly. I finally said to Shirley:

"I've had enough. Let's go for a swim."

She agreed. The score at that time was 4 to 0 in our favor. Walter still carried on and started swearing at me. I realized he had taken a dislike to my presence but I couldn't figure out why. It didn't bode well for the rest of my visit.

After the swim, which was still too cold, we went back to our quarters and changed for dinner. It was to be a cook out by the lake. It turned into a fun time. Dianne sat with me and apologized for her cousin. She told me she would be fourteen in three days and that a big party was being planned for her. The way she was acting I could tell she was a consummate flirt. She had all the boys in the palm of her hands. Jack later told me he found her to be the most fascinating girl he had ever seen. I told him to watch out. Her cousin Walter felt he had priority rights.

The next few days were a mirror of the first. Walter went out of his way to be rude to me. Shirley attempted to organize everything and keep him away from me in all the competitions. It became extremely uncomfortable. The evening of Dianne's birthday was spectacular. A huge bonfire was made, a five-piece band was hired to play Dianne's favorites, a deck was put up for dancing and twenty five kids of her acquaintance were invited. I danced with Shirley most of the time until later in the evening when Dianne and Jack came by, stopped and asked to switch partners. The next two numbers I danced with Dianne. Walter then cut in and gave me a shove saying:

"Leave her alone."

I couldn't help but think how childish this was getting. The evening ended with Shirley and me trying to do a rumba that was beyond my talents. Leaving, we all had to give Dianne a birthday kiss. When my turn came she whispered:

"Come to the house tomorrow morning about eleven."

After going to bed, Jack and I started talking about Walter and Dianne. He was as uncomfortable with Walter as I was. He thought Di was trying to flirt with all the boys but admitted he found her delightful. I told him what she had whispered to me. He laughed and said he wished he had been told to meet her. I confessed to being nervous about keeping the rendezvous and suggested he go in my place. He said no but that he'd go to the house with me. We soon slept.

Eleven the next morning found Jack and me at the main house. Dianne opened the door. We talked for a short time in the living room and then she said:

"Jack, would you excuse us for a minute. I want to take Chuck up to my room to show him the award I won at school."

I said:

"Can Jack come?"

"No. He's not interested in sailing."

"Are you sure it's alright for me to go up there?"

"Sure. Don't be funny."

Up we went. Her room was large. She walked over to a bureau and took down a plaque. It was inscribed:

"1943 Dinghy Sail Racing Champion — Dianne Southerland."

Putting it back, she said:

"See, I told you I was as good a sailor as you. Oh, come in the closet and I'll show you the picture of my dinghy."

We walked in. She turned and put her arms around me and reached up to give me a kiss. The closet door flew open:

"Mamselle. What are you doing? Monsieur, please leave at once."

I turned beet red and fled. The upstairs maid had caught us in the closet. Running downstairs, I yelled for Jack and bolted out the door. Halfway to our lodging, I told him what had happened. He laughed so hard he could hardly run. When we arrived at the carriage house, he blurted it all out to Ron. The two of them laughed even harder. I didn't know what to do. I thought it was time to start packing. When things calmed down Ron chokingly said:

"Chuck, don't worry. That is so typical of Di. She is a little devil. Everyone knows she is a terrible flirt. You are just another of her victims."

I kept a wide berth of her the rest of my visit.

Jack and I left two days after this incident. Aside from that fiasco and petulant Walter, it had been an unbelievable week. It had been fun, beautiful, elegant and enough to boggle the mind. I have never been to another place like it.

CHAPTER 20

THE NEXT TEN days were spent in Scarsdale waiting to go back to New Hamburgh. Having played so much tennis at St. Bruno, Jack and I wanted to improve our games. We decided to use the Edgemont School courts. The day after returning, we were on the courts about 10:15 AM. As we were playing, two girls arrived and started to play on the other court. Watching them, we realized they were pretty good players. When their set was finished, we asked if we could join them in playing doubles. Introducing themselves as Marian Logan and Billie Bailey they agreed. Marian was blonde, athletically built, with blue eyes and a smiling open face. "Billie" was on the thin side, about five foot three, with curly dark hair and an impish face. They were both a year younger than me and were students at Edgemont. The first set was boys against girls. The ladies won easily. We decided it best to change partners. Billie became my partner and Marian teamed with Jack. We lost quickly. In the second set we managed to hold them to a 7 to 5 victory. The sets over, we sat around talking to get to know each other better. When we were leaving, Marian said:

"How about playing again in the morning?

Jack immediately said he couldn't because he had a dentist appointment. Billie said she couldn't play either. That left two young people staring at each other. Marian said:

"Would you be game for singles?"

"Yea. OK. What time?"

"How about 10 o'clock?"

"Sure. I'll see you then, at ten".

So began eight days of tennis with Marian. It developed into more. We also found time for the movies, eating at each other's homes, going to parties and to become the best of friends. By the time I left for New Hamburgh, there was no question in my mind that she was the nicest girl I had ever dated. We enjoyed the same things, were both highly competitive, laughed at the same things and just had fun together. We promised to see each other as soon as I was back in town. For the first time, I wasn't anxious to leave for the island. That feeling left me as soon as I reached town even though I was faced with being tutored in French.

The tutor, Miss Green, lived in Hopewell Junction. To get to her place, I had to ride my bike nine miles. Following her directions, I rode down her road that first day not knowing what to expect. It turned out she lived on her folk's farm. Reaching the house, I leaned my bike against a tree and walked up the front steps. The door opened and there stood a woman in her forties, with dark brown hair tied back into a bun, glasses sliding down her nose, with no shoes upon her feet and a book in her hand. She spoke right up:

"Hello. You must be Charles. I'm Miss. Green. It is so nice to meet you. I didn't know what to expect. Your Dad hired me over the phone. He didn't tell me much other than that you needed to be tutored in French. Did you have any trouble finding our place? Please come in. We'll go in to the room on the right."

She didn't give me any time to respond or even say "Hello".

I walked in to the room, noticed an upright piano, several tables, lamps and a desk with chairs on either side. I moved to sit in one of them and she quickly said:

"Oh. Not there. Please sit in one of the wing backed chairs by the fireplace."

Re-directing myself, I sat in the one opposite the one where she seemed to be headed. It seemed a strange beginning. Very frankly, I didn't know what to make of her. Wasting no time, she opened her French book, turning to a page she had marked, handed it to me and asked me to read it out loud. It was all in French but I read it out in English.

"No. No. No. Monsieur. En Francois, Si vous Plais!"

I read again but this time tried to speak in French. Stumbling along, she interrupted me:

"That is terrible. We have our work cut out. Now, as I read the words out loud, you repeat after me. Listen to my pronunciation and mimic me. Don't be shy. Be bold. I will not laugh at you. We have seven weeks to bring you to the level of a good third year student of French. We shall work hard."

So began the summer of French.

The schedule for working on the hill was changed. The days of French required me to work in the afternoons from one to five. The normal hours were worked on the other days. There was little time for sailing but I tried to make up for that on the weekends. Most of my pals were now in the service. However, a new friend was made — Johnny Costello. His family had moved into town during the winter. They were renting a house directly across the bay from the island. Actually, it was my Aunt Nell who got us together. She thought we would get along and we did.

On the third day after returning to my town, I was at the Post Office picking up our mail when Aunt Nell saw Johnny going into Churchill's grocery store. (Johnny Myers had sold the store to him about three years previously.). My aunt kept looking for John to come out and when he did she called for him to come meet me. Walking towards us, I could see he was about my build, had curly dark hair, a smile on his face and a swagger that told everyone he loved the world. He was an Irishman through and through. Shaking hands, he looked me straight in the eye and said:

"Hi, rich kid. I know all about you. John Scardefield told me you might come from a rich family but you had a reputation of being a hard worker and not stuck-up. I don't particularly like to work, try to get out of anything that might require energy but love to talk to everyone about anything. My Dad says I'll make the perfect politician. We're Democrats. We are one of the few families in town that aren't Republican. So if you can stomach that, I guess we could be friends."

I was taken aback but had to laugh.

"My aunt wanted me to meet you but didn't tell me all those bad things about you. I'll have to give this serious consideration. You are probably even a Catholic, which makes it even more difficult. Why don't we meet at the Yacht Club after supper so we can talk this out?"

"I'm going there right after I take this beer home to my Dad. Come with me and then we'll go to the club."

"No good. I have to work this afternoon up on the hill but I'd like to get together with you this evening."

"Ok. If you have any vegetables ready up there, bring some with you. My Mom sure would appreciate some."

"My God, you sure aren't bashful! I'll see you a little after seven."

173

So ended our get acquainted meeting. As he strolled off with the six-pack, whistling some jaunty tune, I didn't know what to think. He was unlike anyone that I knew.

We met as arranged. I brought some of the last of our peas for his mother. He never once said thanks. As we sat on the Club porch looking at the river, we started a lively conversation. It lasted for hours. What we talked about I can't remember. Admittedly, it was enjoyable. We did have a different perspective on most issues but things never developed into heated arguments. We spent more time laughing than getting into serious discussions. It turned out to be an evening of light sparring and was the forerunner of many happy times. All summer we spent time doing things together. However, he had no interest in sailing, canoeing, fishing, woodchuck hunting, crabbing, hiking through the woods or, in particular, working. He was a city or town guy. He loved going to the movies, dancing with the girls at the community center, eating Italian food at restaurants of questionable reputation, watching others work and occasionally, swimming off the town dock. For that, the temperature had to be in the nineties and the water calm. Our friendship introduced me to an entirely different aspect of life. It proved an interesting education. He never passed anyone without saying hello and attempting to engage in conversation. Everybody liked him and all knew he was lazy. How he obtained his money was a mystery. His family was poor, his father was out of work, his mother was always home, two of his three sisters were too young to work and the one old enough to have a job was never home. Still, he always had more cash than I did.

The summer had other surprising happenings. Captain Drake had bought a new sailboat the previous year. It was one of the old J Boats, like the Endeavor II. It looked huge when it was under sail on the river, It would be on one tack and immediately have to tack again, never reaching its' potential sailing ability. The Captain had hired John Scardefield as crew to help maintain her but now that John was in the service he asked if I'd give him a hand. Because of my working and the French tutoring I didn't have enough time so turned him down. I did sail with him several times and it was a tremendous thrill. By the end of the summer, Captain Drake realized it was too much boat for the river and he had difficulty getting enough crew members to help him sail it. He sold it that fall.

In August, Dad had arranged to borrow a pickup truck to use on the hill. I was allowed to drive it even though I had yet to get my license. The restriction was that I could only drive it in town and from the island to the hill. One day while driving over the railroad bridge, I saw Marian Jensen(?) waving for me to stop. Pulling over, I asked what she wanted. She asked if I would drive her to Wappingers Falls. I immediately said yes. Marian was visiting the Rufs for three weeks. I had met her at the community center one evening. She was rather attractive, very well put together and pleasant. She lived in the Bronx but loved to come to New Hamburgh. I drove her to Wappingers, waited as she did some shopping and then drove her back to town. Feeling like a "Big I Am", my nerve allowed me to ask her to meet me at the community center that evening. She agreed. It was the beginning of many dates over the next two weeks. We danced, walked around town, went to the Yacht Club to watch the evening activity on the river and to talk about our dissimilar lives. It was fun, even though John Costello kept giving us a hard time. One night, John tried to get Marian to kiss me. She wouldn't, so he started pushing me to kiss her. I told him to stop embarrassing us. John never relented and told everyone in town that he'd get us to kiss eventually. He started having people bet on whether we would or not. Finally, it got so bad that during a dance at the center, he stopped the music and said:

"Now, Charles. Go for it!"

All the kids started to yell and egg us on. Marian started laughing and said to me:

"Come on let's give the whole town a treat."

We did. The uproar and clapping was hilarious. John was all smiles. I leaned over to Marian and said:

"That wasn't so bad. How about another?'

She threw her arms around me and we kissed for over a minute. I thought the place would go wild. The evening ended and I walked her home.

The next day, Aunt Nell cornered me in the Post Office and read me the riot act. She highly disapproved of the shenanigans of the night before. She liked Marian but was shocked that I would lend myself to a public display. In no way was I to lead that girl on. No matter what my protestations, she was adamant that it was wrong and demeaning to both of us. Fortunately, three days later Marian was on her way back to the Bronx. I received several letters from her, wrote her once but never saw her again. No, that's not right. We met thirty-three years later at a party. Neither of us mentioned John's bet and his resultant victory.

French lessons with Miss. Green were coming to an end. The departure of Marian allowed me to spend more time studying for the final exam. There were to be two sections of the exam. The first was to be verbal, consisting of a twenty-minute conversation with Miss. Green conducted in French. The second part was to be an hour and a half session of reading a French essay after which I would have to answer many questions. The answers had to be written in French. I approached the exam with confidence. My lessons over the summer had done me much good. The day of the exam turned out to be fun. I was able to converse reasonably well and the reading and writing was easier than I expected. After finishing, she read what I had written and then gave me a big smile:

"Bon, Bon!" She said.

This was followed by a big hug. We sat and talked for a while. She told me she had enjoyed having me as a pupil and that she was sure I would do much better in the subject. Knowing I had an interest in West Point, she tried to encourage me to pursue that dream. Biking back to the island, I couldn't help but think about her. Here she was forty some odd years old, unmarried with apparently no prospects, not that unattractive and certainly educated with a lively personality. I felt sorry for her. A few days later, I wrote her a note, telling her how much I appreciated all she had done for me and that I hoped we would stay in touch. We never did. Her tutoring job was over and I was off to other things.

The third of September saw the end of the New Hamburgh stay. My eagerness to return to Scarsdale was centered on one person — the other Marian. It would be nine days before I had to return to school. Those nine days just flew by. When I left for school, Marian and I admitted to each other that we were well suited and cared a great deal about one another. We pledged to remain that way. As close as we felt, I had not dared request a kiss. On the train back to school, I could have kicked myself for being such a wimp!

Chapter 21

THE BIG NEWS, on returning to school, was that Ron Erskine had been elected Head Prefect and Jack Zimmerman one of the prefects. They were a good selection as were the others chosen. In all there were eight prefects. Events proved they would have their work cut out in maintaining good school spirit and discipline. The Head Master seemed incapable of bringing the student body together or of giving his faculty strong guidance. The war was still overhanging everything. Casualties were mounting, the Nazis had been slowed in Russia, the African campaign was over, General Patton had taken Sicily and the press was in an uproar over his treatment of a soldier. Mussolini had been deposed in Italy and the Badoligio government sued for peace with the allies. Our armies were on the march but the Germans were still a force that most believed would take several more years to defeat, thus insuring a continued high rate of casualties. The Pacific theatre was also turning. The Japanese advance had been stopped but the re-taking of islands was costly. No quick end of hostilities was forecast. Instead, it was believed years would be taken up with fighting. All of us in school were certain we would have our turn at the horrific job of subduing these enemies. For the first time, students became aware of a divergence of opinion among the faculty concerning the war and of the participating nations. New masters, who had been hired over the summer to replace those that had left to enter either the military or take positions in other institutions, were more in tune with the Reverend Langdon. They were much more liberal, anxious to break with tradition, more casual and certainly less interested in preparing us for the rough and tumble aspects of life. Several were enraptured with communism and made no bones that the U.S. would benefit from adopting some of the ideas of that philosophy. Initially, I couldn't figure out why they were so critical of our country. All I knew is that their views made me uncomfortable. I soon learned that many students felt as I did. However, most of our new students found these ideas fascinating. This only increased the division within the school.

Coach Myers started football practice the second day we were back. I made the varsity as the starting halfback, punter and place kicker. In those days we played both offense and defense. Substitution was only allowed at a time out or at the end of each quarter. Many of us played the full sixty minutes. Our first game was the last weekend in September. We won. It was the beginning of an undefeated season. It was the best performance the school had in fifteen years. It was my good fortune to score more points than any player in the history of the school. I've been told it was a record that lasted for thirty-six years. The achievement was possible only because the team had so many good players and our line overwhelmed every other team. With such a good season the normal reaction should have been high morale throughout the school. It did not materialize. Discipline became a major problem. Smoking and even some drinking within the ranks of the sloppy and disgruntled became very noticeable. An attitude of "Boys will be boys" was still espoused by the Head Master. Ron and his prefects were hard put to maintain a well-functioning and happy campus. All of the masters who had been at the school for a number of years were frustrated and the new ones seemed not to care. All in all, it was a bad scene. When the Thanksgiving weekend came it was a welcome respite.

Instead of spending the holiday in New Hamburgh, it had been decided to stay in Scarsdale. I suspected my sister was behind this change. She had big plans for those four days. She and Bob Clauson, who was now at Yale in the V-12 program, hoped to spend nearly every minute of that time together. As for me, for the first time it was agreeable not to be in my town by the river over Thanksgiving. I hoped to spend the days with Marian.

That Wednesday night we did get together. She was as anxious as me. We went to the movies and then returned to her home. Her mother and father were there. As usual, they greeted me warmly. We had fun kidding one another. During our bantering, I learned that Marian had a half-brother that lived in Texas. Mr. Logan, it turned out, had been married before and it was his son.

I gathered Marian did not get along with him too well and it was for this reason she had never confided in me of his existence. He was five years older than her and was about to be drafted, so they were all flying out to Texas on Saturday. I was disappointed she would not be around the whole weekend but understood she had to go. When I left that night, we agreed to get together on Friday. It had been my hope to give her our first kiss as I was leaving but with her parents hanging around, the opportunity never materialized.

Thanksgiving was strange. Scarsdale couldn't compare with New Hamburgh when it came to a feeling of warmth generated by a home filled with family history and stability. It was like play-acting a Thanksgiving with all the surrounding new homes participating in a similar charade. I wished the war had never happened and all my friends were at the Yacht Club with me doing the normal target shooting, kidding each other and enjoying the river, hills, train whistles and the last of the falling colorful leaves. Those were good solid things, not the superficial gaiety and forced thankfulness experienced this day in Scarsdale. Perhaps this difference was a result of all being cognizant of the ever-present war, the worry of losing our friends to enemy fire and the feeling that reality had gone for a walk. My sister's delight in her time spent with Bob had been spoiled by the news received about a boyfriend of old. He had just been reported missing in action in the Pacific. The day was certainly a glum one. I phoned Marian in hopes we could get together that evening but her folks had company and their dinner was to be late, so that was out. I was glad when the day ended.

I called my girl at nine in the morning. It was an unusually warm day so we decided to play tennis. At ten thirty we were on the court with Billie and Bob. It was the beginning of a wonderful day. That night as we were returning from the movies we opened her front door and I reached for her, she started to turn and a voice shouted downstairs:

"Marian, say goodnight to Chuck. You have to finish packing."

Once again, I was foiled in my efforts to get my kiss. We did manage a small hug before I was out the door.

Walking home, I kept thinking what a fantastic girl she was.

Saturday, I kept thinking about her on the plane. It was hard to believe she would be in Texas in a few hours. I spent most of the day with Ron and Jack. They too felt it had been a strange

Thanksgiving. The next day we were on the train going back for the short period before Christmas break.

The day after returning, a school meeting was held after Chapel. The Reverend Langdon had a few announcements of innocuous importance and then stunned us all with his decision to hold a special school election prior to the holiday, to elect four fifth formers to a new group to be called: "The Fifth Form Committee". Its' purpose was to assist the Prefects in carrying out disciplinary action and to devise programs to increase school spirit. Everyone was dumbfounded over the idea. The most surprised were Ron Erskine and the other prefects. The Rev. Langdon had not even discussed his idea with them. It was a direct slap in the face to Ron and his associates. The only student with whom he had discussed the plan was my classmate, Bill Thompson. On learning of this, I knew Bill was scheming to ingratiate himself to the Head Master and had probably conceived of the plan himself. As usual, his duplicity caused much consternation within the student body and the faculty. I learned of the faculty displeasure during one of the Sunday afternoon teas held at Coach Myer's home. His wife, Jo, told me her husband had been taken totally by surprise and that Bill, acting on his own, suggested the plan to the Head Master and none of the faculty had ever been consulted.

The day before dismissal for the Christmas break, the students cast their ballots for the Fifth Form Committee and its' chairman. The masters cast their ballots after we had left. The results were to be made known when we returned.

It was a very cold December. There was no snow in Scarsdale when I got home, but there was thick ice on all the ponds. Skating had become the pastime of choice. As soon as I had unpacked, I called Marian. Her mom answered and told me she was still in school. They wouldn't start their break for two days, but she would be home between three and three thirty. Mrs. Logan also told me that her daughter had expected me to be home and wanted me to call her later. Shortly after three, I was on the phone and she quickly picked up:

"Chuck, it's so good to hear your voice. Let's get together. How about going skating?"

"Great idea. I'll be at your place in fifteen minutes unless you'd rather meet me at Crane's pond. We could save time and see each other quicker."

"Okay. That's a better idea. Billie would like to come also. See you in a few minutes. Oh, I thought you'd never get home. I've missed you."

"You must know you are all I have been thinking about since Thanksgiving. Don't be long."

Grabbing my skates, I hurriedly walked and ran to the pond. A giddy feeling infused every step. I was certain it was love on both our parts. Approaching the skaters, I could smell smoke from the wood-burning bonfire crackling several yards from the pond. Marian had not arrived so I looked for other friends. The first person I saw was Bill Leavitt. We had known each other since fourth grade but had never been that friendly but got along okay. Talking with him, I noticed a young girl hanging around trying to catch our attention. We ignored her. I kept looking for Marian. In a moment she appeared. All other people faded from sight. My eyes only had room for her. Walking toward me, she broke in to a huge smile. I reached out to give her a welcoming hug and she handed me her skates with a soft laugh. I became tongue tied, as did she. Laughing foolishly, we sat on a large log and put on our skates. We were soon on the ice, skating side by side, gathering our thoughts and attempting to calm down. She spoke first:

"It seems ages since Thanksgiving. I so wish you went to our school and not away for so long. Well, you are home now. I hope the next few weeks don't go bye too fast. Do you have any plans?"

"No, not really, just spend as much time with you as possible. I'd like to take you to my home along the river to meet my Aunt Nell and to see that side of my life. It is really very different but it is where I am happiest with the exception of being with you. Do you think your folks would allow you to go up there with me? We'd have to take the train from Tarrytown but I think my sister would drive us to the station."

"I'd love to go. You have told me so much about it all. I have to admit, it doesn't sound like a place that fits your personality so I'm doubly curious."

"Perhaps we can go up on Saturday. Why don't you feel your parents out on the idea?"

"It would be better if you asked them. I think they would like that. Mom asked me before I left for here if you would like to come for dinner tonight. If you do, you could ask them then."

"I'll have to check. Mom may want me to stay home since this is the first night home for me. I'll call you as soon as I can after skating."

On that note, we dropped the subject and concentrated on having a good time. That was easy. I think we were both on cloud nine.

When I got home, Dad had not returned from work. I told Mom the Logan's had invited me to dinner and asked her if it was all right for me to go. She said it would be fine as long as I was home by ten or ten thirty because it was a school night for Marian. I immediately called my girl before my mother had a chance to change her mind. Dinner was to be at seven-thirty so Marian suggested I get there by seven fifteen. When I hung up, my mother called to me:

"Charles, you must be here tomorrow night. Your sister will be coming home from college so we will all be home for a change. We don't sit down together enough, with both of you away. I'm sure you and your sister have much to tell us."

"Okay. I'll be here."

I thought it would give me an opportunity to ask about taking Marian to the country on Saturday.

The dinner at the Logan's was comfortably nice. Both parents made me very welcome, showed interest in my schooling, joked about how keen Marian and I seemed to be about one another, told me about their trip to. Texas to see their son off to the Army and told stories about each other's ineptness on the ski slopes. Apparently, their son was an excellent skier and hoped to get in to the Ski troops. We also discussed the war and their belief that it would last at least another four years. This brought up the question of what branch of the service I hoped to enlist in when old enough. When I mentioned my interest in West Point, they indicated an Army career was not one they admired. They thought I should look at other colleges. Mr. Logan was in manufacturing and even though most of their production was now geared to the military, they looked forward to peacetime and a resurgence of their core business.

After dinner we went in to the living room. Mr. Logan cleared his throat, looked straight at me and said:

"Chuck, You and Marian seem quite interested in one another which is fine with us but you are both young. Your education stretches before you both and you will certainly be in the service for a time. We know you are two fine young people but being close at your age puts many temptations in your way. Our expectations are that you will handle them properly, maintain high morals and keep in perspective the lives before you. Yours is a teenage infatuation. Keep it just that. Need I say more?"

I felt the blood rushing to my face. His comments had been unexpected and hit me like a sledge- hammer. All I could think was: How should I respond? Returning his gaze, I took a deep breath and said:

"Sir, it is obvious, I think Marian the finest girl I have ever met. We get along great, like the same things, enjoy doing things together but I assure you. I will never do anything to hurt her or her reputation. We both realize we are young and have many things to accomplish. We are friends, good friends and want to remain so. Neither of us have any illusions about our relationship. We know the limitations and are determined to abide by them."

"Thank you. I like you young man!"

So ended a discussion I had no idea was coming. Later that evening, I admitted to myself, it was good it had happened. It seemed to make everything a lot easier. In fact, it gave me the courage to ask permission to take Marian for a visit to New Hamburgh. It was granted with enthusiasm. Saying goodnight, Marian smiled in to my eyes, leaned forward and whispered into my ear:

"You handled that so well, thank you."

Sleep came slowly to me that night. There was so much to think about.

Nancy Jane came home the next afternoon. It was great to see her. She looked happier than I had ever seen her. I couldn't help wonder what was up. Before dinner we were alone in the living room, so I spoke right out:

"What's going on? You positively glow. Are you and Bob Clauson a serious twosome?"

"Oh, come on. Bob and I broke up months ago. He's at Yale in the V-12 program and since I've been at Briarcliff College, I've fallen head and heels in love with a cadet at West Point. I think I spend every weekend there. He is a second year man, tall, handsome, brilliant and mad for me. If I can get Dad's car, I'm driving up there tomorrow to spend the afternoon with him. His name is Pete Tisdale, he's from Kansas and wants me to meet his family this summer when he is on furlough."

"Wow! What do Mom and Dad think? Have they met him? It sounds to me you are rushing things. I'd like to meet him."

"No, Mom and Dad haven't met him but Major Pfiffer, who worked for Dad, is now at the Point and thinks Pete is terrific. He's told Dad all about him. I'm sure Pete will have some time off before the New Year and come here for a few days. At least that is what we hope. I think he plans on giving me an engagement ring when he is here."

"Gee, I guess you are serious."

"What's this about you and Marian? I really like that girl. She is not only good looking but also someone with a lot of character. Better watch out, some older guy will steal her from you."

"Hey, we are just friends, good friends. You don't have to worry about us. Anyway, we are too young to get seriously involved. I guess we respect each other too much."

"Listen to Methusala. Let me tell you, things have a way of accelerating faster than you can control."

"Is that experience talking?"

"Don't be smart. Just watch yourself."

Dad's coming home broke up our heart to heart conversation.

As soon as Dad had changed and washed up we sat down for dinner. It was the first family meal in a long time. Questions flew to both my sister and me. Answers were hedged in phrases obscuring the full story only to be delineated by my father's cross-examination. His legal background had a way of ferreting out that which we hoped to gloss over. He spent an inordinate amount of time on my scholastic achievements, clearly making known his disappointment that I had not yet made the honor roll. My athletic and extracurricular activities impressed him little. My sister, always known as "Monk" by Dad, escaped the dissection of her dismal scholastic efforts and instead was interrogated about "that boy from West Point".

I marveled how adroit she was in handling the deposition. By the end of the meal, she had both parents eagerly planning a coming visit from the paragon of West Point. She then wormed the car out of Dad for the trip to the Point in the morning. And this was during gas rationing. Amazing! On cue, I slid in the fact I wanted to take Marian to New Hamburgh and that "Monk" had agreed to drop us off on her way to her beau.

"Not on your life, young man! There is no reason for you to take that girl there."

"Dad, she has heard me talk about our home there, Aunt Nell and the island so much she is really interested to see what I've been talking about. Last night I asked her folks if they would allow her to go up with me for the day and they gave their permission."

"You asked them before checking with me to get my permission?"

My sister jumped in:

"Dad, I could drive them up, drop them off at Aunt Nell's, then spend the afternoon with Pete at West Point and pick them back up on my return home. Charles loves it there and I'm sure Marian is curious. She is a very nice girl, her folk's are good people. Even Mom thinks Marian and her parents are among the nicest people in town. I can't see anything wrong with Charles being allowed to take her there."

At that, Mom broke in:

"Reg, I think it would be all right for them to go. They are good friends and seem very responsible."

Dad laughed:

"I guess I have been out maneuvered."

Going to bed that night, I stopped at my sister's room and thanked her for making it all work out so satisfactorily. Earlier, I had called Marian and arranged for us to pick her up at nine.

Saturday was very cold, windy and cloudy. On the drive to New Hamburgh, Marian and my sister kept a constant exchange of stories centered on all of my shortcomings. It was excruciating to see myself in the light of feminine ridicule. By the time we arrived at our destination, I wasn't sure that Marian even liked me.

As usual, my Aunt was in the Post Office. Walking in, my sister shouted:

"Aunt Nell, we came to see you especially to introduce Charles' new love. Come say hello."

At that, my Aunt peered through the gated opening and gawked at my girl.

"So this is the girl that keeps my nephew full of sighs? I'm so pleased to finally meet you. I can see why he is so infatuated. Be careful of him, he chases all the girls."

As my Aunt opened the gate, Marian seemed tongue tied but finally reached out and took my Aunt's hand.

"Hello, Aunt Nell. I have heard more about you than of any other member of his family. You are very special to him. I hope to get to know you more. He says, you are his best friend."

My Aunt teared up and huskily said:

"Oh, you are so sweet to say that, he is like a son to me. Charles, you and Marian go explore the town. I'll be finished here by two and would then like to return home so I can prepare an afternoon tea for us. Be back to my house no later than four. Now, I would like a few minutes alone with Nancy Jane. Marian, it's wonderful to meet you."

As we started to leave, my sister said:

"Charles, I should be back from the Point around five-thirty or six. I'll meet you at Aunt Nell's. Be ready, we are all to have dinner with Mom and Dad at seven -thirty."

The next five hours, or so, were spent showing Marian my real hometown. From the island to the hill, the Yacht Club, the schoolhouse, the old family cemetery, sandy bottom, the town dock, the lumberyard and the long walk to the old family homestead which was now a Noviciate. I proudly unveiled my roots. We visited with Uncle Le and Aunt Gertie, Captain Drake, Bill Ferris, Charlie & Jenny Wicks and Captain Robinson. None of my friends were around, most being in the service. The River was full of ice but the ice-breakers had kept a channel open. Large chunks of ice were piled up along the shore. The only skating was in the bay between the island and the mainland. I introduced her to some of the kids skating but didn't join them because we hadn't brought our skates. I pointed out how we used to skate up and down the river and where the ice boating had been the best. It was a happy afternoon. Before going back to Aunt Nell's, we walked through the woods behind the Mahl Pond to "Lovers Leap", the legendary high rock cliff where it was said an Indian squaw had jumped, killing herself, because she was not allowed to marry her Indian lover. Standing at the high precipice, I reached out to my girl. She smiled and stepped to me. It was our first kiss. It felt so right. We laughed, held hands and walked back to Aunt Nell's. I don't think my feet ever touched the ground.

The tea prepared by my Aunt was delicious and we had fun telling Marian of all my adventures that had kept my Aunt in a state of fearful anticipation of my drowning or in some way getting lost. It was obvious Marian had made a very favorable impression. My sister came for us nearly on time. On the drive home, I kept wondering what Marian really thought of it all. It was certainly different from anything to which she had been exposed.

Dinner that night went very well. Dad had never been home when Marian had eaten with us. This time, it was obvious he was taken with my date. He regaled her with stories of his boyhood in our river town and when it was time for me to walk her home, he gave her a big hug and told her to come visit anytime, whether I was home or not. Both he and Mom liked her. On the way to her house she started talking:

"Chuck, this has been a very special day. I loved everything and everybody. They all were so warm and friendly. I visited a world I never dreamed existed. It explains an awful lot about the way you are. You are different from all the other boys I know. I have wondered why before but after today I think I understand. You are very lucky. It is difficult for me to visualize living in New Hamburgh but it certainly makes you more interesting than ever. Thank you for sharing so much and making the day so happy."

I didn't know whether she genuinely liked what she learned of me but did know she conducted herself beautifully in a strange environment. Saying goodnight to her was not the usual kiss-less affair. Our second kiss was even more thrilling than the first. I thought her wonderful. We dated most days right through Christmas. I gave her a scarf, which my sister thought appropriate for me to give. Two days after Santa had been, an incident occurred which changed everything. Dumb me!!

CHAPTER 22

ON THE EVENTFUL day mentioned, Marian agreed to meet me at the Pond for skating. Arriving about one half hour before we were to meet, I saw a group of twelve or so skating in a circular motion going faster and faster and then spinning off the end skater who would travel at high speed across the ice. This we called the "Whip". After putting on my skates, I pushed off to join the fun. Fifteen feet, or so, from shore, the latest whipped skater came crashing in to me. Down we went in a tangle. Scrambling up, I reached down to help the offending skater. A smiling face looked at me, rose and threw her arms around my neck.

"Hi, Chuck. You don't know me but I was determined to get to know you. I'm in Marian's class and all she talks about is you. I thought it time you noticed me. You'll find me a lot more fun."

Laughing, I responded:

"The way you careened in to me was no fun! You could have arranged a different introduction. We'll probably both be sore for weeks."

"I like to make memorable appearances."

"Weren't you down here the other day with Bill Leavitt? I think I remember seeing you peeking at me from behind him. I thought you were just a little kid."

"I'm not so little. I'll prove that."

She then grabbed my arm and continued:

"Come on. Skate with me."

Off we skated, around and around the pond, arm in arm, laughing and daringly keeping up a banter of innuendo. As we approached the shore near the bonfire, I saw Marian staring at us with daggers in her eyes. I dropped my partner's arm and skated

189

to my date's side. No warm, happy greeting was offered. Instead she said:

"Lucy, I see you are stalking another trophy. Don't you ever give up? You are becoming the talk of the town."

"Marian, I'm not the person talked about, it's you mooning over Chuck. Miss Proper, who doesn't know how to have real fun. You are such a dull goodie, goodie."

All I wanted was to escape the embarrassing spat which was becoming silly. I took Marian's hand and pulled her further on the ice. We started skating but I soon realized she was very upset and had lost interest in skating. She quietly said:

"Let's go. That girl always gives me shudders."

We took off our skates and started walking home. At the top of Old Army Road, she abruptly stopped and looked deeply into my eyes saying:

"Lucy is a terrible flirt. None of the guys she puts in her sights seem able to resist her. It will be interesting to see if you can. Don't think she won't keep trying to corner you. She loves to hunt but once she bags her prey she quickly loses interest. The two of us have always been at odds. Actually, I don't dislike her but do think she flaunts her charms too openly. I don't see myself as a prude but certainly believe there are limits on the way you should act. I hope you can understand what I am saying."

We continued walking to her house, both thinking and rarely talking. I realized the afternoon events had unwittingly changed our relationship. Her attitude towards me had changed to one of watching rather than of enjoying. The rest of the Christmas holiday we continued to date. There was no doubt in my mind that I was totally smitten with her. It seemed that Lucy's interest had withered, which suited me fine.

Returning to school, a whole new chapter in my life unfolded. The results of the election were made known. I had been chosen as the chairman of the Fifth Form Committee. This was an honor I did not want. It placed me in an awkward position vis-à-vis Ron and the other sixth form prefects. Elected to the committee were Bill Thompson, Jack Vigneron and Ed. Nash. Jack and Ed. were straight forward guys with whom I could easily relate. Bill Thompson was difficult. My first step was to meet with Ron Erskine. I impressed upon him that it was my desire to only support his and the other prefect's goals and to do those things which, if they tried to handle, might compromise their effectiveness with the bulk of the students. Our first full meeting was held with Ron and his group. It was decided our roll was to make recommendations to the prefects, enforce their programs and to attempt opening a conduit for all students to make their gripes, desires and frustrations known. The committee did work hard to raise moral and to quiet the rumblings of the dissidents. Success was minimal. Five months of frustration ensued. By the end of the year, Ron and I were still friends, Jack Zimmerman proved himself a rock of good sense, Bill Thompson exposed himself as being nothing but a schemer and it was my strong recommendation that the Fifth Form Committee be abolished forever. The whole fiasco showed that the school was extremely divided and that the newer students were different than those who had been enrolled before the Reverend Langdon became Head Master. The philosophy of the school was changing.

Studies remained a difficult pursuit. My scholastic average never seemed to rise and yet I felt improvement in nearly all my subjects. French was still my nemesis and Physics swung from great to tragic depending upon the segment. Most masters were very encouraging over my progress but it never seemed possible to send high grades home reflecting those sentiments. My relationship with most members of the faculty was very comfortable. I really enjoyed Coach Myers, Mr. Keur, Mr. Tappert and many others as well as the wives of those who were married. My problems were confined to the new breed of masters. Most were very liberal, did all possible to avoid military service, had soft spots for communism and never seemed enthusiastic about America. Mr. Feruski, one of the history instructors, spent more time praising Stalin than Churchill. Unfortunately, or fortunately, History was my best subject. This occasioned some interesting discussions between Feruski and myself to the delight of my classmates. One positive thing was I don't think these disagreements influenced my grade.

While studies always came first and the Fifth Form Committee consumed an inordinate amount of time, athletics brought happiness in abundance. This winter, I was really in to ski jumping. I never missed a meet and never came close to ever winning. It was just thrilling to try. Our school hockey team was undefeated until the next to last game. Kent school loomed as the major threat. The week going in to that game, our goalie, Ted Lilly, was taken ill. Coach Myers tried a number of players at that position, but none were happy or any good. On the Friday before the game, the coach and Ron, the team captain, asked me to fill in at the position. I quickly said no but was finally persuaded to give it a try. It was awful. At the start of the game I stood blocking the goal and watched the face -off and the puck being passed from one Kent player to another while they came down the ice. Ron swooped in, stole the puck, passed to Campbell and away they went to the opposite side of the rink. I started to relax. It was too soon. The puck was re-stolen and down they all came. Twenty-five feet from the net the Kent player made a slap shot towards me. The puck came fast, looked huge and sped by my gloved hand into the net. It was the beginning of a disaster. We lost 13 to 3. As our school paper noted, the score sounded more like that of a football game. My one and only time as a hockey player had ended as expected. The performance insured Ted Lilly,s fame as Salisbury's best goalie!

Easter vacation snuck up on us.Going home on the train I was thinking of Marian and how things would go between us. Our correspondence had been less frequent and decidedly cooler. I still wanted her to be my girl but was unsure of a reciprocal desire. Lost in deep musings, I failed to notice that we had stopped at Pawling, N.Y. to take on some passengers. My reverie was shattered by the commotion from questioning chatter. Was that Presidential candidate Tom Dewey and aide Herbert Brownell who had boarded the train? Excitement grew. One of our more venturesome students walked forward to the next car and shortly returned with an autograph from Mr. Dewey. We all rushed forward and asked for one for ourselves. Standing there, watching him scribble his name, he started asking us questions. First, what school were we from and then whether we were of voting age. Obviously, none of us were but he made us feel older and perhaps more important. He then commented he supposed most of us would soon be in the war and what did we hope for after the victory. None of us gave him any cogent answer but he insisted we should think seriously upon it because it was a very important question. At that, Mr. Brownell made it understood we should depart. As we were leaving, he requested we tell our parents to make sure they voted for Tom Dewey. It was my first brush with a politician. My biggest memory is that Mr. Dewey was smaller in stature than his voice let you believe. Back at my seat, my mind returned to thoughts of Marian.

CHAPTER 23

As soon as returning home, I called the girl who dominated my thoughts. We arranged to meet after dinner. With the last swallow of the food on my plate, I asked to be excused from the table and walked/ran to Marian's. When I knocked on the door it was quickly opened. There stood my blue eyed, blond beauty. She took my breath away. Her smile was radiant. Thoughts of coolness evaporated. We held hands, said "hi" and then I threw my arms around her and sought her lips. The kiss was like a surge of electricity. Breaking away, she whispered:

"My parents are in the living room."

We gathered ourselves and walked in. We spent a good half hour talking with them. It was easy because they were so friendly and happy to see me. Nevertheless, I craved to have Marian to myself so we could talk about what and where we were with each other. Mr. Logan seemed to sense my impatience. Smiling, knowingly, he said:

"Marian, why don't you take Chuck up to the game room so you can talk about all those things you'd rather not share with us?"

We both laughed and probably turned red and excused ourselves.

Entering the game room, we sat in chairs on either side of the upright radio/victrola. I leaned forward and looked at her. She returned my gaze and all of a sudden, it all seemed awkward. Finally, I blurted:

"Marian, you are more beautiful than ever. You have always been good looking but since we were last together you have really blossomed. Maybe, it's just that I've missed you so much and was afraid that the Lucy episode had changed things. Anyway, you are spectacularly gorgeous."

"Come on. You are over doing it. Obviously, Lucy is still on your mind and you are trying to appease me."

"You've got to be kidding. Lucy didn't turn my head. You are everything."

"So you say but I know you haven't seen the last of her. I call her the predator. She'll arrange something to turn your head."

"Hey, let's drop the subject. I'm here. You are here and all I want is to see you as often as possible. How about tennis in the morning? Maybe, Billie and Bob could join us."

"I've got school tomorrow. Our vacation doesn't start until Good Friday."

"Can we get together after school? Come to dinner tomorrow night and then we can catch a movie. I'm sure Mom and Dad would love to have you."

"Okay, that sounds good. I'll see if Billie and Bob can meet us at the movie."

We then started to play ping-pong and listen to music. Our conversation resumed a more normal pattern and things seemed to return to happy companionship. When it was time for me to leave, she walked me to the door. We kissed again but she soon pushed me out the door and said she'd see me tomorrow afternoon. Going home, I wondered if we were really back to normal. Perhaps she had another guy who had caught her interest. I decided to ask her.

The next afternoon found me at her school eagerly waiting her appearance. She came out the usual door with five or six other students. She seemed surprised to see me.

"Hey, what are you doing here? I thought you'd meet me at home."

"Couldn't wait. Hi, Billie, where's Bob?"

"He's at baseball practice."

Marian then introduced me to the others and then she, Billie and I walked to her home. Mrs. Logan was there so it was okay for me to go in with them. Entering the kitchen, Marian's mom looked up, saw me and gave me a big hug and kiss. I couldn't help but wonder why her daughter seemed so reluctant to follow her example. The three of us teenagers went upstairs to play table tennis and other games. The afternoon went quickly. Before going to my home for dinner, Marian changed into a dress that made me realize she had really matured. Wow! I thought she looked fantastic. When we got to my home, it was plain my Dad was of the same opinion. Dinner was easy, happy and quickly over so we could get to the movies on time. Afterwards we had ice cream sodas at Nielson's and then went home to Marian's. Leaving her that night, I asked:

"Are you interested in some other guy?"

"Oh Chuck. You are so dense. No. No. But I do get frightened over our relationship. I know it could get out of control. I realize that every time we kiss. I'm afraid neither of us would want to stop there and that would be terrible. We are too young and must be sensible. I want the best in life and to do things right no matter how difficult it becomes. Please try to understand. Of all people, I think you really do. That is only one of the reasons I love you so much."

I reached for her, gave a gentle hug and kiss and said:

"God Marian, I know you are right but I sure would love to kiss and cuddle you more."

"Chuck, Please. It's so difficult. Please go."

I found myself outside staring at a door. Walking home, I didn't know whether to scream, laugh or cry. One thing for sure, I knew I cared for her deeply.

The rest of the Easter break went by with the two of us together most days or evenings joined by either my friends or hers but no further discussions of that nature took place. I couldn't help but think of Lucy's portrayal of Marian as "Goodie, Goodie". Still, it was Marian that consumed my thoughts. On the train back to school, I realized I hadn't asked her to come up for the spring dance weekend. I wrote her that evening. A week later, I received a letter saying that she and her folks were going to her grandmother's over that weekend so would be unable to come. She ended by saying she couldn't wait for my return at the beginning of summer. Nothing seemed to be going smoothly for us.

Back at school not much had changed. The atmosphere was one of disinterest and waiting for the year to end. Studies did become more intense. Homework was piled on and the weeks rolled quickly along. Sports, again, were the bright spot. In early May, we all woke up to the fact that our Crew team was having a spectacular season. In their first three regattas they had been undefeated, beating all opponents by large margins. No group of students worked harder at conditioning themselves nor spent more time improving their skills. As week after week went by and victories accumulated, the whole school became enthusiastic fans. This, more than anything else, helped improve overall morale. The last regatta of the season pitted four schools against one another. Salisbury and Pomfret were both undefeated. The day of the big race saw the largest gathering of spectators along the banks of the lake to see the regatta. Salisbury handily defeated all the other crews. The thrill of that race gave pride to the school and cemented a happy ending to the year.

Our baseball team was not so successful. We won more than we lost and saw the development of some new talent that gave hope for next season. Because of the new talent, I was moved from centerfield to second base. It was a move that satisfied me greatly. My arm was never strong enough for the outfield.

Exams were the usual tense affairs. I thought I had done fairly well. Waiting for the results, my energy was directed to the track meet. I entered the usual events and finally achieved my goal of winning all I entered but didn't break the ten-second mark in the 100yard dash. It was my best track meet.

Two days before the graduation exercises, the final grades were posted. I passed everything respectably but again failed to make the honor roll. Ron Erskine and Jack Zimmerman both graduated. Jack had been accepted at all five universities to which he applied (Princeton, Yale, Harvard, Pennsylvania and Cornell). To say that he was brilliant is an understatement. Over the years, we had become best friends. Seeing them graduate made me realize how much their friendship had meant to me.

The day after returning home a momentous event occurred. We all awoke to the news of D-Day! The radio was kept continually on so we could catch any news concerning success. Besides the joy, there was a great fear of casualties. We all knew men who would be involved in the invasion. Even though we respected the strength of the Germans our hatred of the Nazis cannot be overemphasized. The false hope of the Dieppe raid, carried out by Canadian troops in mid-August 1942 with horrendous casualties (nearly 60%), helped make this invasion a greater cliff-hanger. That evening, we all went to church and prayed for success. I had arranged to meet Marian and join some friends but our get-together was cancelled so we could go with our families to the churches of choice. The next day was a continuation of waiting for news. A group of us, including Ron Erskine and his girlfriend, Debbie, gathered at Bob Naylor's home to follow the news reports and talk about those we knew who might be in the units storming the beaches of Normandy. It made those of us nearly old enough to join up for military service anxious to reach the age of enlistment. Ron was and enlisted later that month rather than wait to be drafted. His two older brothers were already in England and thought to be in the thick of it.

As the days passed and the success of the invasion seemed more assured, the general pattern of teenage living returned. The war was always there but we partied, listened to music, dated, played ball, went to the beaches and when we could afford it, took our girls to the "Log Cabin" in Armonk or the "Glenn Island Casino" in New Rochelle. We'd listen to the Big Bands, dance some and drink CoCa Cola or some other soft beverage. None of us tried to drink alcohol. It was something we were not into. Perhaps a few of the older teenagers drank beer but not many. It was an exciting time.

I had hoped to get some kind of job in New York City for the summer. Dad quickly shot that hope down. It was back to New Hamburgh and working on the hill for me. My disappointment was great only because I wanted to have the whole summer to court Marian. From the time school ended until going to the island, I had three weeks in Scarsdale. The first ten days were spent with her but then all changed. Her Dad received word that her brother had been wounded in action and was being flown back to the Walter Reed Hospital in Washington D.C. Marian and her folks went down to visit him for five days.

The first day of her absence, I just moped around, tried to read but was too upset in not having her around. Late that afternoon, being bored, I decided to walk downtown. Going in to Schonmocker's Drug Store, I bumped in to John Van Norden. We sat at the soda fountain talking for a few minutes and then started walking home. On the way, we were passing his home and he invited me in. We sat on his back porch chatting. I soon heard the screen door open. Looking up, I saw his next-door neighbor running towards me. It was Lucy McKewen! She flung herself into my lap, pressed her body to me and planted a moist kiss on my lips. I could feel all her curves, which were more than ample.

"Lucy, you better get off, you are darn near suffocating me!"

She giggled and held on more tightly, murmuring:

"I told you I'd capture you. What's the matter, why are you so red in the face?"

I pushed her and tried to stand. She slid down and grabbed me around the legs.

"I'm not going to let you go until you kiss me in return."

197

Trying to dislodge her, I could hear John laughing his head off. I started to get mad which only made him laugh more and Lucy to attempt pulling me down. Realizing it was hopeless I bent down and gave her the kiss. She let go, stood up and pulled her sweater in place accentuating her body more. I tried not to look. Taking my seat again, she sat in a chair opposite. She was damn pretty, had a beguiling smile and eyes that seemed to sparkle with warmth. Looking at one another, neither of us spoke. I was too confused and she probably calculating her next move. She spoke first:

"See, that wasn't too bad? I enjoyed it. Been thinking about you a long time, so when I saw you and John turning in to his place I decided it was now or never. When are you taking me out? I know Marian is in Washington to see her brother and won't be back for a few days, so why not escort harmless me to the movies? Tonight would be great."

"Lucy, you are too much. I'm not taking you out."

"Gee, you are afraid of me! Miss. Goodie, Goodie sure has you under her thumb. Be a man. Enjoy life. Don't spend your days pining for someone that runs dullsville. Be daring. Take me out."

"Sorry Lucy. I'm going."

"John good to see you I enjoyed our talk, you take Lucy to the movies."

"Chuck, she won't give me the time of day. We have lived as neighbors for too long."

When I walked away from his house, Lucy called to me:

"Chuck, perhaps tomorrow night would be better. You can't get away this easy. See you."

All the way home I kept thinking to myself: Why not take her out? Would Marian really dump me for one date with Lucy? There is no harm in taking someone to a movie. She is full of life. Her kisses left me cold, not the way Marian's made me feel. I'm strong enough to hold her at bay. What am I? Frightened of a girl? Perhaps I'll give her a call. It would certainly be better than hanging around doing nothing. Maybe I should go up to New Hamburgh early. Ops, then I wouldn't be here when Marian gets back. Oh well, I'll see what tomorrow brings. Going to bed that night, I could still feel Lucy sitting in my lap.

I got up early the next morning and walked down to Louie's pond. I hadn't been there in months. As I jumped across the stream leading to the pond, I heard someone chopping wood behind the house. Rounding the corner of his home, I saw Louie wielding the ax. He was stripped to the waist, sweat pouring off his glistening back and he looked gruff.

"Hey Louie, how come you are splitting wood in June? That's a fall job."

He looked up, put the ax down and slowly walked towards me. I thought I saw tears in his eyes.

"Hey Charles, long time no see. I'm pretty down. Last week we heard Henry was killed by the damn Japs. I'm gonna miss that boy. He was such a quiet, gentle young man. If I weren't so old, I'd go fight them bastards. Excuse me for swearing but I'm too undone to watch my language. Come on in the house. Mary Jo will sure love to see you. We often talk about you foolin around the pond. Remember that little alligator you thought you'd keep? We got a kick out of seeing you and Johnny digging a separate little pond for him. Those were the days. We hardly ever see kids down here anymore. I think they are scared of us black folk. Hell, what a world. White or black don't matter when a Jap shoots ya."

Stepping through their door, Louie called out to Jo:

"Hey Sweet, look whose come visit."

"I didn't dress for visitors."

"For this one it don't make no difference. He's like lost family."

"Why didn't he ---Oh my, is that Charles?'

She ran to me and swamped me with a hug.

"Honey Chile, where have you been? It has been too long since we seen you. Sit down. There's coffee and I have some biscuits. Sit, Sit. Now tell us all you're up to."

I spent the better part of the morning with them. It was like old times. They hadn't changed a bit. In fact, she looked exactly the same. Louie had some gray in his hair but still had the happy guile-less smile. When I left, it occurred to me they were the nicest couple I had ever known.

When I got home, I went out on the porch to read "Oliver Wiswall" by Kenneth Roberts but soon found myself toying with the idea of calling Lucy. Procrastinating for the better part of an hour, I finally went to the phone and called.

"Lucy?---"

"Chuck, I knew you would call. When?"

"What makes you so sure it's when?"

"'Cause I know we have to get together. You need to prove you're not afraid of me and I need to show you I'm not that bad girl you think I am."

"Okay' how about the movies tonight?"

199

"What time will you pick me up?"

"Six thirty for the seven o'clock show."

"No good. Let's make it at eight for the nine o'clock show. I want you to meet my Mom and Dad. I'm sure they are curious after hearing so much about you."

"Okay, I'll be there. See ya."

Hanging up, I wasn't sure I was doing the right thing but the die was cast.

Eight o'clock found me on Edgemont Road pressing the McKewen's door bell. The door opened and there stood a tall, rugged man giving me a penetrating once over.

"Good evening, Sir, I'm Chuck Van Anden. I have asked Lucy to join me at the movies."

"Young man, relax. I know who you are. You have been the subject of this household for weeks. My daughter can be tenacious, flirtatious and a handful. Come on in, she'll be down in a minute. He led me in to their living room and offered me a chair. I no sooner sat down than in walked Mrs. McKewen. Rising, I offered my hand and introduced myself.

"Chuck, you don't have to be so formal. I'm so pleased to meet you. I have heard your mother play the piano so many times. She is marvelous. Do you have her talent?"

Before I could answer, I heard Lucy coming down the stairs. Looking up, I became speechless. She looked more prepared for the opera than for a local movie. She laughed coming towards me:

"Mom thinks I'm over dressed but I told her I have never been out with someone so special."

I turned crimson. All I could mutter was: "Hi."

We all sat and my biography was explored. Lucy's life was also reviewed. But what else do you discuss with parents of a date? I was relieved when it was time to walk to town. I did think her folks were nice and they certainly tried to put me at ease. Lucy held my arm all the way to the theatre. She was easy to talk with and we started to enjoy each other.

After the movie, we went to Nielson's for the traditional ice cream. As luck would have it, Billie and Bob were there. Making the best of a bad situation, I immediately went to their table and asked if we could join them. The look from Billie was not pretty. The tension eased as time passed and we actually ended up having a nice time. As we parted, Billie whispered:

"How could you? Marian will be devastated."

When we got to Lucy's house she asked if I'd like to come in for a moment. I told her I had to be getting home. She thanked me for a great evening and told me she hoped we would go out again. There was no kiss. I wondered if, as Marian had said, the hunt and capture was the important part for Lucy and now she could set her sights on another.

At nine the next morning, my reading on the porch was interrupted by a phone call. It was Lucy.

"Chuck, it's Lucy. I know it's wrong for a girl to call a boy but I had such a wonderful time last night. How about going in to New York tonight? Dad has given me tickets to a radio show featuring Frank Sinatra. They are real good seats and I'd really like to see him. Please say yes."

"Oh Lucy, I don't know. Frank Sinatra is not one of my favorite singers and I'm not sure we should make a habit of going out together."

"Spoil sport. Please say you will. I'm not that bad, am I?"

My mind started whirling. What was happening? Marian will kill me. I'm only seventeen and I shouldn't let one girl prevent me from going out with others. Hopefully, she will understand and know she is number one, but with Lucy? She'll be livid. Why is it all so confusing?

"Lucy, the answer is ----??--Great, let's go!"

"Oh, I think I love you."

"What time is the show?'

"Nine o'clock at the ABC studios."

"Let's have dinner first. Nowhere too fancy, my pocket book can't stand much. Why don't I pick you up at five. We can catch the five-forty train in, have dinner and have time to get to the show."

"Yes. Yes. Yes. See you at five. Thanks."

Meeting her at five, I was overwhelmed again. She was beautifully dressed, looked as good as any movie star and absolutely glowed. My guilt over Marian kept pushing between us. Both girls were really something: one so blonde and classic and the other so dark and intriguing. I had to pinch myself to make sure it was not all a dream. What a quandary I was in!!

CHAPTER 24

STEPPING OFF THE train in Grand Central Station, we walked up the runway to the open gate. I noticed that most of the men couldn't help but give my date that particular glance indicating their envy over my good fortune. Lucy was very aware of the impression she was making. Holding on to my arm she murmured as we walked:

"Chuck, I so love being out with you. I'm so glad you agreed to come."

"Lucy, you are shameless. You just like being ogled by all the men. I'm just the crutch. You are really oblivious of me. It's fun watching how you gain so much attention, seemingly without a conscious effort."

"Oh, you are mean. I do like being with you. I thought it might never happen."

We made our way to a small restaurant just off First Avenue. It was her choice. Her Dad and Mom had taken her there several times. Actually, it was an Irish Pub. The food was good and best of all it was within the confines of my budget. It turned out to be a delightful meal and she was happy to be the center of the furtive looks aimed in her direction.

When we left the Pub we walked to the ABC studio. Over dinner, I had learned that her Dad was a VP at the station and that is why we got the tickets. Arriving at the show, we were ushered to second row seats directly in the center. When time came for the broadcast, a man popped out from the side curtain with cue cards for the audience. As the curtain opened, we duly followed our instructions: applauding, whistling, laughing, etc. The band started playing then faded as the announcer spoke into the microphone. If I remember correctly, it was the Lucky

Strike commercial. Then the female vocalist appeared, reached for the tall microphone and gave her rendition of "I don't want to set the world on fire". She received enthusiastic applause. (If not mistaken, the girl was Helen Forest). This was followed by the announcer trying his best to raise the anticipation of the audience for the introduction of Frank Sinatra. When he walked on stage I saw a very skinny man of medium height, with an adam's apple that kept bobbing up and down, wearing a suit too big for his frame. His hair was swept up in a greasy pompadour. None of that mattered. The audience went wild. The noise was deafening. The song he sang escapes me. All I can remember is that the audience was spell bound and when he finished there was no need for a cue card. It was a fantastic show. My opinion of the singer had changed. Lucy was more than enthralled and when it ended she took my arm and said:

"Let's go back stage. Dad has arranged for us to meet Frank."

"You go, but not me. I have no interest in pushing around him. In my opinion, he is a funny twerp with a reedy voice and a great publicist."

I was being stupid and really didn't mean what I was saying. The look she gave me should have warned me of the approaching storm. She dropped my arm and raced backstage. A half hour later she was back.

"Sometimes, you are a real jerk! You could have escorted me back there. He wouldn't have even noticed you and you wouldn't have had to talk to him. He had so many fans trying to reach him. It was only because of my Dad's authority that I got the opportunity to speak with him. He's nice. I gave him a kiss. I'm not saving any for you!"

At that, we made our way to Grand Central to catch our train. We hardly spoke during the trip back. We sat at least a foot apart. I kept thinking: "Well, I guess that's that." Walking from the train to her house, things started to thaw. At her front door, she took both my hands and looked at me:

"Chuck, you are mean and selfish. I never expected that of you, don't ever be that way again. Not with me or with anyone. It makes you out to be a complete jackass. Part of me wants to say: 'Get lost'. Another part wants me to give you a big slap, followed by a small forgiving kiss. Why did I ever want to get mixed up with you? What do you have to say?"

Upset with myself and embarrassed, I tried to think how I should respond. Finally, I summoned a few words:

"Lucy, you are right. I did not act properly. There is no excuse for my behavior, so I'll not offer one. I enjoyed all the other aspects of our evening. I even liked Frank Sinatra. You are very different than I expected. You are a nice, good and happy person. A lot of fun to be around and extremely interesting in the way you approach things. Our friendship, at times, confuses me. Let's not delve too deeply into our actions, rather, let's continue to be friends."

She stared at me for a long time and softly said:

"Ok, call me in the morning. I need more time to think. Goodnight, you exasperating idiot."

The door closed behind her and off I walked, wondering about the evening, my behavior, Lucy and what would happen. Marian was due back in two days. I had come to enjoy Lucy but ---- Oh well, time would tell.

The next morning, before I could call Lucy, Ron Erskine called. He asked if I'd like to go to the beach at Rye with him and his latest girl, Debbie Swanson. I told him I thought I was getting together with Lucy and was about to call her. He then said it would be great if I could have her join them also. At ten, I called Lucy.

"Hi Lucy, are you talking to me today?"

"Of course I am. It was difficult sleeping last night thinking about what a clutz you were yesterday. I still can't believe it was you. One of the things that attracted me to you from the start was your thoughtfulness and enthusiasm for just about everything. Let's try to forget it. It couldn't have been the real you."

"Thanks. I'll try to climb back in to your good graces. Anyway, Ron Erskine called me a few minutes ago and asked if we would join him and Debbie Swanson at Rye beach today. Debbie said she would pack a picnic. What do you think?"

"I'd love to go to the beach but not at Rye. We belong to the Westchester Country Club and I would love it if they would join us there. Mom is going in to the city today and I'll ask her if we can borrow the car to drive to the Club. I'll call you back in a couple of minutes after I've talked to her. Is that okay with you?"

"Sounds great, I'll call Ron and tell him what we are thinking."

When I called Ron, he was enthusiastic. By ten-thirty, Lucy had called back and said her Mom would let me drive their car and that she wanted us to eat at the Club snack bar charging it to the McKewens. They wanted the charges to help with their minimum.

By twelve-thirty we were at the club. It was the first time Ron, Debbie and I had been there. It sure beat Rye Beach! We found a likely spot on the beach and spread out our towels on the sand. The girls took their beach robes off and I thought Ron's eyes would jump out of their sockets when he looked at Lucy. She had on a one- piece suit but it certainly showed off her figure. I think Debbie felt the need to put her robe back on. The competition was too steep. Stretching out side by side we started talking. In a moment, Lucy rolled on her stomach, reached out with the Noxzema and asked me to rub it on her back. Being a good boy scout, I complied. She moaned sensually as I rubbed the sun lotion in. As I started to put the top back on the jar, she quickly turned over, clasped me around the neck and pulled me down to her, planting a warm kiss on my lips.

"That's for doing such a good job."

I became all flustered, looked at Ron gawking, saw the shocked expression on Debbie's face and didn't know exactly what to say, I inanely stammered:

"Should we go for a swim?"

"Chuck, why are you so embarrassed you know I love to kiss. Come here, let's do it again."

Ron and Debbie both jumped up and ran in to the water. Lucy laughed and said:

"I thought that would make them leave. Now I have you all to myself."

"Come on Lucy, don't make things so awkward. Ron is one of my best friends. I don't want to ruin his day with Debbie."

"Oh, all right. I'll behave but I've decided to kiss you, hug you and make you want to be with me all the time. I know who is coming back tomorrow and I'm not going to be pushed aside. I've never had so much fun."

"Is your fun stalking and sliding in between Marian and me, or is it just nice being friendly? You have me so confused."

"That's good! Now I'll try to behave but watch out."

"God, you are such a tease."

The rest of the afternoon, she acted demurely and we all had a great time together. I did notice that Ron could not keep his eyes from her. Whether Debbie noticed or not, I never found out. They continued dating for months. She was a very nice girl and probably had never come up against anyone like Lucy.

That night, Lucy and I went to the movies. When we got home to her house she invited me in. Sitting in the living room we started talking. The subject of Marian was on both our minds. She broached the subject first.

"Well, what's going to happen? Are you seeing Marian tomorrow? If so, what are you going to tell her? I'll bet Billie will say something before you can get to her. Poor Chuck. Two girls and you have to make a choice. I don't feel sorry for you at all. In the long run we will probably both dump you for someone better. You're not perfect by any means. Tell me your plan."

"I'm going to see her first thing in the morning. I don't want her to hear about our going out from anyone else. There is nothing wrong in my seeing you. I like you both. You are very different but I consider you both special. We are all too young to get involved so I don't see why we can't go on seeing whoever we want. I'm sure as soon as I go to New Hamburgh you'll have other boys to date and I'm sure she will also. It is a long road ahead before any of us can tie ourselves to just one girl or boy. A lot can happen between now, school, military service and college. I hope when I do get a chance to be around I can see either of you. We have to be sensible."

"You are a dreamer. That is not the way things work. We'll either bust up or continue our relationship. I don't want to bust up now. This has got to be played out."

"You are not making things very easy."

"I don't want to."

"Well, I better get going. Remember we are friends, just friends and I think that is the way we should keep it. As I have said, we're too young to be anything but friends."

"You can't leave yet. Kiss me."

"No. I like you a lot Lucy. We have had fun together. I'm seeing Marian tomorrow and in a few days I'll be in New Hamburgh for the summer. We'll see how things stand after that."

She got up and ran over to me and sat on my lap as she had at John's. Kisses came fast and furious. I could tell I had better leave in a hurry. I pushed her down, got up and said:

"Lucy, you are something. I have got to leave. I'll call you in the morning."

She held on to me and received another kiss before I could get out the door. But I did make it. I couldn't make up my mind if I was glad or sad.

Chapter 25

It was a sleepless night. I tossed and turned, was anxious but nervous to see Marian and very fearful she would be mad at me. Lucy's laughing face kept intruding. By early morning, I hadn't decided on how best to approach my returning girlfriend. All sorts of scenarios traveled through my mind. Around five o'clock I got up and went for a long walk up Fort Hill, back down to Crane's pond, over to the railway station and finally back home. Dad was just leaving for work. Seeing me he said:

"Boy, what's up with you? Where have you been? Is something troubling you?"

"Marian came home late last night and I'm going over to see her this morning. I don't think she will like the fact of my going out with Lucy these past few days."

"Why should that make a difference? You haven't been silly enough to lead her to the belief that she is the only girl you'll go out with? Both of you are just kids and should certainly have many girlfriends and/or boyfriends. Going out with her doesn't mean you are serious. I like Marian but put things in their proper perspective. You are only seventeen and she sixteen. You both have a lot to experience before tying yourselves into knots. Relax and enjoy these formative years. Just remember to always acquit yourself in a proper manner. I have told you before that we expect you to behave with decency and to handle relationships with the opposite sex in a correct and morally sensible manner. It's the boy's duty to be restrained. I've got to leave to catch the train. I expect you to do right!"

I knew what he said was true but it didn't make my task any easier.

At ten, I called Marian. She seemed pleased to hear from me and asked me to come over to her place as soon as I could. Feeling more confident our meeting would go all right, I changed into casual but nice clothes and hurriedly walked to her house. Her door was opened as soon as I knocked. I was surprised to see Mrs. Logan.

"Hi, Mrs. Logan, how is your son? Is he very badly wounded?"

"Not too badly but they don't think they will be able to save his left leg. He is taking it all very well. Says he's just glad to be alive. The doctors say they will make the decision on his leg within a couple of days. My husband is staying there for a few more days. He seems more upset than our son. Anyway, thanks for asking. Marian is up in the game room. You can go on up. It's nice to see you."

I hurried up the back stairs and there stood Marian. One glimpse told me she was the very best. She looked so beautiful, so serene and yet so vibrant.

"Hi. I've missed you."

"That's not the story I've heard."

"Okay, I have had dates with Lucy but that doesn't mean I didn't miss you. I ran in to her at John Van Norden's and one thing led to another. Before I knew it, she challenged me to take her to the movies."

"Go on. I know it wasn't just going to the movies. Tell me it all."

"Her Dad gave her tickets to the `Hit Parade' show staring Frank Sinatra and she asked me to go with her, which I did."

"Go on, there's more."

"We went to the Westchester Country Club with Ron and Debbie one day."

"I heard you were making a spectacle of yourselves. That you and Lucy couldn't keep your hands off one another and shocked a lot of people on the beach."

"Wow! You certainly have been filled in with all my foibles. What else have you heard?"

"That, that tart, has you drooling over her."

"Oh, come on, Marian. That's not true. I have really missed you. Lucy puts me on edge but with you I just feel happy."

"Don't try to get around me. Let's face facts. You enjoyed yourself with that, that hussy. If it had been anyone else, I wouldn't have minded so much but Lucy ---- what made you give in to her? I know how she operates and I thought you would see through her onslaught. You are nothing but a typical lecherous male, charmed by oversexed females."

"Marian, I hope you don't really think that of me. I admit I found Lucy fun to be with, admittedly forward but someone I could easily keep at bay and not succumb to her advances. In many ways she is a nice girl."

"Oh, my Lord you have really been taken in."

"Come on, let's talk about us. I think you are very special. There is no one I think more of or want to be around. Right or wrong, I think of you as more than just a friend. So often I just want to hold and cuddle you and feel the warmth and happiness of you. You once told me you really felt the same about me but were afraid it would start something we couldn't control. With difficulty, I agreed we should keep things from boiling over. We have to. I do realize that. However, I do think a little kiss and hug would keep us both happier. I know we are young but I think I really love you — just you."

"Chuck, stop it. You are making things so difficult. I care for you and I'm very jealous of your time with Lucy. Really, I think we must give ourselves a break from being together. You are going to New Hamburgh pretty soon and I'll be back and forth to Washington throughout the summer. Perhaps before you go back to school we'll get together. We'll just have to wait and see. I do like you more than you realize but I'm not going to ruin your life or mine. I think if we kept seeing each other things could be dangerous. I know myself. So please, let's slow down and see what happens. You can date anyone you want and, if asked, I'll date other guys. It will be a good test for us."

"I can't believe this! You indicate you want to be with me but won't be with me. I'm confused. If that is what you really want, I guess there is not much I can do. Remember, you are the girl I want to date. I care and respect you too much to make a big scene now and assure you, I am determined to have things turn out right for us. I guess that's it. I hope it is not for too long."

She nodded, smiled weakly and with moist eyes pushed me gently towards the stairs. I descended in a haze and let myself out the front door.

The next few days saw me really in the dumps. I didn't call Lucy but just kept to myself. I did play tennis with Bob Naylor several times. He had heard all about Marian and me from Billie and He asked if I was going to see Lucy to tick Marian off. I told him I hoped that she had joined the past. Little did I know the artfulness of that young lady.

A few days later, I was back in my river town. It was like surviving a storm and finding my way to the security of my homeport. There was work aplenty. When the spring thaw occurred, the heavy ice in the river started to move with the tide. There was so much of it and the spring tide so strong that it tore our bridge down. We were back to using boats to reach the island. Bill Ferris had already been instructed by Dad to start preparing for the rebuilding. The day after my return, we began. Since Bill was working on the railroad and I had things to do on the hill, our work time was limited to late afternoons and the evenings. We used oil lamps at night so we could continue until eleven. Weekends we worked fourteen or fifteen hours a day. If nothing else, it kept my mind from dwelling on Marian. Aunt Nell was very upset that I had allowed that "wonderful girl" to get away.

We finished the bridge in less than three weeks. It was much stronger, heavier and wider. We had also built ice breaking triangular shaped buffers on each side. The gate we made was far superior and my mother appreciated the greater security.

The summer also proved lonely. All my usual friends were in the service. Work was plentiful. I was very much in demand. I was kept so busy I stopped delivering vegetables through town, much to the annoyance of customers who had received produce free.

In mid-August, I received a letter from the Reverend Langdon at Salisbury School advising me that I had been elected Head Prefect. He congratulated me and hoped that we could work together to make the school year a memorable one. He also requested I return early so we could have a few days before opening to discuss various programs and responsibilities. The letter included a list of the other Prefects elected to assist me. I was pleased to be honored with the position but wondered if I could get along with the Head Master. In my response, I thanked him for his kind congratulations and said I would return to school two days early and that I would like to have the prefects return a day early, if that would meet with his approval. I never heard back. At the end of August, I wrote each of the prefects requesting their return on the day prior to opening. I heard from them all but Bill Thompson. The two silences did not bode well.

When my parents learned of my election their reaction surprised me. Instead of being thrilled, they merely said they expected it. I couldn't help but think of all that had happened since attending the school. I knew it had changed me far more than if I had continued in the Scarsdale schools. I hoped I would do a good job and instill a happier climate on campus.

On Labor Day, we left the island. It was the last full summer I would spend there.

CHAPTER 26

THE MORNING AFTER returning to Scarsdale I called Marian. Her voice seemed to indicate she was pleased to hear from me but she turned down my request for a date. I was devastated. We talked about many things and I told her of my being elected Head Prefect. She said she was very happy and proud of me and wished she knew more about that part of my life. I made it clear that was her fault because she had never accepted my invitations to come for a dance weekend. The conversation became more stilted. We soon said goodbye, promising to stay in touch.

That night I went out with Gordon Ferguson to the movies in White Plains. After the show, he mentioned he had heard that Marian and I were no longer going out and that it was because of another girl. According to him, that girl was supposed to be a real catch and he was anxious to meet her. I told him there wasn't any chance of that because I wasn't seeing her any more. When I asked him if he was still dating Sue Waterman, he admitted he was. Driving me home, (he had his folk's car) he asked if I'd consider joining he and Sue for dinner at Maxell's on Friday night. He suggested I be brave and ask "that Girl" Lucy. I finally said, I'd call her in the morning and then let him know.

I did get my nerve up and called.

"Hello"

"Mrs. McKewen?"

"Yes"

"This is Chuck Van Anden. Is Lucy at home?"

"Oh, Hi Chuck. She's downstairs. Let me call down and tell her you are on the phone."

"Thanks, Mrs. Mckewen."

"Hello, I knew you couldn't stay away. When am I going to see you?"

"How about going out to dinner with me tomorrow night? Gordon Ferguson has asked me to join him and Sue Waterman and bring a date. Are you game?"

"Who are Gordon and Sue?"

"Gordon is a long -time friend of mine, goes to school with me and is currently dating Sue, a girl from Larchmont. They are both nice people. Will you join us?

"Yes, of course. I've been hoping you would call. I only wish we were going to be alone."

"Lucy, this is to be just a friendly date. Okay?"

"Uh,Uh, but we'll see about that. What time should I be ready?"

"I'll call you back later once I know all the arrangements."

"Don't hang up, talk to me. There, I just blew you a big kiss. Get prepared."

"Lucy, it's just a friendly date."

"Okay. I'll be waiting for your call. Bye."

Hanging up, I was sure I had made a mistake. She certainly knew how to keep a fellow off base. I was beginning to wonder how she would act in front of our dinner partners.

Arrangements were finalized. I called Lucy back, told her I'd pick her up in my parent's car around seven the next evening and was surprised how normal she sounded, not the flirty thing as before. I stayed in that evening. My sister had come home. She and Pete Tisdale still were not engaged. After dinner we sat and had a good catch up talk. I learned all about her dreams with Pete, how Mom and Dad were not too thrilled with him, which only made things difficult. I gathered Mom was the biggest objector and Dad, as usual, was taking it easy on her. Nancy Jane then launched in to the bust up between Marian and me. She took Marian's side and had nothing good to say about Lucy. When I told her I was going out to dinner with her the next evening, all she said was:

"Watch it boy. I've said it before, that is one designing girl with plenty of ammunition. I'd hate to see you get too involved. I know she has all that a guy dreams about but that is not necessarily good."

"You too? She is really not as bad as you think. In fact, she is darn nice perhaps a little forward but certainly nothing to worry about."

"You are so innocent."

"Let's drop the subject, okay?"

"Yea, but be careful."

On that note our brother/sister chat came to an end.

I arrived at Lucy's right at seven. As I got out of the car, she opened her door, raced down the front walk and threw her arms around me:

"You're back. I knew Marian couldn't take you from me."

"Lucy, it is not about Marian. It is just you and me joining friends for dinner. Don't make something out of this that it isn't."

"You'll see. Come in the house and say hello to my folks. Dad really likes you. Thinks you are the best boy I have dated."

We had five or ten minutes of chit chat with her Mom and Dad and then left, with instructions to be home by mid-night. I thought it would be more like 11:00PM. Driving off, I soon found Lucy snuggled up close to me.

"Lucy, give me breathing room. You'll have me driving off the road!"

"Spoil sport."

She slid inches away and we talked of what we had done all summer. According to her, it had been very dull. I found that hard to believe. One thing, she wasn't a person surrounded by dullness. When I told her I was going back to school early, her only comment was:

"We'll have to squeeze a lot in over the next few days."

She was incorrigible!

Arriving at Maxell's, I noticed Gordon and Sue had already arrived. Entering, I looked around and saw Gordon and Sue by the window, waved, took Lucy's arm and guided her towards the table. Gordon stood up, stared at Lucy, ignored me and said something inane. I bent to give Sue a peck on the cheek and then introduced her to Lucy. They shook hands politely but I could feel the atmosphere turning to ice. Sue regained her composure as Gordon focused more attention upon her. The meal was good, reasonable enough and as the evening wore on the music became more pronounced and festive. We danced, watched others trying to do the Polka and had a very pleasant time. On the whole, Lucy acted very demurely and Sue was her usual "in control" self. A little before mid-night, we said goodnight and each couple drove off. No sooner were we in the car than Lucy was back snuggling.

"Lucy, please. Let me drive, it has been a nice evening and I don't want it to end in a disagreement. You come on too strong you scare a guy. If we are to be friends we must try to act more like adults."

"That's what I want. Let's act as adults."

"Lucy, you know what I mean. Now stop this foolishness."

"You really are a chicken, aren't you?"

"I'm not answering that!"

"Okay, I'll be good if you promise to take me out tomorrow. Is that a deal?"

"Yes, but just a local movie. Maybe we can get Bob and Billie to go with us."

"Oh, my God. You are really afraid of being alone with me. Too bad."

Thank goodness, we had reached her house. I walked her to the front door, we had a friendly kiss and I was on my way back to the car. She called out:

"Chuck I had a wonderful evening. Call me in the morning."

I had escaped unscathed!

In the morning, I decided to call Marian. Two more days remained before returning to school. I hoped she would agree to get together and go to the movies with me. When the phone rang, I crossed my fingers, hoping she would answer and not her mother.

"Hello."

"Marian, it's Chuck. Don't hang up. I want to talk with you. First, I miss you. Second, in two days it's back to school for me. Third, will you go to the movies with me tonight?"

"Oh, Chuck. I miss you also, but we talked about giving ourselves some room so we'd keep things on an easier footing. It is difficult but something tells me we really should."

"Is that a no?" I'll be away for months so that should give us the room you are talking about. I'd just like to see you before I go back."

"Oh, alright, let's go to the early show."

"Great. I'll pick you up around six thirty. Thanks."

Hanging up, I started to believe everything would work out. I hoped so anyway. Now I had to call Lucy. I didn't want to and certainly felt our relationship should end.

"Hello."

"Lucy, it's me."

"I knew you would call. Are we seeing each other tonight?"

No, Lucy, I'm taking Marian to the movies. I think we should call it quits. You are a great girl but I think we both should give our relationship a rest."

"Oh, my God! That iceberg has gotten to you again. You know we have more fun together than you have with her. I can't understand you. I'm not taking this for the end. You'll see, in a few weeks you'll be calling me and probably wanting to get together over Thanksgiving. I'll be here. I'm not that proud. Tell that prude she'll never beat me."

"Lucy, that's it. I think the only reason you go out with me is to show Marian she can't compete with you. It's not that you think so much of me. Instead, it is all about your ego."

"You'll see. I know you find me more than fascinating."

"You are right. You are a lot of fun. Have a good year. You are really something. Bye."

I was glad that was over.

Six thirty that evening found me at Marian's door, nervous over what to expect. The door opened and there stood my girl. I wanted to grab and kiss her. But all we did was say" "Hi." Walking to the theatre, we talked about everything but us. The movie is a blank. I spent almost the whole time looking at her. At Nielson's we had the usual sodas and still kept the conversation light. She did let me hold her hand as we made our way to her house. Opening the door, we found that her parents had already gone to bed. The living room was ours. I started to speak:

"Marian, I care only for ---"

She quickly turned and rushed to me, threw her arms around me and kissed as I had often dreamt she would. Our kiss lasted for minutes, each holding on to the other as tightly as we could. I didn't want it to ever end. We finally parted.

"Oh, Marian, I have longed for that from the first week we met. I'm in love with you!"

"Chuck, I've loved you from the very beginning. You must have known."

We held each other again and kissed more fervently. My heart was racing and I could tell she was in the same state. Parting again, she quietly said:

"There, now you must know. Don't have any doubts. This is why we must give everything a rest. We are far too young to feel so deeply. I know that if we continued it would only lead to a very big problem. The only way we are ever going to avoid disaster, is to break away until we are older. If in a year, or so, we get together and still feel this way we can let things happen normally. I have talked to my parents about us and they agree but wish it were different. Do you remember my Dad talking to you one night after dinner? Do you recall what you told him? He remembers and has told me it was then that he realized you were an exceptional young man."

"God, Marian. I don't want to go so long without you. I like being together. You are different than any girl I have ever known. We are happy together."

"Chuck, that's not the point. If we are ever going to have a chance, we must give it a break. Please, I have thought about this. It is not what emotionally I want but I am determined to do things right for us. Knowing you, that is what you will come to realize."

We talked more but found no other path to take. How we came to say goodnight I can't remember. I know we hugged and kissed again and then I found myself walking home.

On the day I was leaving to return to school, my sister asked:

"What's gotten in to you? Where is that smile and joyful outlook? You act as if you are fearful in returning to school."

"I never could fool you. No, it's not school. It's all about Marian and me. She insists we must break it off for a year. You'd think I was an uncontrollable fiend. She says, it's wrong for us to feel this way at our age. I just can't figure it all out."

"You worry too much. You have to go back to school. Don't let the relationship with her interfere with what you have to do there. I shouldn't tell you this but I'm proud of you and thrilled you are the Head Prefect. Do the best job you can. Somehow, it will all work out with you and Marian. She's a neat girl, has a lot more sense than most. I think she's great."

The pep talk helped little.

CHAPTER 27

TAKING THE TRAIN to school gave me time to re-adjust my thinking to what lie ahead. The responsibilities of being Head Prefect were daunting, particularly when into the equation was thrown the Head Master and my wariness. From the start we had seemed to view the school in a different light. I realized he had every right to set the tone and it was my function to help the student body adjust to his new ways. Could I follow his lead if it was so diametrically opposed to my beliefs? For weeks my mind had been wrestling with this question. Up to now, my conclusion had been that it was my duty to do so. After all, I was only a student: He was the ultimate authority. I had seriously toyed with the idea of not accepting the position but convinced myself that it would test my ability to handle an awkward situation and ultimately make me a better person overcoming my tendency to be unreasonably stubborn.

The cab ride from the train station to the school seemed faster than normal. Arriving, I made my way to the Head Master's office. I knocked on his door:

"Come in."

"Good afternoon, Sir. It is great to be back."

"Welcome, Chuck. I appreciate your coming back early. There is much for us to discuss. I want this year to be the start of a very good relationship between us. The voting of the students and the faculty clearly showed the confidence they have in your leadership. Their support is vital. I know many still view me as the new Head Master and think of you as a strong product of the school's traditions. Hopefully, we can show that the future is a continuation of tradition building, as in the past. Changes are always inevitable and must be expected. I have instituted some and desire to continue with others. Your cooperation is essential in their being established successfully. I am counting on your cooperation."

"Sir, I'll do my very best."

"Thanks, I'm happy you understand. Now, go get settled in your new room and come to the house for dinner. Say, around seven-thirty."

The rest of the afternoon, I did get settled and also walked around the campus. It was very quiet without the other students. Passing Coach Myer's home, his wife, Jo, called out:

"Chuck? Won't you come in and say hello?"

"Hi. Mrs. Myers. It's good to see you. Is the coach around?"

"Of course he is. Come in. He's in the living room."

As I entered he shouted:

"Chuck, I heard you were coming in today. Congratulations on being elected Head Prefect. All of us wish you the very best. Please sit down."

For over an hour we sat and talked. It became clear he was not too happy with the way things had been going and was counting on me to help make all run a little more smoothly with greater school spirit than last year. By the end of our discussion, I wondered if it was going to be so easy and if the majority of the Masters where unified in their support of the Reverend Langdon.

My next stop was at Mr. Keurs. He gave me a warm welcome and congratulations on my election. As usual, he didn't let me forget our past conflicts. In his view, they were instrumental in bringing me to my senses, even if they didn't produce a top scholar. No mention was made of what the Reverend Langdon planned. He seemed more relaxed than I had ever seen him.

When these visits were over, it was time for me to shower, dress and go over to the Head Master's house. When ushered in by the maid, I heard a familiar voice in the other room. Anger and disappointment swept in upon me. It was Bill Thompson. Entering the room, I saw him sitting with the Rev. and Mrs. Langdon. They all rose. Mrs. greeted me with her usual phony smile and the Reverend turned from Bill and said:

"Chuck, I have asked Bill to join us in our discussions after dinner. He has been here for the past two days and we have had some very successful meetings which have helped outline plans for the year."

I was stunned! How could they be so underhanded? I had been elected Head Prefect and Bill, as one of the Prefects, supposedly worked for me. Obviously, he was up to his old tricks trying to maneuver his agenda behind my back. It was all I could do to be polite. I couldn't help but feel the Head Master was deliberately trying to shove me aside regardless of the election. The evening and the school year were off to a terrible start. Admittedly, dinner was delicious, the conversation evasive and stilted, while Bill preened over his successful fait accompli as the great politician. I had never trusted him and now realized he was out to subvert me at every turn.

At five AM, I was up and walking through the woods to the cabins. I needed to walk off steam, adjust my thoughts and decide what to do. Again, I thought seriously of resigning. In the end, I came to the resolve that I would never let them get the better of me. To hell with them both! I would do the very best I could to ignore Bill's interference, support the Head Master when I could but never give in to those things which involved my core beliefs. I was not happy but became very determined. The walk lasted for more than three hours but when it was over, I felt better.

That day we had two more meetings. At the first, Bill showed up. He tried to dominate the discussions and was allowed to drone on and on. At the end, I told the Reverend I had come back to meet with him on a one to one basis and that under no circumstances would I participate in any further sessions if Bill was to be in attendance. I emphasized that I was the Head Prefect and Bill worked under me. The room went quiet. I just sat and waited for the Reverend to comment. He finally did and agreed to meet with me alone from then on. It was a small victory but, to me, essential.

We met later that afternoon. When I arrived he greeted me but not too warmly. An attitude of annoyance seemed to surround him. He started by saying:

"Chuck, I'm the Head Master and my authority is to be unchallenged."

"Sir, I understand you are the Head Master and have every right to run this school as you see fit. I also fully realize I am just one of many students here for one purpose — to get an education. My being elected as Head Prefect was unsought. This is my fifth year at this school and I have come to love it for a variety of reasons. As the new Head Prefect, I view my job as the main person within the student body whose responsibility is to help implement those policies you desire. I also believe it is my responsibility to advise you of the reception those policies are receiving and offer suggestions as to how they may be made more understandable if some resistance is encountered. Secondly, my job is to help in maintaining discipline while doing everything possible to generate an `esprit de corps`. The other Prefects are there to assist us in accomplishing those goals. Giving the appearance that you favor another as Head Prefect or that there are two Heads, will only dilute my effectiveness and indirectly yours. Bill Thompson was not elected Head Prefect, I was. Your show of confidence in my leadership is essential. If I do not have it, I respectfully resign. The choice is yours."

"Oh, You are, as always, blunt! No, I don't want your resignation. It is important we work together but I also intend to keep communications open between me and the other Prefects. In that way, I will maintain a more rounded picture of the feelings of the students. I need the cooperation of all, including the faculty."

"Sir, I have no objection to your discussing anything with the other Prefects. That is as it should be. What I would find difficult are discussions occurring without my being informed of the relevance they have to my responsibilities. If decisions were reached by you and other Prefects and implemented without my knowledge or input, it would subvert my effectiveness and, in the long run, yours. I hope you understand. Not to be pushy, but do you agree?"

"Yes, I can see your point. It is essential we cooperate. Are you sure I can count on your cooperation?"

"Of course, that is why I was so eager to return early so we could start on the right foot."

Our first confrontation ended on that note.

The next day, the five other Prefects arrived. Bill Thompson had made himself invisible until we all met for our first meeting. The group was enthusiastic, confident and happy to be singled out. All were good friends and we made a great effort to bring Bill into the fold. We accomplished a solid understanding of how we would operate together in gaining the trust, confidence and good will of all attending the school. Our first priority was to make certain all were warmly welcomed, particularly the new boys. As the days progressed we felt things were off to a very good start.

The new school year brought more new masters who had been hired over the summer months. Many were replacements for those who had been called into the service. War was still raging. The allies had landed in Normandy back in June and were pushing the Germans back, the Soviets were relentlessly pushing the Nazi army back and the Japanese were taking their lumps in the Pacific. However, they made every island and atoll we captured a place of dead and broken bodies. Our flame- throwers were rousting or roasting them from their caves. War was showing the brutality of mankind and all of us at school were certain the future would find us in the thick of the carnage.

Classes started the day after all had returned. I knew it had to be a good year for me scholastically if I ever hoped to be accepted by West Point, which was still my choice. One subject loomed as the "toughie" — chemistry. Mr. McEnery was the master teaching the course. He was new, young, had an Irish temper, liberal, 4F and a conscientious objector to boot. His quick wit made him popular with a large segment of the student body. He chose me as a target, calling me: "The FBI tyrant trained to thwart the forward march of history by subjugating a large segment of the students." He, like Mr. Feruski, was ultra- liberal, enraptured by communism. We spent the better part of the year poles apart.

Football became a passion with me. The previous year my performance had proved record breaking. I wanted this year to be a continuation but it soon became obvious we had lost many good players from graduation and that our team was about twenty pounds lighter per position. Our spirit was good. We had speed but lacked a good passer. These facts underlined that my past record was due to the team not to my abilities. As our first game approached, we suffered the loss of our best end to a knee injury. The game turned to be a real frustration.. We lost 20 to 12. Our second game we were slaughtered 38 to 6. The third game we won 19 to 13. Our fourth turned out to be pivotal. At half time, we were behind 12 to 0. The coach of Gunnery told our coach at the end of the halftime break that it was the best his team had ever played against us. Coach Myers just smiled. He had seen a weakness in their defensive unit and told me to run every other play through their right tackle. That meant Tom Hewett, our left tackle, would have to knock his opposite out of the way on every other play. Tom had never been much as a player but this day he excelled. He knocked the guy off consistently, allowing me to run through the resultant hole, gaining ten or twelve yards a play. They never recovered. We won 33 to 12. Tom became our hero and the team melded in to a good unit.

The school was excited over our win. Driving on to campus, we were greeted as returning heroes. Tom was boosted on the shoulders of some of the happy students and paraded to the gym. As we all entered, we were stopped by Bill Thompson. He was editor of the school newspaper. Even before Tom was handed down to the floor Bill yelled above the cheers:

"Tom, I hope you can have the story of the game on my desk before dinner."

"Gee, Bill, I played the whole game and didn't have time to watch, take notes and think about a story for the paper."

"You are our sports reporter. I need that story."

I couldn't resist:

"Bill, Tom played a spectacular game He's the reason we won. It will be very difficult for him to write you up a story of the game, he was too busy to accurately describe all that happened. Why don't you interview those who were there watching, some of the other players and the coach and get your story that way?"

"Chuck, stay out of my business. Tom's my reporter and he should quit if he can't do the job. I've a paper to run."

"Get off it Bill. Give Tom a break. Let him bask in the praise he so well deserves. He was really good out there. Don't you think winning the game is more important than writing a story?"

"God, there you go again, always giving me a hard time. You really are a bastard!"

It was all I could do not to hit him. Instead, I grabbed Tom by the shoulders and said:

"Come on, let's get cleaned up, believe me, we are all proud of the way you played."

Unfortunately, that was not the end of this most ridiculous confrontation. Later that evening, Bill had another row with Tom. At the time, no one knew of it but it all came out in tragic circumstances.

Monday it was back to schoolwork and football practice. Things seemed to calm down after our successful football victory. That night I got to bed shortly after ten, exhausted. At two-thirty in the morning, I heard running feet coming from the main building to my dorm, then a loud knock on my door and Harry Bartley calling:

"Chuck! Wake up! It's Harry. Tom's missing!"

CHAPTER 28

IT WAS A hectic night. Opening the door for Bart, I said:

"What do you mean Tom's missing?"

"Something woke me up about an hour ago. I thought it was Tom leaving the room to go to the bathroom. After thirty or forty minutes, I went looking for him to see if he was all right. He wasn't in the bathroom. I looked all over our dorm but he was nowhere to be found."

"Has he ever done anything like this before?"

"No, Tom has always been very predictable. You know, he's quiet, a bit of a loner but very thoughtful. A nice guy even though he does give the impression, at times, of being somewhat effeminate. Actually, I don't believe he is. His interests are of a more gentle nature, like poetry, art, music and reading. Personally, I think his family has probably sheltered him too much."

"Well, that's not telling us where we can find him. Has he been upset about anything recently?"

By now, I was fully dressed and my mind was whirling around trying to guess what Tom was up to.

"Bart, let's divide up. You search the main building, the furnace area and check your room again and see if he has returned. If not, check to see if he has taken any clothes, other than what he would normally wear. See if he has left his pajamas anywhere. I'll check this dorm, the classrooms downstairs, the gym and the ski barn. Meet me back here as soon as you have checked everything or found him."

Out the door he ran and I started my search. It took only a few minutes to check the sleeping quarters of the Dorm. I went next to the basement where most of the classrooms were. As

I approached the chemistry lab, I could see the door was ajar. Switching the light on, I found nothing. Closing the door, I smelled something unusual. I walked further down the hall and came to the small lavatory. I tried to push its' door open, something was blocking it. I pushed and pushed and finally got it opened enough to put my head in. The light was on and looking behind the door I saw Tom hanging from a rope around his neck. A stool under him had turned over and was wedged against the stall, blocking the door. Also on the floor, in the far corner was a chemistry beaker with liquid in with smoke or heavy vapors rising from it. I yelled:

"Tom! Tom! Tom! Please say something!"

There was no answer. I backed off and then slammed myself at the door. It moved a little. I slammed again and heard the stool make a scraping sound on the floor. Again I slammed. The stool moved a little more and I had just enough room to slip through. The stink was awful. Tom's bowels had erupted, his urine was mixed in the mess and the stink from the chemicals was suffocating. I reached for Tom, tried to push him up to take the pressure off his neck and kept shouting his name. At this point, I felt a hand on my back.

"Chuck? Oh, Jesus! Let me help."

It was Bart. He had returned and not finding me in my room had fortunately come looking for me. Together we were able to raise Tom up enough to loosen the rope so Bart could slip it from his neck. We carried him into the hallway. As we laid him down, I was sure he took a breath of air. We gave him artificial respiration the best we knew how and in a few minutes we were rewarded with coughs from him and eyes that fluttered. Bart ran into the chemistry lab and found some towels which we wrapped around Tom. In a few minutes, he was weakly responding to our voices. I became more confident that we had reached him in time. I wondered what to do. There was no way I wanted him to be seen by other students. I decided to ask Bart to run over to the Head Master's house, wake him and tell him what had happened and get him to come to where we were. Fifteen minutes later, He was back informing me that the Reverend wanted us to carry Tom over to his house as surreptitiously as possible. We did. Bart grabbed Tom's legs and I put my arms under his shoulders and up over his chest. We struggled while carrying him but we kept shouting at him the whole time in an effort to make him respond. It was a hard trip but we made it. Thankfully, Bart was a big guy — six foot two and about 175lbs. As we walked, he pushed Tom's legs to either side of him so he could take more of the weight. We never would have made it if it hadn't been for him.

By the time we got to the Head Master's house, we were sure Tom was going to pull through even though he failed to talk. He just looked at us and refused to say anything. Even when the Head Master talked to him he didn't respond. The Reverend called the nurse. She was with us in minutes. Giving him a quick check over, she said she was very optimistic. She was sure he would survive and that in time he would talk but not to push him too hard. It was her opinion, based on other suicide attempts she had seen, that he would adjust his mind and talk guardedly but refuse any acknowledgment of what he had done.

Now that things seemed under control, we were told to go back to our rooms, try to get some sleep and come back to the Head Master's house in the morning. As we were walking back, I thought of the mess in the lavatory and asked Bart to give me a hand in cleaning up and putting things to right so none of the other students would see, which would surely arouse their curiosity. He agreed. It took us a better part of an hour. We finally got back to our respective rooms as daylight was breaking. I went to bed but couldn't sleep. Instead, I started to shake. It was difficult to erase from my mind the scene of Tom's hanging. I kept asking, why did he try to do such a terrible thing?

Breakfast in the dining room was difficult. Bart and I took different tables so we wouldn't be tempted to talk about the night's event. After chapel, Langdon stopped us as we walked out. He asked us to go over to his house for a meeting. He did this in a rather loud voice so others could hear. He later explained, he wanted others to know he had called for us to meet so no mystery would surround our absence from classes. When we arrived, Tom had been cleaned up and been given a pair of the Reverend's pajamas to wear. He seemed to look through us but did manage a listless "Hello". That over, Langdon asked us to step in to the study off the front hall. As we entered, he said:

"Chuck, Bart. I can never express enough of my gratitude for what you two have done. You acted in an exemplary fashion and have saved the school a very tragic occurrence. I will never forget your alertness and thorough manner in which you acted in saving Tom's life. Bart, would you be kind enough to return to your room and select some clothes for Tom and bring them here. I would like him to be dressed properly when his family arrives."

Bart left and the Reverend clasped my hand.

"Chuck, Thank God you acted so promptly and so discreetly. I am forever indebted to you. I now know why you are so popular and so trusted by the faculty and students. I'm glad you are the Head Prefect."

That sentiment lasted for only a few months.

After Bart returned with Tom's clothes, we were allowed to join our classes. Admittedly, it was difficult to concentrate on the subjects and involve myself in discussions concerning them. Football practice that afternoon helped to bring things back to a more realistic venue.

Back in my room after practice, I had no sooner settled down to study than there was a knock on my door. After calling: "Come in", the door was opened and in walked Mr. Hewett, Tom's father.

"Chuck, I will always be in your debt. You saved my son's life. Why he tried what he did, I can't understand. Do you know of anything that may have triggered this tragedy? He has always been such a good son. He has always been sensitive but a very happy boy. You have known him since the third grade. Can you understand what has gone wrong? Tell me if you know of anything. We just can't imagine what made him take such a drastic action. It is so unlike him. Do you have any ideas?"

"Sir, I am and was as shocked as you. As you say, I have known Tom for years. We have never been close but always considered ourselves friends, not close but friends. This is so unlike anything I would have thought he would do. He is really liked by everyone. I can't think of anyone who has ever been knowingly mean to him. He is a very good student, has had a good year on the football team and is involved in many other activities. It's all really beyond me."

"Chuck, if you ever learn of anything that may have caused this, please let me know. We are taking him home with us for a few days. Hopefully, he will return to his old self. I don't want him to be away from school for too long. I think that might cause more problems. When he returns, I would appreciate your keeping an eye on him and do all you can to make everything as normal as possible. He knows you were the one who saved him. He might be resentful. I hope not but we don't know for sure. It may prove to be a difficult time for you but I am confident you will handle it well."

He reached out and took my hand:

"Thank you from the bottom of my heart. We can never repay you enough. Mrs. Hewett and I have agreed that you will be remembered in our wills. We owe you so much."

"Sir, please, you don't have to do anything for me. I'm just glad we found him in time. "

We shook hands and he departed.

The next morning after chapel, Reverend Langdon called a school meeting. We all filed in wondering what to expect. He made a few announcements concerning some minor schedule changes and then announced that the day was a declared special holiday in appreciation of the Head Prefect and the other Prefects. He said since he had become Head Master he had never been so impressed with the boys in those positions. It caught us all by surprise and the students gave us a resounding ovation. They always thrilled to an unexpected holiday.

Another more surprising thing quickly followed. The last Saturday in October, I received a note in my mailbox from Mr. Keur. It asked if I would please meet with him at his apartment on Sunday afternoon at 4:30PM. It was a most unusual request because the Masters rarely interrupted the free time we had on Sundays. I couldn't help but wonder what it was all about. Our relationship had developed from total warfare, to an advisor to student and recently to an acknowledgement of mutual respect and friendship. He, more than any Master, changed my attitude toward learning and helped to develop the manner in which I viewed and approached the conflicting choices life threw at me. On that Sunday, I was prompt on knocking on his door. As I entered, he appeared to be nervous.

"Chuck, find yourself a seat. I'll have tea made in a jiffy. Help yourself to those cookies on the piano."

I took some cookies and sat. In two minutes he was back with the tea. Sitting across from me, he leaned back and smiled nervously.

"I have something of great importance to ask of you but first, an announcement. I have proposed to Jane Tyrell, she has accepted and we are getting married here in the chapel the second Saturday in December, right after school breaks for Christmas vacation."

Jumping up, I shook his hand and said how delighted I was for him and Jane. I knew her fairly well. She was the sister of a student who had graduated two years previously. Many times she had been up to see her brother and on several occasions I

231

had seen Mr. Keur take particular notice of her but had no idea that things had progressed so far. She was an attractive girl with a lot of energy and an outgoing, happy personality. I thought the match would be wonderful for them both.

He glowed with happiness once he had made the revelation. We sat back down, relaxed, talked about his intended and savored our tea. He then became more nervous.

"Chuck, I have two favors to ask of you. As I mentioned we are to be married here in the chapel. Reverend Langdon will officiate. The service is Episcopal and I have never been baptized. To be married in the Episcopal Church, one must be baptized. The second Sunday in November, the Bishop is coming to baptize a number of students and he has agreed to baptize me in a private ceremony later that afternoon. I very much want you to be my Godfather."

I almost fell off my chair. I think I actually burst out laughing. To say I was overwhelmed is an understatement. I groped for the proper words with which to respond.

"Sir, I am nearly speechless. I'm flattered but can't help but ask: Why me? Surely the Church would not allow me to be your Godfather. You are thirty-four and I'm only seventeen."

"Chuck, I have already discussed this with Rev. Langdon and the Bishop and they, nor the Church , have any objection whatsoever. There is no one I would rather have than you to do that honor for me. For nearly five years I have known and watched you grow and mature. Truly, if Jane and I are fortunate enough to have children, I would like my son to be as you are. Please, accept the responsibility."

I felt as if all being said was unreal. How could I refuse his request? Stalling for time, I said:

"Sir, why not ask one of the other Masters? I'm sure they would be honored. If I say yes, how will it look to the other students? I'm deeply honored but surely someone else would be more fitting."

"Chuck, I have considered others but you are the person I want to assume the responsibility. As for the other students, you are no longer in any of my classes and frankly I don't care what they think. It is not their decision."

I could see his determination and the disappointment in my evasion. My decision became easy.

"Sir, I would be honored. You have my hand on it. I accept."

That handshake was one of the most emotional I had ever experienced in my young life. When we sat down, he smiled and said:

"Now, my second request. I would like you to be the usher at the wedding. Mr. Tappert will be my Best Man and Maggie Wright, Jane's closest friend, will be the maid of Honor. We would all like you to be the usher. It will be a fairly small wedding so there is no need for more."

"Are you sure? I can think of many others — Masters and friends — who would be very pleased to be part of your wedding."

"Chuck, I want it to be you and so does Jane."

"Again, I'm honored. It will be my pleasure. You can count on me."

The next half hour or so we talked of other subjects. In a way, I felt awkward but kept thinking how very much the school had changed me. The man who was to become my Godchild had played a large part in that transition. How I used to fear him. Surprises seemed to be forever thrust from the unseen path of living. Our "tea" soon ended.

"Chuck, thank you. Now get out of here and go study. Oh, incidentally, I consider you a close friend. When we are not doing school business, please call me,'Wim'. Thanks."

Walking back to my room, I couldn't help but wonder why this all had to happen to me. I wasn't too sure it would go down too well with the student body. Mr. Keur was not very popular and many made fun of him. He and John Myers were all that were left from the Quaile years — with the exception of Mr. Tappert who was never forceful in his views. I often wondered why he stayed at the school.

CHAPTER 29

BESIDES THE PREVIOUS goings on, a number of us were involved in preparing for the fall dance week-end. It was to be held on the last weekend in October. Unfortunately, at the beginning of the year, I had been prevailed upon to assume the chairmanship of the Dance Committee. There were five of us on the committee: Bert Wright, Harry(Bart) Bartley, Ed. Nash, Bill Thompson and myself. It was our job to select and hire a band, arrange for accommodations for the girls, enlist chaperons from Master's wives, select the menus for all meals, coordinate the serving staff with the kitchen personnel, install the decorations, provide corsages for the girls, which hopefully would not clash with their gowns, and enlist bachelor students to attend, to insure "cut in" personnel for our delightful partners on the floor. We expected the usual number of dates to be between fifty and sixty. In preparation, dance cards and programs of the weekend had to be printed, prizes selected for the several ridiculous events and a photographer found to record the merriment. Our greatest worry, as usual, was to make certain all couples clearly understood the rules and regulations, particularly for the Sunday luncheon at the cabins. It consumed an inordinate amount of our time.

My enthusiasm for the weekend was muted. I dearly wanted Marian to be my date but knew it would not be so. Our late summer discussions had put a final period to that. My mind reviewed all the girls I knew who might be willing to come. Seventeen days before the dance, I decided on Lucy with doubts, fear and anticipation. I wrote her and received her reply in five days. She accepted with glee. I became fearful she would turn the school on its' ear and worried that her seductive manner might overcome my weaknesses and cause embarrassing results. The die was cast and I looked forward to the weekend with trepidation and dread.

All these concerns dwindled on the arrival of the big dance weekend. The day was picture perfect with a blue autumn sky and a balmy temperature of 66 degrees. There wasn't a cloud in the sky. Our dates were scheduled to arrive at eleven on that Saturday. All of us were waiting eagerly. When the taxis arrived, there was much pushing and shoving to open the doors of the vehicles. Admittedly, my anticipation was not as high as most. I still wished it were Marian I was greeting. Then I heard my name called:

"Chuck. Over here! I thought we'd never arrive. This place is really in the country. All you can see is mountains and trees. No wonder all you guys are gawking. You live like hermits!"

"Hi Lucy, you're right. We are all gawking. We don't get a chance to see or be with girls very often. In fact, there is not much social contact. It is why these weekends are so important for us. You look wonderful. It's great to see you. Thanks for coming."

"Are you kidding? I was thrilled when you asked me. Are we going to be alone together?"

"Lucy, stop it. Forget those thoughts. This is a weekend to be spent with friends and having a great time together. It is not a time for lover assignations and other foolish romantic notions."

"You want to bet? I didn't come all this way to share you with others."

"God, you are such an artful flirt. Let's just have a good time. You do look fabulous. You'll be swamped by admirers."

"That's what I want, to be swamped and admired by you. Don't I even get a kiss?"

Making no answer, I located her suitcase, took her arm and led her to the stairs leading to the accommodations for the girls.

"Go up and get settled and I'll meet you here in about twenty minutes. We'll take a quick tour of the campus and then have lunch. After lunch I have to go to the Gym and get ready for the football game. You and Harry Bartley 's date can come to the game together, If that's okay with you."

"Okay, I'll be down in less than twenty minutes. You better be here."

When she came down, the gallery was assembled. It had actually grown in size. Many guys, even without dates, were there. Apparently, word traveled fast about my date. She was with Harry

Bartley's date, talking avidly and pretending to ignore the audience. I knew otherwise. Of all the girls I had known, she knew how to handle admiration better than any. It was a real skill. It was also fun to watch and admire. She ignored all others, reached for my arm and gave me that smile that was such a tease.

"I knew you were Head Prefect but had no idea you were such a big cheese. Show me around campus. I'm sure there is a good quiet corner where I can receive and get that delicious welcoming kiss."

"Lucy, please. This weekend should be fun but it must be achieved without breaking all the rules of decorum."

"You are such a stuff box. Why can't we relax more, enjoy every opportunity and not worry whether you are doing what is right or wrong? Life is meant to be fun."

"I do enjoy all aspects of life but people can't just do as they please. I think to truly enjoy things you must be responsible."

"Oh, come on! Don't climb into the pulpit with me. At times you are unbelievable. You act like an old man."

"Okay, okay. You are right. Let's stop being serious. In fact, I really love having you here. You are gorgeous and have a way to make all seem happy. I admit, I'm not sure how to handle you."

"With passion Dummy!"

"You are something."

On that note, I showed her the campus. I couldn't help but notice others keeping their eyes on her. We didn't find that quiet corner.

Luncheon was full of hilarity. Harry was with his girl Norma, Bert with Jill and Ed and Jean where at our table. All the girls seemed to get along and had decided to come to the game in a group. I was glad of that, I feared Lucy to be left on her own. She would have been the target of all the single guys not playing in the game. I realized I was becoming jealous.

Pomfret was our opponent. They had been undefeated and were expected to pummel us. At the start of the game we lost the toss of the coin. Pomfret elected to receive. My kick off was deep and their return was stopped short of their twenty-yard line. We held them for three downs and on the fourth they punted. It came directly at me, I reached up, caught the ball and Wham! I was tackled. Two minutes later, I came to my senses. Through bleary eyes, I saw the coach bending over me and heard him say:

"I'm taking you out of the game until next quarter."

I shook my head and said:

237

"Please, leave me in, I'll be all right."

"How many fingers am I holding up?"

"Four."

"Now, how many?"

"One."

"Okay. I guess you are with it. But if you feel at all woozy, you must take yourself out. Promise?"

"Yeah, okay."

Play resumed. We got two first downs before I had to punt. It was short. Pomfret ran one play then fumbled on the second. Bill Osterhout recovered it for us. By now, I was feeling much better. I called for an end run. The ball was snapped, I clutched it and took off. Ed. Hotchkiss threw a terrific block and I was off to the end zone. My extra point was good and we took the lead 7 to 0. That was the last we scored. The final was 38 to 7. It was one of the worst defeats we had experienced. Salisbury had no hero's that day. And it happened in front of our girlfriends!

After the game and a shower, I met Lucy at the main building, where the after game tea was being held. She saw me come in, ran to me and planted that delicious welcoming kiss on me.

"I thought I'd lost you for the weekend. When that guy hit you, it sounded as if every bone in your body had been broken. It was sickening. How do you feel now?"

"Great; after receiving that kiss! I guess we'll be excused for it."

"There had better be plenty more."

The coquettish Lucy somehow made even the loss, not so tragic. I could have hugged her with joy, if it hadn't been for the frowns on the faces of those Master's wives present.

After tea, we spent the rest of the afternoon with a whole group of other couples, talking a lot of nonsense, sprinkled with jokes, good and bad. We all had a good time and then it was time to part and dress for dinner and the evening. Escorting Lucy to the steps to her accommodations, she held tightly to my arm and said:

"This has been fun but aren't we ever going to be alone? I came up to be with you, not with a lot of cackling girls. I've decided you are not very romantic."

"Go up and get dressed for the evening. I've got to do the same."

"Oh; my God. Will you ever learn?"

An hour or so later, spruced up and attired in our tuxedos, we were all at the foot of the stairs to the girl's accommodations with corsages in hand, eagerly anticipating the appearance of our weekend partners. I should have guessed. The first to appear was Lucy. She seemed to float down. Unrestrained whistles erupted from many of the guys. She was in a cream colored gown, that was somewhat demur but well fitted, accentuating her striking figure. She kept her sparkling eyes fastened on mine. Her smile was radiant and her dark hair glistened with lights. It was, a "Grande Entrance". I never noticed the other girls following and I doubt any of the other males did either. I held out my arm and she lightly placed her hand upon it as she softly whispered:

"Will I do? You must know — I am all yours."

I couldn't help the blush that arose in my neck and face. I'm sure others heard her whisper. Unsteadily, I escorted her to our table, held her chair as she seated and then stood behind mine to look at the others arriving. There was no question but that Lucy was the most fetching.

After dinner, we adjourned to the sixth form room for coffee, while unattached volunteers set up the dining hall for the dance. The band arrived while we were having our coffee. I had to excuse myself to meet with them. It was the Bob Halprin Dance Band from Hartford. We had used them before so my meeting with them was short. They knew the procedure and the type of music preferred. Returning to the coffee, I spotted Lucy in the center of a gaggle of males. She was in her element. When she noticed me, she broke away and quickly approached. I was certain she was going to give me a kiss in front of all. I suddenly realized, that was part of her allure to others. Taking her hand, I fended her off and said:

"Don't you dare."

"Why? You are mine, you know."

"Come on, Lucy. This is a school dance and nothing more. Lighten up."

"Just you wait. I'm not one to be denied."

This was all getting to be too much. I liked her but was beginning to wonder where this was all heading. I felt the prey of a voracious predator. The words Marian used when she first saw me with Lucy, rushed in to my mind. Was all this a big game? The warmth of Marian's presence seemed very real and I fervently wished she was actually there. She was a girl who made all seem right.

Lucy's dance card was full within minutes after receiving it. I had the first and last of the ten dances on the card. The purpose of the card was to have it filled with a variety of guys to make the evening more interesting and to break the ice between people. The number of applicants for a position on her card would have kept her dancing for a week but Lucy insisted she dance almost exclusively with me after her duty from the card had been fulfilled. To say we danced is a misnomer. It was swaying to the music, while standing in one spot, pressed together. The dance was over at 12:15 AM. By tradition, we all walked our dates to the stairs leading to their quarters. Parting, Lucy gave me such a sensational hug and kiss, the singing abruptly stopped and loud laughter and whistles made me extremely embarrassed. It was her way of grabbing the center of attention. I knew then, she was using me to establish herself as the femme fatal of the weekend.

After paying the Band and helping to clean the dining hall, I went back to my room for the night. Once in bed, I spent hours tossing and turning. I kept thinking how impossible Lucy was. My thoughts moved to a contemplation of terminating our relationship. In truth, I missed Marian. She was so different than Lucy. Her beauty was both outward and inward. I couldn't ever remember her doing anything to make herself the center of attention. She was what she was. Her thoughtfulness of others was second nature to her. She had a smile for everyone, which was open and friendly. She radiated interest in all things. As the night drew on, I wondered if I could convince Marian that we should continue to see one another and not try to cool things for a year or more. I had a difficult time understanding why she was so fearful of our relationship. Before I fell asleep, I had decided to be straight with Lucy before she left for home. I liked her, admired her beauty but knew it was time to break off our dating.

Breakfast on Sunday was later than normal. Usually, less than half the girls attended. This time, nearly all showed up, including Lucy. I met her at the bottom of the stairs and we went into the dining hall. She seemed more subdued than normal and a little unsure. There was no public good morning kiss and no reaching for my hand as we entered. As we left, she did catch my hand and gave it a little squeeze, asking:

"Do I have to join you in going to Chapel? I'm still tired. I was awake most of the night thinking of you — us. We must find time to be alone together. There is so much we have to discuss. Can't we get away by ourselves for a little while?"

"You don't have to come to chapel. When we go to the cabins, we'll try to find a way to go off to a secluded spot so we can talk. I agree, it is important we talk about everything. But please, don't get any romantic ideas. Right now, I have to go back to my dorm and then to chapel. I'll see you in about an hour or so."

When chapel was over, I made my way to the common room. There was Lucy, holding court, surrounded by seven or eight guys. She had changed into an outdoor outfit that somehow made her look ravishing. The young men drooled over every word she spoke and followed all her sinuous actions. There was no doubt — she knew how to hold their attention. I finally caught her eye and she immediately broke up the court and held out her hand to me.

"I thought you'd never get here. These guys have all been telling me all about you. You get more intriguing all the time."

We said goodbye to her enthralled and went to meet Harry, Ed. and their dates for the walk to the cabins. The lunch and sing along was fun, everybody seemed to be having a great time. At an opportune time, I told Harry I was taking Lucy for a short walk on our own so we could have a talk. He looked at me with that knowing grin and said:

"Bet you can't resist her. Be careful. I'll cover for you."

"No, Harry, believe me, it is only for a walk. We have a lot of things to sort out."

We tried to slip away unnoticed. We went towards Wolf's Ledge. Hearing voices, we detoured and made off for the "Crows Nest". About a quarter mile from the cabins, Lucy pushed me into the bushes, threw her arms around me and huskily said:

"Please hold me tight. Run your hands all over my body."

"Oh, my God, Lucy, please be sensible. It can't be that way. You are a sweet, beautiful, enticing young lady. It is so tempting to do as you ask but it would also be wrong of me. How do I tell you this? As desirable as you are and as fun as it is to be with you, it can't be like that. I respect you too much. You are a wonderful girl but I know I'm not in love with you. Tempting? Yes! But it just can't be. We have had a great time dating but it is time for us to put a stop to it now. I will not take advantage of you. I think too much of you. Try to understand."

She clung to me more tightly and showered me with kisses.

"Chuck, you are what I want. We have had such good times together. I don't care if you love me. I just want to be with you."

241

"It is no good, Lucy. It really is time we stopped seeing each other. It is best for both of us."

"I'll bet you are going to run back to Marian. What does she have that I don't. I know she is not as much fun and is too much a goodie, goodie."

"This is about you and me, not about Marian. Please, let's end things as friends."

At that she broke down and started crying loudly. I thought all the others in the woods would hear her and think I had tried to take advantage. Her crying became louder. Taking her arm, I started pulling her back to campus. She came but continued crying. When we got back she ran up to her room and didn't come down until the taxis had come to transport them all to the train. Getting in to the taxi, she turned and sobbed:

"I do love you but I hate you more!"

So ended my unusual and exciting time with the girl who, I first noticed on the ice, found running into my lap at John Van Norden's and who I disappointed at Frank Sinatra's radio show. It was destined to end. I felt terribly it had ended in the way it did. I never saw her again.

CHAPTER 30

THINGS QUICKLY RETURNED to normal after that roller coaster weekend. The worry over the situation with Marian intensified. I became determined to meet with her. She just had to agree to see me again so we could reach a more sensible compromise. Too much of each day was spent ruminating over these things. My studies began to suffer. By Thursday of that week, Coach Myer's pulled me aside after practice and said:

"Chuck, you are not concentrating. It shows in your class work and you are running plays during practice in a dreamy manner. Snap out of it. I hope you are not mooning over that girl you had up for the dance. Get a hold of yourself. You have responsibilities."

"Yes Sir. I hear what you are saying. I'll be okay."

Saturday arrived and we had the traditional game with our archrival — Hotchkis. It would be the last game I would play for Salisbury. I wanted to play a lot better than I had in the last two games. Just before kick-off, my concentration seemed to return. We had won the toss and elected to receive. The ball was kicked directly to me. I caught it on the run, broke right and sprinted down the field. No one laid a hand on me. Ed. Nash had thrown a beautiful block, which allowed me to run into the end zone. The extra point was missed and we led 6 to 0. That run did more to restore reality than anything else could have. It was the start of one of the most frustrating games I had ever played. We lost 25 to 6. Our season ended with more loses than wins. I was thoroughly dejected.

Coming off the field at the game's end, the coach called me over:

"Chuck, we did our best, they were just too big for us. I would like you to meet Dean Hermansk from Princeton University. He is the director of admissions and he would like to meet with you after you have dressed."

I looked at the Dean, shook his hand and said I'd be happy to meet with him. Then asked where we would meet and told him I'd be there in about forty-five minutes. Leaving them, I wondered why he wanted to meet with me. I hadn't applied to that University and really still hoped I might get in to West Point. I thought he couldn't possibly be interested in my going to Princeton, not with my scholastic record.

The Dean had been given the Head Master's office for our meeting. Knocking on the door, I wondered if Reverend Langdon would be there as well.

"Come in."

Entering, the Dean was alone. He stood, thrust his hand out and said:

"Chuck, that was a splendid game you played. Your speed had them off balance all afternoon. They out weighed you by 25lbs per position and yet you all played well and never gave up. I understand you are the Captain and also the Head Prefect of the school. The Masters to whom I've spoken, also tell me you have been a student here for five years, ever since the second form. We think highly of this school. We have accepted a number who have studied here and they've all done well. What are your thoughts about college? Do you have any preference?"

His warm greeting and enthusiasm startled me.

"Sir, thanks for the bright spin you've put on the afternoon. It was pretty awful. Our whole team played well today. We really wanted this one. As for college, I have long thought of applying to the Academy at West Point. With the war and all, I think the training would be very beneficial. It is also on the Hudson River, close to where I was brought up."

"According to the sheet I have on you, your home is in Scarsdale. Isn't that correct?"

"Yes Sir, my family live there. I was born along the Hudson River and spent the major portion of my life in the town of New Hamburgh. I really consider that more of my home. My folks have an island there and when not in school I work on a farm near town."

"That sounds interesting. Tell me about yourself, a short biography, what you would like to accomplish in life and what drives you."

For a minute or two I said nothing, trying to gather my thoughts. Then I responded. When I finished, he said:

"Very interesting. I can tell you really like that town along the Hudson. It seems you have always worked more than other boys. Do you like to work?"

"Yes, I guess I do. But I also love many sports, like sailing, canoeing, tennis, etc. For some reason, I've always liked to be busy. Loafing makes me irritable. Most work seems to turn into fun."

"I think you are one of the few boys I've ever interviewed that has told me that. Don't you like doing things with other boys?"

"Sure I do. It's just that I don't like to hang around."

Do you want to make the Army your career? That is what West Point prepares you to do. This war, both in Europe and in the Pacific, will be over within a few years. Have you thought of what a peace time army would be like? From what I have learned about you and listening to your responses, I doubt it would be something which would suit you. I think you should look at the longer view."

"I'm not so sure the war will be over that quickly. Perhaps in Europe, the Nazi will be defeated for lack of supplies and men but the Japanese are a fanatic people and will take a long time to subdue. I dread thinking of what it will take to invade and take over that island. As far as I can see, it will take many, many years."

"Well, you may be right but I'm more optimistic. We are a strong country and are just now getting in to full swing with our industrial might and well-trained troops. Now back to your higher education. What do you know of Princeton?'

"Sir, not a great deal. One of my closest friends started there last year and he loves it. He's very, very smart."

"Why don't you consider Princeton?"

"Sir, I'm not a top student. I struggle to get through. Once you look at my scholastic record, you'll see."

"Chuck, I have looked at your record. Why are you so hard on yourself? All the Masters with whom I have spoken, tell me you are a plugger. I happen to like pluggers. They also tell me you are smarter than you let others believe. You have something else. According to those I've talked with, you are a born leader. Not everyone is Head Prefect, Captain of both Football and Baseball teams and thought so highly of by the manner in which you treat others. You shouldn't try to undersell yourself. I would like you to consider Princeton. Come down for a visit, attend a few lectures and classes, meet students, talk to some of the coaches and then come see me. I'm not promising anything but I do want you to look us over. We are open over Thanksgiving, come then."

"You have given me much to think about. Yes, I'll be down then. I can stay with my friend, Jack Zimmerman"

"Good. I look forward to your visit. When you get there check in with my office first. Oh, I meant to ask earlier. What do you think your main interest in studies would be?"

I became tongue- tied. For the better part of a year I had been debating with myself that very question. In honesty, no conclusion had been reached. I took a deep breath and said:

"Sir, in all honesty, I don't know. I have asked myself that question many times. Perhaps that is another reason why I was thinking of West Point. Going there, it'd be ordained that the military service be my career. I have thought of other possibilities but have decided on none. My Dad wants me to study law and combine that with chemistry. The law might be good but I really don't know. Business fascinates me. As a kid, another fellow and I formed the McVan Photo Company and it was fun trying to make it grow. He had the talent but I could bring in the business. My problem is I don't know what business I'd like to go into after college. I've also thought of coaching. I love sports and a lot of my friends think I would be great at it. But, I don't know. It might bore me in a few years. As I've said before, I like to keep busy. Right now I have no overwhelming desire to pursue any particular field."

"Do you think that's unusual? It's not. Very few entering Princeton, or any college, really know what they want to become. As you grow older, mature and learn more of the world, those decisions will become easier. It has been a most interesting meeting. I appreciate your forthrightness. I hope you will come down over Thanksgiving as you have said. Don't forget to check in to my office first. I'll have a suggested itinerary prepared, to make sure you see and talk to a variety of people. I've enjoyed meeting you."

The rest of the day, I walked around in a daze. It was hard to believe that a place like Princeton would be interested in me.

The Thanksgiving weekend was soon upon us. I had alerted my folks of my discussions with Dean Hermantz and that I would be spending most of the holiday weekend at Princeton. To put it mildly, they were shocked. Mom was pleased but Dad didn't think I had a prayer and it was all a big joke. The first night of the break was spent in Scarsdale. At dinner, Dad told me the tuition costs would be prohibitive, so advised against my getting too excited. My sister, who was still hoping to be engaged to her cadet, insisted I should keep trying for West Point. My thoughts were on Marian. I wanted to tell her what I was doing and hoped she would see me when I returned from the college. I decided not to call her, in case I didn't get back in time. If I didn't, things in that area of my life would have to wait until the Christmas holiday.

Wednesday morning, I took the train from New York City to Princeton Junction , then caught the PJ&B (the "Dink") to Princeton. Jack met me at the station. He seemed thrilled to see me and told me of the plans he had made to ease my introduction to the University. Walking through campus was like a dream. It was one of the most beautiful places I had ever seen. I was smitten with the architecture, the well maintained expanse of lawns, the friendliness of the students and the palpable vibration of learning. After dropping my bag off at his room, he took me to Nassau Hall where Dean Hermantz had his office. He was not there but his secretary was expecting me and gave me a packet from the Dean with appointments he had scheduled and some suggestions of things I might want to do and see. The college was in full session. All was on an accelerated schedule due to the war. Students wanted to get in as many credits as possible before being called up for service. Thursday, Friday and Saturday were whirlwinds of activity. I attended four lectures, sat in on five precepts, talked with Charlie Caldwell, the Head Football Coach, Jim Travis, the Track Coach, toured the whole campus, ate in the dining hall and then had a finishing visit with Dean Hermantz. His first question was:

"How do you like Old Nassau?"

"It's great! I'm overwhelmed. My only concern is can I handle it if accepted? It would be a real challenge."

"Good. Go visit West Point and compare. Here is a folder all about Princeton and our curriculum. Study it. There is also an application to fill out. Do that if you have an interest and I'll take it from there."

247

On that note, I left. There was so much to ponder. Riding back on the train, my mind was in a state of turmoil. The challenge would be daunting.

Sunday, I went to church with the folks and then caught the train back to school. My family had very little to say after hearing my recitation of all that had happened at Princeton. Dad said that I should give it serious thought. He would not influence me in any way. He let it be known he would review the costs involved after all the facts were on the table. My world seemed to be traveling too fast. How I wished I could talk it all over with Marian.

CHAPTER 31

BACK AT SCHOOL we settled in for the three weeks of intensive study before the Christmas break. This time of year always seemed to have extra emphasis on the subjects we were studying. Sports were less consuming because interscholastic competition was over until the New Year. This void of physical exertion always increased the incidents of disciplinary infractions. Coach Myers wanted to run a physical conditioning course structured around the Army's Ranger training program but Rev. Langdon was opposed to the idea. I remember him saying:

"The boys have been involved in sports all Fall, they should now have time to pursue other interests. They need a break from physical exertion."

The coach had a different philosophy:

"We need to exert these students with good workouts, tire them physically, it will keep them fit and hold down disciplinary problems." The Head Master's ideas prevailed and the students proved the coach right. At no time during my years at school did so many students find trouble. Langdon's responses never varied:

"Boys will be boys!"

My job, as Head Prefect, became almost intolerable.

Several days after returning from the Thanksgiving holiday, Ed. Nash, Prefect on the third floor dorm of Payson Hall, came to me. He was upset with a group of students on his floor. He had unexpectedly caught them smoking in one of the classrooms in the basement. He broke the session up but found they only returned to carry on later that night. Smoking had always been classified as a major offense. Our insurance did not permit it. Fire was always a major concern because so many of our buildings were constructed with wood. Theoretically, students who broke the no smoking rule were to be expelled immediately. I asked Ed. to call a meeting of the offenders and I would talk to them. The meeting was held and my little speech on the seriousness of their infraction was greeted with smirks and snide remarks. Alan Brennan, the apparent leader of the smokers, smugly told me:

"I don't give a damn what you say. The Head Master will never toss any of us out of school. He needs the revenue from our tuition to keep the joint afloat."

I reiterated why it was against the rules and that there would be consequences if they continued. He and others just scoffed. I did eventually get their promises that there would be no more smoking before the holiday break. Those promises lasted two days. Their new sessions became so raucous many other students heard them. Some joined in and others left in disgust. Ed. learned of them and investigated. To his surprise, they were not only smoking but someone had produced a bottle of "Jack Daniels", which was being passed around. The affair was shut down with much swearing back and forth. Ed. sought me and reported all that was going on. I immediately went to Alan's room, confronted him with his broken promise and further rule breaking. He was not contrite. Instead, he snidely said:

"Go shove it. Langdon won't do a damn thing. My family has lots of money he is counting on to help build the school. You'll see, he's easy to get around. He always backs down"

My response was:

"Don't bet on that! Alan, I like you and believe you can contribute much to this school. You are well liked, a better than average student so it is difficult for me to understand your rebellion. Why are you attempting to cause trouble?"

"Van Anden, you'll never understand. I hate this place, the rules, no girls around and having to cow tow to the masters and you prefects. Life here is too structured. I like smoking and drinking and we should be allowed to live a more normal life."

"Alan, we will all probably be in the service in another year or two. If you think this life is tough think what the military will require of you."

"I doubt I'll be drafted. I have medical problems you are unaware of."

"Well, it's up to you but I'm hoping you will cooperate and be a better citizen."

250

He did not cooperate and was found smoking and drinking more.

I had hoped to handle the problem without involving others but decided it was time all the Prefects were apprised of what was going on and a common plan developed to defuse the situation. I did not yet want to go to the Head Master because I was sure he would do nothing. A meeting was called and the infractions discussed. All, but Bill Thompson, agreed we had to stop the smoking and drinking, discipline those involved and keep the Reverand out of it. We established menial work programs that kept the offenders so busy there would be no time for parties. Each Prefect set up different tasks. Bill refused to cooperate. The rest of us spent the next two weeks, before the break, running "convict gangs" that cleaned every area of the school, whether it was needed or not. We were successful because we stuck together and supported each other in reigning in the culprits. The faculty soon caught on. Some liked how we were handling the recalcitrant but others wondered why. We tried to keep the substance of the infractions a secret.. Thankfully, the two weeks ended without further confrontations. For more reasons than one, I was delighted when the break arrived.

Wim Keur's wedding was three days later. It snowed for two of those days. We began to wonder if the guests would be able to get to the church and reception. There were at least sixteen inches of white stuff on the roads and everywhere it was very slippery. The day of the wedding the sun broke through. It remained cold but the wedding was able to proceed. It turned out to be a very joyous affair and a great deal of fun for me.

The wedding took place at four in the afternoon of a very cold and blustery day. As the only usher, I was kept busy fitting all one hundred and ten invitees into a chapel that only seated ninety comfortably. At the appointed hour, Jane was at the back, on the arm of her father, who was dressed in his naval uniform with Captain stripes. She was radiant. At the nave, nervously erect, stood Wim and his best man. As the couple finally met, he broke in to a broad grin, matching her smile. Jane passed her bouquet to her maid of honor. Watching, I got a glimpse of Maggie, the bridesmaid. She could not be called beautiful but she exuded charm, poise and maturity. The evening before had been the rehearsal dinner and we had hardly spoken. In my mind, I had categorized her as plain, destined to be an old maid and uninterested in giving me the time of day. The wedding took twenty minutes and then we were all off to the reception at the White Hart Inn.

Scrambling to the head table, I found my place was next to Maggie. Conversation, at first, was forced. Then it came time for the toasts. She poked me and said:

"Chuck, I hope you realize you have to give one. After all, you are his Godfather as well as his Usher."

I thought she was kidding. It had never occurred to me to prepare for such an eventuality. Ed. Tappert, the Best man, gave the first. It was as dry as one would expect of a Latin scholar. Then Jane's father gave his toast. It was full of humor and wistful expressions concerning his loss of his prized daughter to such a grumpy Dutchman. Maggie again poked me and said:

"It's your turn."

With knees shaking and blood rising to my face I stood, the room went quiet with expectancy. Faces turned to me, my mouth opened and I hesitated. Maggie reached for my hand and whispered:

"Go on. Say just what's in your heart."

Somehow, that helped.

"Jane, Wim, may your marriage always reflect the happiness we all share in your union. As Wim's unusual Godfather I am proud he showed the good sense to find such a wonderful life's partner. Let's all raise our glasses and wish them well."

I sat down before I fell down. Maggie leaned over, gave me a little hug and said:

"Perfect."

All I could think was that I hoped she was close to being right and thank God that was over. The cake was cut, dancing started and I tried to make myself scarce. Walking in to the men's room, I bumped into Jack Vigneron. He had been invited because his home was in town. Wim had not invited other students because they all lived far away and he didn't want to interfere with their vacation. Jack said:

"What are you doing after it's over?"

"I have no idea. Probably go back to my room at school."

"It's a full moon. Why don't we go skiing through the woods?"

"That sounds good to me. Maybe I can coax Maggie to join us. I think she is a pretty good sport. She sure has helped me a lot."

"Let me know when the married couple begins to leave. Don't forget."

I went back to the reception and was immediately caught by Mrs. Myers. She wanted to dance. On to the floor we went. Surprisingly, she was all a glow. The music was an easy fox trot, so I didn't mess up too badly. Around the floor we went and soon the questions started coming.

"What is really going on at school? We've heard there is much unrest among the student body. How are you and Reverend Langdon getting along? Are the Prefects unified behind you? What are you doing about Bill Thompson? Is everything making your studies suffer? My husband and I want to help you in any way we can."

I tried to be as non-committal as possible. When the music stopped, she leaned forward, gripped my arm and said:

"The coach would like you to come back to school early after the Christmas recess. He desperately wants to spend a day talking about the school."

I told her to tell him, I'd be back one day early. It all made me feel in the middle of a tug of war. I couldn't imagine what he wanted to discuss. It was the beginning of my anxiety over finishing school and getting on with a normal life. Then it struck me. Maybe this was what was considered normal.

I perused the dance floor for Maggie, spotted her dancing with Ed. Tappert and cut in. I said:

"Hello. Thanks. You saved me from much embarrassment. I have an off the wall question for you. How would you like to join Jack Vigneron and me skiing through the woods in the moonlight? This is not an irreverent proposition but an invitation to see the wonders of this place. We could stop at the cabins, build a fire, brew some coffee or cocoa and get to know more of each other. I know I'm just a kid to you but I assure you we are harmless and would just like to show you a different world than your home in Brooklyn."

"What a proposition! It's the nicest I've ever had. I'm not much of a skier but if you can find the skis and equipment I'd love to give it a try. Oh, I'll need some ski pants and warm clothing."

"Great. Jack lives near here and I'm sure his sister has clothes and equipment that will do. As soon as Wim and Jane leave, I'll come for you."

We danced some more, waiting for the bride and groom to depart. I learned she was madly in love with a guy she had never dated. I thought this strange but her sincerity prevented me from telling her it sounded like a dream which had no chance of coming true. She was twenty-three and desperately wanted to get married. Her frankness and happy outlook charmed me. She wasn't just a plain girl but a very vivacious one with a personality that proved infectious. Jack then cut in. They danced and I talked to Mr. Tappert. I soon detected, he was well on his way to intoxication. I couldn't help but think: "Poor, middle aged bachelor, in love with Latin, lonely, unpopular, probably misunderstood and afraid of the future". It made me see him in a new light and feel very sorry for him. From that moment on, we became friends. Buying him another drink, I heard commotion behind us. Wim and Jane were leaving. I rushed, Tappert stumbled to the door and we threw rice, with the other guests, at the departing couple. Turning, I saw moisture in his eyes.

Jack, Maggie and I soon located each other and we were off to school and skiing. The moon was so bright the trees threw shadows on the snow. Maggie did her best to glide along with us. We could tell she was having a glorious time. She fell on several small slopes but kept laughing and marveling at the winter wonderland. We reached the cabins without accident and built a fire. The good hard wood was dry and blazing before we found the cocoa. Settling down in front, catching the warmth of the flames, Maggie started to sing. She had a gorgeous voice and knew all the tunes. Jack joined in and I tried but couldn't compete. The cocoa made, without milk, we sipped our drinks and talked. It was just small, comfortable talk. Then Maggie said:

"I wonder how the soldiers in Europe are doing. I hear it's very cold there. The man I love is there. I pray the good Lord is watching over him. I only wish he knew how I felt."

Jack and I said nothing but each thought of those we knew who were overseas. In another year it could be our turn. We changed the subject and spent another hour in front of the fire, taking turns holding Maggie from behind to keep her as warm as she was from the flames before her. We finally doused the fire with snow and skied back to school. We found that the temperature outside was 6 degrees. It had never seemed that cold. I drove Maggie back to the White Hart Inn where she was staying. Leaving her at the door, she said:

"Chuck, this evening has been one of the most wonderful in my life. You and Jack are real gentlemen and made me feel like a Princess. No wonder Wim and Jane think so highly of you. Goodnight sweet Prince."

That was the first and only time I saw her. She eventually married her unsuspecting soldier, was very happy but died of cancer when she was thirty-seven. Knowing her has always been special. She was a fine person who made life sparkle.

The next day it was back to Scarsdale.

CHAPTER 32

WHEN I GOT home, only six more days remained before Christmas. My sister was also home so we spent a few days shopping together. Being with her was always a happy time. During those days, things were not going too well with her cadet. He was a staunch Catholic and was insisting she turn to that church before he would consider marrying her. This bothered my sister. He would not consider her remaining an Episcopalian and refused any discussion of the reasons for her intransigency. This extremely upset her, to the extent she thought him unreasonable. Listening to her, I could see an end to the affair looming on the horizon.

My situation was in a shambles as well. Although not as imminent, it seemed crucial to me. Marian was still the girl I wanted. Mom didn't like me moping around. She took matters in her own hands. I was informed that Amy Lu Huser was without a partner for the cotillion and since I was at loose ends, she had offered me to be her escort. I could have screamed! It was to be held three days after Santa Claus had come. I dreaded the thought.

The big night of the cotillion arrived. The dinner party before the dance was to be held at Amy Lu's. I arrived late. When the door opened, there stood Amy Lu. She did look nice and was certainly pleased to see me. Shedding my coat and hat, we walked in to the living room. I was introduced to people I'd never seen before. Shaking hands to typical Scarsdale couples, exuding false interest, I began to feel the hairs on the back of my neck rising. The power was so strong that I glanced from the couple in front of me and turned. My eyes were drawn to the far corner of the room. My heart lost a beat. There, looking directly at me was

Marian. My knees seemed to buckle. My eyes clamped on to hers, she smiled and actually blew me a kiss. My throat went dry and breathing seemed impossible. The rest of the room faded from view and all I saw was Marian. From a distance I heard Amy Lu say:

"Chuck, I'm not your date tonight, Marian is."

Incomprehensibly, I muttered:

"Oh God, how?"

"Never mind go say hello to your date."

Somehow, my legs took me across the room. When I reached her, I clasped both her arms, looked with moist eyes in to her equally moist eyes. The world went silent. Finally, never taking my eyes from hers, I quietly said:

"Oh, Marian, my fantastic girl I have so wanted to call you but have been so afraid you'd say no to our getting together. There are so many things I want to discuss with you, so much aching to relieve by holding you and many things yet for us to sort out. I can never express how terribly I've missed you. How did all this happen? What made it possible for us to be together again?"

"You won't believe it. My mom and yours arranged it. They both think we are crazy not to see one another."

"What do you think?"

"Oh, Chuck. Not now. We can't discuss all that here. Let's have a great evening and think, talk about it and decide later when we are alone."

"God, I don't ever want to lose you again. Stay with me all evening. It's a night, just for us."

""You'll never lose me. That's a promise.""

We then joined the others. It started an unexpected cotillion evening.

The dinner party was great fun. The other couples were full of laughs. Some directed at us with knowing winks and subtle remarks. All seemed to know one another and have that particular Westchester trait of "informed condescension". Besides Amy Lu and Marian I didn't know a soul and could have cared less. To me, all was immaterial but Marian. I was with the girl of my dreams.

When it was time to go to the Club for the dance, Marian and I ran to my car and drove off before others could hitch a ride. As we approached Crane's Pond, Marian asked me to pull in to the parking lot. I did, put on the brakes, switched the lights off, stopped the motor and reached for my girl. The kiss was long and ever so needed. It was all we could do to separate. The warmth and joy was near overwhelming. We found each other again and the kisses became more fervent. In a few minutes she mumbled:

"We must stop this. We have got to go to the cotillion. They will miss us and start imagining all sorts of things."

"Who cares? I just want to be with you. A few minutes won't make any difference."

We embraced again and happiness glowed through my whole being. She pushed gently against my chest and whispered:

"Stop, we must go. Let's enjoy the dance and then when we leave we must stop somewhere and talk about us. I've missed you. It is all so difficult. Come on, start the car, we must not be any later."

I behaved, started the car and drove to the Club.

The dance turned out to be more fun than expected. We danced together most of the time. Other guys tried to cut in but we were able to shoo most of them away. Our table was dominated by laughter and teasing couples making so much noise it brought the dowager — Miss. Covington — over to quiet us down. To my amazement, she recognized me and insisted I dance with her. Refusal was unthinkable. I tried to remember all her instructions from the past. I must have succeeded because when the music stopped, she thanked me and said:

"That was very nice. Give my regards to your mother."

That duty over, Marian and I resumed our dance floor clutches. At mid-night, refreshments were served. We ate and danced the last numbers. I was hoping with all my heart that this was the beginning of a new chapter for us. It had been such a wonderful evening. We found our coats, put them on and said our farewells to those with whom we had spent the last hours. Amy Lu came up to us and said:

"Being the foil for bringing you together again was exciting. It was a panic the way your mom's enlisted my mom in to their little scheme. Do you realize, it was in the middle of Gristede's grocery store that they worked up this whole plan to bring you together? They really think you two are something. Bye. I've had a ball."

With that, she pecked each of us on our cheeks and left.

We held hands walking to the car. Marian pushed in to me and said:

"Now, where can we go? Not some place too far but it must be where we won't be disturbed. We have a lot to decide."

I drove to Louie's and pulled in to the old barn where his brother, Henry, used to have his taxidermy facility. It was far enough from the house so I felt comfortable we would not be heard arriving. Turning the motor off and dousing the lights, I reached for Marian.

"No, Chuck, wait, we have to talk. You must know I'm in love with you. It has been that way ever since we first met on the tennis courts. No one else has ever come close in appealing to me. When you are away, I'm miserable. I have gone out with other boys but it's not the same. It's always you I want to be with. My folks know how I feel and Mom, particularly, thinks I'm being foolish to keep us apart. I don't think they understand. The existence of my half- brother has always impressed upon me the unhappiness that can result from slipping up in a relationship. You should know, Dad never did marry his son's mother. Once she became with child, both of them knew they were not suited for each other. They decided not to get married. The result has been misery for my half- brother, expensive for my father and awful for his girlfriend. She never married. I think, she really did want to marry Dad. Mom and Dad have a wonderful relationship but I know Mom resents the old girlfriend. My feelings for my brother are complicated. We are certainly not close. All of this has made me frightened over our relationship. Forbidden thoughts surge in to my mind when we hold one another. Try to understand. I love you but want to remove those temptations for now."

"Silly love, I'd never do anything to upset or compromise you. You mean far too much to me. I even promised your Dad I'd keep things proper and never do anything to hurt you. I meant it and still do. I know there is temptation but firmly believe we can handle it. We are young, far too young to lose control of our desires. I may be naïve and can't really believe we are having this conversation. I want us to continue dating. In that way we will learn more about each other. It is the normal way to strengthen a relationship. We'll find different things in ourselves, share much more, probably have disputes and find ways to handle problems unseen by us today. By seeing each other we can prove we are right together and will grow into decent people. Oh, God, come here, that's enough talk!"

I put my arms around her and pulled her close. We kissed and kissed some more. She clung to me and murmured, "Yes. Yes" I held her more tightly. I could hear the blood rushing through my ears. My hands moved from her back and slowly cupped her breasts. She moaned. We kissed more fervently. It was heaven. Then I heard her whispered cry:

"No. Oh God, No. Yes, I want. We can't. Chuck, No. Please just hold me. Oh, we've got to stop. Kiss me again."

I did. We held on in youthful fright and desire. Minutes flew by. The world seemed to be swaying. We came up for air. She spoke so softly, I barely heard:

"Chuck. Oh my love. See what I mean? I don't want it to ever stop. Please help us be strong."

Somehow, I pulled away, reluctantly. She straightened up, tidied her hair while looking at me as she did so and then smiled.

"Thank you. I couldn't have let go. What are we going to do? I still think the only way is to cool our relationship and the only way that can happen is for us not to see each other for a while. As difficult as it will be, we should wait to see one another until I'm eighteen. That will be in twenty months. I promise I'll come running back to you."

"Why? We just proved we could contain ourselves. I don't want to stop seeing you. Too many things can happen over the next two years. I'll be going to college, into the Army or Navy and then who knows what. You are what I want. Not seeing you leaves wide open the door for unwanted possibilities. I'll be back at Salisbury in a week and except for the Easter break, away until June. If we have to remain aloof, let's just use that period and resume being together after my graduation."

"No. I think we must wait longer. Trust me. It will be easier that way. Now, it's very late, you better drive me home."

In confusion, I did. At her house, we slowly walked to her front door. We kissed again, held each other for a minute or two and then I turned and started for the car. After a few steps, I heard her say:

"I'll come back to you, I mean it with all my heart."

The evening had ended with my heart in pieces.

CHAPTER 33

THE FOLLOWING MORNING I was up before sunrise. The night had been spent tossing and turning. How to change Marian's resolve occupied all my thoughts. The only conclusion seemed to be to accept her decision. Were her fears justified? Why couldn't we continue dating? Couldn't we control our desires if we both realized how necessary it was to do so? Other couples our age surely must confront similar stresses and succeed. I knew she had a very strong will and I thought I did as well. Then what was the problem? The more I thought, the more convinced I became she was wrong. How could I change her mind? In frustration, I threw on my warm clothes and went for a walk. It was too early for breakfast and no one else was up. My feet took me down to Louie's pond. I walked out on to the ice, tried sliding as if I had skates on and kept reliving the night's discussion. Looking down the dirt driveway to the barn, I heard a door open. Glancing toward the noise, I saw Louie. He raised his hand in greeting and shouted:

"You're up and about early. Why don't you come in for coffee and some of Mary Jo's biscuits? She'd love to see you."

"Hey, friend, that sounds inviting. Good morning to you."

I walked over to him, gave him my usual pat on the back and we went in. His wife was sitting at the kitchen table. She looked at me and said:

"Come give me a kiss. How come you are moping around so early?"

Giving her the required kiss and hug, I answered:

"Have a lot to think about."

"It must be a girl then."

"You know me too well."

"Yeah, but I've seen lovesick boys before. They all act the same. Instead of fumbling things through your mind, take action. Nothing a girl likes more than a decisive pursuit. The timid always lose."

"You are something. I feel better already."

"Sit. I'll get you some biscuits. They should be warm. Help yourself to coffee. You don't take cream or sugar, do you?"

"You remember everything too well."

"Chuck, honey, I've known you most of your life. You're special. Wish we'd had a boy like you but the Good Lord denied us that. Now, tell me about her."

I sketched out my courtship of Marian, our joy when we are together and the problems she fears might arise if we don't slow down and wait for the future. That did it. She burst out:

"Lordy, Lordy, what foolishness. You can't predict the future. Live for today and trust in the Lord. You got a problem. Don't let it sit there, control the situation. You remind me of the whip-poor-will Louie and I used to hear in the evenings as we sat outside taking in all the wonders of the warm spring weather. It always sounded mournful as if it was crying over a lost love. Go after that girl if you don't want to lose her. I can't say more. Now, how's that biscuit?"

"Delicious. You have always been a good cook."

Louie smiled and said:

"You got that right. She keeps me too heavy. Now let me say something. I heard you drive in last night. Wondered who was in the barn, so walked down to see. Soon as I saw your Dad's old LaSalle, I knew it was you. I peeked in to make sure and saw you and your girl. Weren't talking then. I backed off and came back in the house. Didn't say nothing to Mary Jo. Didn't mean to pry. Not too sure you should use our barn for a love nest. Might go hard on us if people found out and it became a popular spot. Know what I mean? Anyway, hate to be fussy but hope you understand."

"Louie, I won't use it again. I'm sorry. Marian and I needed some place private to talk and that was the first place that came to mind. Okay?"

Yea, I know you'll live up to your word."

We spent another half hour or so talking about old times, what they were doing now and about his job at the fire department. He was so very proud of what he was contributing. When I left, I was glad they had called me in. What great friends they were!

Back home, Dad was just leaving for work as I walked in.

"How was the cotillion? Your mother heard you go out this morning and has been fretting ever since, wondering what happened. She'll be down in a minute. I've got to go. See you tonight?"

"Yea, I'm planning to be here. I'll pick you up at the station when your train gets in. Have fun."

He no sooner left than Mom came down.

"Well, tell me all about it."

"Mom, you and Mrs. Logan are fantastic! I couldn't believe it when Amy Lu told me she wasn't my date and then I saw Marian. It was wonderful. We both know we have great parents. The evening was too short. We danced together most of the time. Afterwards, we spent an hour or more talking everything over. As you know, we are crazy over each other but Marian is afraid it will get out of hand. I don't feel that way. Both of us are sensible and dating will show how good we are together or blow everything up. It has me flummoxed. That's why I went out this morning. I couldn't sleep last night, so tried to walk my confusion away. What do you think? both you and Mrs. Logan seem to feel we should be able to enjoy each other or you wouldn't have arranged last evening."

"Charles, I guess we really don't understand you two. You are both good children, have each done well, are thought of highly by your peers and seem to enjoy one another's company. Certainly, we expect you to behave yourselves. I can't imagine you 'going too far' as the saying goes. If there is a question of that, then you should stop now. You have no idea how much unhappiness you would both create. I had no idea you both were worried about that possibility. I'm sure Mrs. Logan doesn't either. Are you suggesting there is some cause for our concern?"

"Mom, I don't know. I can't believe we would ever be so foolish. Marian is not so sure."

"Are you telling me she has reasons for doubts?"

"No, Mom. We have never even come close to crossing that line."

"I should hope not! Perhaps you should cool things off. We had no thought things had progressed that far."

"Mom, they haven't!"

"You and your father will have to have a talk. Now, let's have breakfast."

No more was said. I knew a lecture was coming that evening.

I called Marian late that afternoon and got Mrs. Logan. She was very friendly but told me Marian didn't want to talk yet. She asked me to call the next day. She also told me she knew of our discussions and felt very sorry for us. God, what a mess it was!

Dad's train was on time. While I had been waiting, I thought of the days when I sold the Saturday Evening Post to the men leaving the train. Those were certainly simpler days and everything seemed so easy. It made me wonder if things became more difficult in direct proportion to your age. When he climbed in to the car, he said:

"How did it go with Marian? I know how Mom and Mrs. Logan arranged things. I told them to leave things alone. It was up to the two of you to sort things out. Did you have a good time?"

"Yea, it was great."

We dropped the subject and instead talked about the war. From all reports, there was a big battle raging with the Germans. Apparently, they had launched a surprise counter attack and things were rather dicey. The reports talked about the extreme cold and the snowy condition making the fighting more miserable. Casualties were said to be high. It made us wonder how long the war would last. Dinner was served shortly after we got home. Somehow, Mom had gotten the word to Dad about the results of the cotillion. He informed me, he would like to have a discussion in the basement after we had eaten.

When we met, it was short and to the point.

"Boy, we have talked before about the proper relationship between the sexes. If there is any doubt in your mind, or Marian's, that you can't conduct yourselves according to what is right, then terminate the means for that temptation. The consequences of a misstep are too great. Do I make myself clear?"

"Yes sir. We will not disappoint you or the Logan's."

"Then, that's it. You can go upstairs. I'm surprised. I really liked Marian."

"Sir, it's no fault of hers. It's just that we find each other irresistible."

"Nonsense! You must be the strong one. I'll not tolerate any foolishness! Now, go upstairs, I have some bills to pay."

No more was said for years. I did call Marian the next day, talked to her at length but things remained the same. We would somehow find each other in a few years. It was a decision I long regretted.

New Year's Eve was dateless. I got together with Gordon and Sue. Several other couples joined us and I felt miserable the whole night. In fact, I was looking forward to returning to school. The day before my return, a trip to New Hamburgh was made. The time spent with Aunt Nell brought back so many good memories. However, her main interest was Marian. When I told her of what was happening, she said:

"Phew. Don't let that girl get away. She is right for you."

That's all of what was said on the subject but I knew she still had hopes for us even though we were so young. Leaving her that night was very difficult. For so many years she had been the backbone of my existence. Never once had I experienced her questioning my judgment, honesty or hopes for the future. She was very special and I sensed life was, of necessity, removing that closeness a little further away. I hugged her tighter before I walked out her door.

CHAPTER 34

I LEFT FOR Salisbury the following morning. Getting off the train at Millerton to catch a cab back to school, I couldn't believe how much snow had accumulated. It was also bitterly cold. Harry Applahadian, the cab driver, said it was the coldest he could remember but he understood it was much colder in Europe where the fighting was very severe. His son was in the Fourth Infantry Division and he hoped he wasn't in the thick of it. He dropped me off at Coach Myer's home. I had promised I would come back early to spend some time talking with him. When in the house, they made me welcome and out came the tea. Mrs. Myers had made a chocolate cake, which was delicious. Their home was the old farmhouse that had sat on the property since 1790. It was one of the most comfortable homes I had ever been in. I couldn't help but think' it was the kind of home I hoped to own one day.

After tea, the coach started talking about the problems we were experiencing at the school. He took great pains not to criticize Mr. Langdon but did make plain his frustration over the way students were flaunting the rules. As Head Prefect, he wanted me to continue enforcing the regulations even if support was not forthcoming from the administration. It was his contention that the Board of Directors also wanted the same. I assured him, it was my intention to do all I could to maintain discipline and all other Prefects, other than Bill, were in agreement. He warned me that my commitment would only lead to unpopularity but that I must try to avoid letting that alter my determination. He then said a strange thing:

"Chuck, some people will be vicious. I'm sorry you will be the one burdened but remember I and the majority of the faculty will be supportive. This school has a very fine reputation and we do not want to lose it. If Mr. Quaile were still alive he'd want you to stay true to our school's traditional principles."

That is the nitty-gritty of our conversation that afternoon.

Studies started off pretty well with the exception of chemistry. I thought I was learning and my experiments were received well but my grade seemed stuck at a barely passable level. Mr. McEnery, the master teaching chemistry, enjoyed deviling me. I finally went to him and tried to have him explain why we were having such difficulty. He bluntly told me:

"You are too big a deal in this school. Someone has to take you down a peg. Don't worry, you'll probably pass but I'm not going to make it easy."

I had no response. There didn't seem any avenue to take that would make him ease up.

The winter weather was spectacular. It remained cold all through January and into the first two weeks of February. Snow was in abundance. The first week in February was Parents weekend. My folks came up. I was anxious to show them my jumping. On Saturday afternoon there was another meet. They came to watch me compete. When it was my turn, I pushed off from the tower with all the strength I had. The down track was fast, at the lip I sprang to get maximum distance. Flying through the air, bent forward over my skis, the right one came loose from my foot. I landed on one foot and tried to keep my balance. It was all going well, when all of a sudden the ski, which had come off, slammed in to the back of my head knocking me unconscious. I crumbled to the snow and somersaulted to the bottom of the hill. I awoke shortly, seeing my mother bending over me.

"Are you all right? You are never to ski jump again. You'll kill yourself."

Dad appeared and looked at me:

"Get up! Go to the top and jump again. Don't try to show off, just jump properly."

Up I got and gathered my skis. Jack Vigneron helped me climb the tower and to fasten my skis on. Down I went again. At the lip, I sprang once more, flew through the air, landed and didn't fall. It wasn't a long jump but it was good enough. At the bottom, I was all smiles but quickly became embarrassed. Mom and Dad were having a very public argument. I intervened and we left the hill. All soon calmed down but none of us were happy. That evening things turned to a happier mood. Mom played the piano for all students who were interested. Soon a large gathering surrounded her at the piano. She changed the music to popular songs and the whole place rocked with happy voices. This impromptu sing-along lasted until lights out. The day certainly ended on a more positive note.

That weekend over, my attention was directed to the winter dance to be held at the end of the month. I had no date lined up. As Chairman of the Dance Committee, that was unthinkable. Gordon Ferguson finally got me to consider a blind date. I hated the thought and only wanted Marian. He came to me with a suggestion from Sue, his girlfriend. She knew a number of girls who would love to come for the dance. With two and a half weeks to go, I reluctantly agreed. Sue picked a girl, also from Larchmont, by the name of Betty Riegel. No picture was sent. I only received a lot of verbiage on what a great girl she was. I became fearful I was being setup. Arrangements were finalized even though I was not very keen on the idea. My fears for a pending disaster multiplied.

All of this turmoil was quickly overshadowed by the terrible news of casualties sustained by members of our recent alumni. Four had been killed in action and three others wounded. The biggest shocker for me was Birks Erskine's death at the Battle of the Bulge. I had known him for many years, he was one of Ron's older brothers and one of the very first to greet me when I came to Salisbury. The war suddenly seemed very close. I remembered the night when Maggie, Jack Vigneron and I went skiing after Wim's wedding. She had told us then that she had heard there was fierce fighting that night and prayed her unsuspecting soldier was safe. Apparently while we were having the time of our lives, Birk's was fighting for his and lost. The thought almost made me cry.

We also now suspected our turn would be here quicker than it was comfortable to contemplate.

The week before the dance, I received another shock. Steve Davies had been killed on a training mission in the Air Force. My buddy from Camp Wampanoag, Scarsdale and rock climbing along the Hudson was no longer with us. It was very hard to accept. We had always been very close and had remained friends even after he and his family moved to Pittsburgh. It seemed the war was getting worse not better. Unfortunately, more casualties were yet to come.

The dance weekend also arrived, as did my blind date. On that Saturday morning, the cabs arrived with the girls from the New York/Westchester area and the usual group of anxious boys was out front eagerly waiting for the first glimpse of their sexual fantasies. I hung back knowing mine would not be there. Instead I was grabbed by Gordon and pushed forward. Sue stepped out of the cab all smiles and waving at us. A rather thin, tall, dark hair girl followed. Sue pointed at us and I knew the other was my date. They walked toward us as we approached them. I noticed my date was talking a mile a minute, smiling happily and looking me over with skepticism. Introductions were made and Betty gave me a firm and warm handshake, saying:

"Hi, I'm not that bad, am I? I thought from what Sue said you would be taller. I guess we'll both have to adjust our thinking. I've really looked forward to meeting you. I have heard so much about you, not only from Sue but also from Natalie Hugh. By the way, she says to say: `Hi'. My suitcase is over there. Where are we going to stay? I'd like to freshen up before we do anything. Hi, Gordon. Good to see you again. Wow, this is quite a place, the scenery is spectacular. I hear you are a ski jumper. Are we going to see you jump? I love to ski but never tried jumping -----"

On and on she rattled. At that moment I could have strangled Gordon and Sue. We finally got them to the stairs leading to their accommodations. When they went up, I turned to him and said:

"Does she talk incessantly or does she eventually wind down? One thing for sure, I won't have to say much all weekend."

The following two days was an experience unlike any I had participated in before. Betty had energy, particularly of the voice. You could hear it from any corner of any room. It was not because of loudness but rather from its' constant action. It was happy, funny and clever. Her mind at times had trouble keeping up. At the dance, her movements reflected her monologue. I teasingly called her, "perpetual Betty". I really didn't know if I wanted to shout: "Shut up!", laugh or keep quiet and marvel. She was different than any girl with whom I had ever gone out. The dance finally ended and as we parted, she said:

"I have had a wonderful day. I'm so looking forward to tomorrow. Thank you for being so patient with me. I know I'm hard to get used too. It's just because I'm nervous. Other girls are more demure and better looking, which puts me on edge. Good Night and thanks again."

I watched her ascend the stairs and felt relief. I admitted to myself, she wasn't that bad and in her way fun to be around. I sure missed Marian.

The rest of the weekend was full of surprises. Betty was eager to attend Chapel with me, knew all the prayers and the hymns by heart and never tried to talk. Afterwards, she quickly changed into a ski outfit and begged me to take her skiing. She was better at it than me. When we got to the cabins for luncheon and found places by the fire, she sang with everyone else all the old songs, never forgetting a word and ended up leading the others in songs she knew which were different. Her singing voice was admittedly good. After lunch we went back to the main building with Gordon and Sue. For some reason, her talkative nature had left her. She was so quiet I thought I must have offended her. The girls packed and came down to take the cabs back to the station. I walked with her to the cab, thanked her for coming and started to leave. She put her hand out and said:

"Chuck, I've had a wonderful weekend. It is such a beautiful school and you have been very gracious. Thank you for putting up with me. I hope we can get together sometime. You are different than I expected but it's been fun being with you. Bye."

The cab drove off and we all waved. I thought: "It was different but I'll never see her again. Marian, Marian, why wasn't it you? We have got to work things out".

Monday, school returned to the normal routine. Problems soon emerged.

Ed. Nash had again found the usual misfits smoking, drinking and being rude to those who would not participate. Upon learning this, I took immediate action. I confronted Alan Brennan that evening. He told me to "Go f--- myself". He'd do as he pleased. I tried to remain calm and talk sense into his head but to no avail. Subsequently, I called a meeting of the Prefects to discuss appropriate action. Bill Thompson, as usual, was all for letting the matter drop. He believed that if we took no action, it would not become a problem but if we did, it would become a major issue and lead the school into turmoil. My response was that it was already an issue and, if left alone, it would become more than a major issue. The student body would feel they could do just as they liked without censure. The rest of the Prefects agreed with me. We voted to recommend that Brennan be suspended.. It was time for me to approach the Reverend Langdon and lay the whole situation before him. The next day I requested a meeting. We met right after classes. When I told him what we were faced with, he said he already knew. He had discussed it with Bill Thompson and had decided to turn a blind eye. I was furious. Controlling my temper, I told him it was my recommendation that Brennan should be suspended if not expelled.. He shouted at me:

"No! That is not a decision for you. I'm in charge here. Don't try to force me."

"Sir, it is your decision. As Head Prefect it is my responsibility to bring to your attention things that are violating rules, the security of the facilities and the well- being of the students. I believe this is such a case and my recommendation stands. The decision is yours. You certainly can do as you like."

"Chuck, don't you have empathy for your fellow students? You are all boys. It is natural to break rules. We must always forgive, not punish."

"Sir, the problem will only get worse if they are permitted to get away with whatever they want. It will surely lead to serious problems for a number of students. Doing nothing shows weakness and invites trouble."

"That's your ill- advised opinion, not mine. Do nothing and the problem will dissolve. This discussion is over."

How upset he made me! I knew the problem would end up in my lap again. Why had Mr. Quaile died? He would have taken action, explained why to the culprits and the school would have been a lot better off and happier. He ran the school on expecting and believing in a system of honor between students and the Administration. It was very important to him that honor between people be a solid basis for the well- being of society. Not excusing the lack of it. Graduation couldn't come soon enough. I so wanted to get away from this new way of thinking.

Not much has been said about Wim and Jane since their wedding. I had purposely left them alone so they could enjoy their life together. However, one evening after the Christmas break we did have dinner together. They were on cloud 9. Wim had never acted so happy. Obviously, their honeymoon had been a great success. On their return, the school had provided them with larger quarters and they were spending all available time fixing it up to make it theirs. Now that more than a month had passed, I felt it acceptable to bother them a little more. The school situation was troubling me so much, I felt in the need to discuss it with someone whose judgment I trusted. Saturday evening, I knocked on their door. Jane answered:

"Well, it's about time! We thought you were purposely avoiding us."

"Hi, I was. The last thing you needed was me hanging around. Boy, your place looks great. Wim has never lived in such luxury. You'll turn him in to an old softy."

"Don't just stand there, come in. The grumpy old goat is in his study. He'll be pleased you came. Wim, Chuck's here."

In he lumbered with a big smile splitting his face.

"Well, well, look who has finally come to pay us a visit. I have seen you around campus and you never seem your usual happy self. What has you looking so miserable? You had a date for the dance and you never introduced her to us. What happened to Lucy? She was something hard to keep your eyes from. What was this new girl like?"

"She was a very nice person but different from any girl I've ever been out with. I didn't drop in to discuss my sad situation with the opposite sex but to discuss my concern over the things that are happening around school. Do you have any idea what I am referring to?"

"No. Not really. Besides my classes, I have spent most of my time with Jane putting this place to rights. I'm afraid my involvement in the daily routine at school has suffered. There is a faculty meeting Monday night and I suppose I'll hear all the latest then. What are you referring to?"

"Oh, I shouldn't bother you. It's just that I'm upset over some disciplinary problems. It shall probably all work out in the end but it has me wondering why I'm Head Prefect. I don't think my year will be remembered with pride."

"What's this? I've never heard you feeling sorry for yourself."

"It's not that. It's just that I'm frustrated. We'll talk about it some other time. It has been great to see you both. Jane, as I said before, your Maggie is one wonderful lady. Jack and I keep talking about what a great sport she was that night. When you talk to her, give her my best and let her know we thought she was special."

"I will, but I don't like to see you so down. Don't keep it in. Come see Wim when you think it would help. Thanks for coming over."

I left disappointed not being able to discuss what was on my mind. Then I realized, it was a problem I had to work through on my own. It came with the territory of my position in school.

Twenty-four hours later, the school became a zoo, a comedy and a near tragedy. It was still very cold with much snow still on the ground. After chapel on Sunday, a group of us went cross-country skiing to the cabins. When we approached ours, we saw seven or eight students running away. Entering the cabin, we saw it had been trashed. Leaning against the fireplace was a poorly drawn picture depicting me as Adolph Hitler with the words: "The Dictator will be eliminated! The people have risen!" We cleaned everything the best we could and returned to school. Opening the door to my room, I saw it was all upside down and written on one wall, with toothpaste and shaving cream, was the same epitaph. The rest of the day I was subjected to more of the same. Students, hiding from sight, shouted rude remarks and ridiculous slogans as I passed. My popularity was at an all-time low. Going in to dinner that evening, I was greeted by Brennan and his followers, standing at the entrance to the hall, arms extended in the Nazi salute. I noticed the Reverend Langdon smiling with glee.

Dinner over, I returned to my room to study. Lights out was at ten-thirty. Somehow, I slept even though the ridicule hurt. I thought of what Coach Myers had said when I returned from the Christmas break. He had been so prophetic. About one- twenty, I woke with a start hearing loud screaming and the sound of feet running up and down the stairs of the dorm. Jumping out of bed, dressing quickly, I rushed out to the corridor. Ed. Nash came bounding up the stairs shouting:

"Fire. Fire!"

Then Jack Vigneron came up from the basement, took one look at me and said:

"Chuck, Two students in a class below are as drunk as lords. One has been cut badly. I need help in getting them to the infirmary."

Out of the corner of my eye I saw Art Gossner arrive. I asked him to go with Jack to help with the injured student and asked Ed. to accompany me to the basement to see about the fire. We reached the smoky room only to find Brennan slouched in a chair in front of three trashcans that were burning away. He was trying to pop popcorn over the flames while slurping some booze and intermittently singing some dirty ballad in a very slurred voice. Bottles of booze were scattered on the floor, one with a small pool of blood underneath. In a way, the sight was comical but dangerous enough to set the whole building on fire. I grabbed the drunk and dragged him across campus to the Head Master's house. Shouting at the top of my lungs and banging on his door finally aroused him. He opened the door and I shoved Alan in to him, saying:

"Here's your friend. He and his group have been having a party. There is a fire in our dorm, a number of students are drunk, one is cut badly and has been taken to the infirmary and the school is awash with laughter, meanness and stupidity. I have got to go back and arrange to clean everything up and make sure we have an accounting of all students. Boys will be boys but my advice is still for you to dismiss the bums!"

As I walked away, Langdon shouted:

"Come to my office first thing in the morning, right after chapel."

When I returned to Payson Dorm, all the Prefects had gathered except for Bill Thompson. Two Masters had arrived, Mr. McEnery and Mr. Corbin. The cleanup was well underway and all involved in the party had been given cold showers and sent to bed. No one in the dorm had missed the events and most were dismayed or ashamed of what had occurred. It was well after three o'clock before things quieted and all were in their rooms with thoughts of their own. Mine was one of fury. In my view, the Head Master should have come to the scene of the trouble, taken charge and meted out discipline on the spot. Instead, he was coddling the perpetrator.

Chapel the next morning was very subdued. Word had traveled through the whole student body about the eventful night. I went directly to the Head Master's office after the service. Who was there? You guessed it, Bill Thompson. I thought to myself: the Reverend needed his sycophantic supporter by his side.

Langdon avoided looking directly at me and said:

"Chuck, I have called Mr. Brennan. He and his wife will be here shortly after noon. I have requested them to take Alan home while we sort out what is to be done. I don't want to do anything hasty. We have a young boy who must be given every chance to mend his ways."

I just looked at him. Minutes ticked by. Finally, I said:

"Sir? Will that be all?"

He nodded and I left for class leaving the two of them huddled by his desk. I was in total disbelief.

Classes went by in a fog. After all that had happened, I couldn't believe the Head Master was still thinking of keeping the constant trouble maker in school. The place could have easily burned down if Ed. Nash hadn't been thorough in his responsibilities.

What a message this was going to send to the students. That afternoon I spent on the ski slopes. I don't think I ever went at it with such vengeance. I did down- hill skiing, slalom, jumping and a difficult cross-country run. Ed. Nash, Harry Bartley and Jack V. accompanied me on the latter. They were almost as upset as me. That night, while studying, I heard the Masters returning from the faculty meeting that had been called. A few minutes later, there was a knock on my door. It was Coach Myers. When he came in, he said:

"Chuck, I wanted to speak with you. We have just had a faculty meeting over the tragic disturbances of last night. The discussion was very open and the majority strongly recommended the dismissal of Brennan and that those other students involved, be put on notice for suspension for any other infractions. Of course, the final decision will be Reverend Langdon's. I don't think he will take our position lightly. As for your response to the event, we believe you handled it all extremely well and support you and your staff completely. That does not include Bill Thompson. We, very frankly, do not like the relationship that has developed. You have a difficult job. Don't give up on it. Now, I hope you can get some sleep tonight."

I did. I was tired.

Alan Brennan was dismissed. The Head Master called me in to his office to inform me of his decision. However, he did intimate that he might consider having him return the following year. I hoped that would not happen. From that day to graduation, disciplinary problems diminished to a few minor infractions. As far as all Prefects could tell, smoking and drinking disappeared from campus. School spirit gradually returned. A few times, I laughed when I heard Bill Thompson comment to his entourage of young students:

"There goes, My Fuhrer. Sig Heil!"

In the middle of these trying days, I heard from Dean Hermansk that I had been accepted at Princeton with a small scholarship. I was to enroll on June 7th into an accelerated program. Two weeks later, Harry Bartley was notified of his acceptance. We were both thrilled and hoped Jack Zimmerman would still be there and not in the service, so we could once again be together. When I called my folks about my acceptance, they were pleased but concerned over the small amount of scholarship.

Another unusual thing was happening. Since the dance weekend, I had received four letters from Betty. No one had ever written me such long letters and so often. She could rattle on in a letter just as much as she did in speech. I didn't answer any. It was a relationship I had no interest in pursuing. Easter vacation started the last few days in March. All I could think about was how to get Marian to agree to spend time with me.

CHAPTER 35

THE FIRST DAY home, I called my girl. Mrs. Logan answered and seemed very happy to hear from me. After going through the niceties of the day, I asked to speak with Marian. I heard her call out and tell Marian that I was on the phone. My heart was in my mouth. I was afraid she would refuse to come to speak with me. Then I heard her voice:

"Oh Chuck, I've so missed you. I thought you might get home today. Not a day goes by without wishing we were together."

"Marian, please say you'll go out with me tonight. It has been awful wondering if you have relented and realized how right it is for us to get together. I've really missed you."

"Chuck, I still think we should keep apart. I still have the same fears. I do love you. You must know that."

"Yes, I believe you do but not seeing me is a strange way to show it. I have never heard of anything like it. It is all so damn frustrating!"

"Please. Don't get angry."

"Well, I still find it hard to understand. I've been accepted at Princeton and start there on June 7th in an accelerated program and I sure want to see you before then. I'll have only these eight days now and then three days between my graduation and starting college. Please say you'll go out with me sometime real soon."

"Oh, I'm thrilled you have been selected! I'm so proud of you."

We talked for nearly an hour but I still was unable to change her mind or get a commitment on a date. I was crushed! How could she be afraid of us? It made no sense. I became mad. Before hanging up I shouted in to the phone:

"God Marian, You can't really care for me! This is ridiculous! I want you! You say you want me and we can't see each other! Something is wrong in that equation. Please see things from my point of view. I don't like being set adrift and only retrieved when you have lost your hang-ups. Think about it. I'll keep calling."

"Chuck, it's difficult but it really is best for us to stay apart."

"Then, I don't think you really care."

"You are wrong, Very wrong. If you don't come for me, I'll find you. I do love you."

We hung up. I was mad, hurt, confused and very much aware that she really mattered to me. Whenever we were together, all seemed right with the world. That was the last I ever, knowingly, heard her voice. It resonated through my mind for more than ten years.

The Easter vacation looked like a bummer. I searched for things to do. Out of the blue, Ed. Nash called to say he was in Scarsdale. His Mom had just moved to an apartment on Garth Road. We made plans to meet that night. We decided to have dinner at a small restaurant in town. Our conversation turned to finding things to pass the days before heading back to school. He hit upon the idea of asking Harry Bartley, Jack Vigneron and Bert Wright to come to town for a few days. We'd also get Gordon Ferguson to be part of the group. Later that night we called them all and invited them. We worked out the accommodations with Gordon. Bert would stay at the Ferguson's, Jack and Harry at my home and Ed. would stay at his Mom's. She didn't have room for a guest. All arrived two days later. In to New York City we went. We caught a movie at Radio City, had a cheap dinner and then went to Nick's in the Village. The Jazz was always good there. What a great night we had. Bert and Harry had never been to the City before and were awed over everything.

The next day, Ed. called to say that Mr. Corbin, a master from school, had phoned and asked him to meet him and Mr. McEnery in the city for a night on the town. When he told them we were all in Scarsdale, he said to bring the bunch. We all agreed. It was a most unusual night being with Masters on a night of frolic. They tried to treat us to dinner but we all said we'd pay for our own. We went to a place called: Sweeney's Grill & Sauce. The food was marginal but we enjoyed ourselves. Piling into two cabs, after our meal, we went to the Cafe' Society Downtown to listen to the fabulous music. Later, we were uptown on 52nd street at a club where Billy Holiday was holding forth. She was obviously under the influence of something but still enraptured us with her singing. It was so crowded we had to share chairs at our table. It was the closest I ever got to Mr.McEnery. He kept pushing me off the chair and saying to everyone that I was drunk. I wasn't even drinking liquor but he tried to make all think I was pie eyed. It was a hilarious evening but it didn't help my chemistry average.

The Saturday before Easter, I went to New Hamburgh. The town looked as wonderful as ever to me. Compared to Scarsdale, it was downright poor but it was home to me. I visited with Aunt Nell and we had a wonderful day reminiscing. Aside from that, she wouldn't let the subject of Marian drop. In her opinion, that girl was perfect for me and repeatedly asked me to keep after her and not lose my great opportunity for real love. I agreed but could see no strategy that would produce the desired results. Going home, I went over and over the problem of Marian. Nothing I visualized dissolved the reality.

CHAPTER 36

AFTER RETURNING TO school, eight weeks remained before final exams and then five additional days before graduation. It became quickly obvious that students were in better spirits. The tragic disciplinary problems of the last semester were over, the students seemed to have had positive thoughts over the outcome and all were eagerly looking forward to the summer. Spring was usually upbeat. Studying gained top priority because the year's results would determine what the future would hold. Baseball and crew allowed all of us to burn off steam and feel better about ourselves and concentrate on those things that were important. Study, study, study. All was going well for me with the exception of chemistry. Mr. McEnery was threatening to flunk me. At least twice a week he'd say in class:

"Chuck, how Princeton ever picked you is beyond belief. I'm determined to show them how wrong they are. I'll give you a failing grade. That will certainly make them realize their mistake and withdraw their offer."

I felt he was happy over my discomfort and intent on blocking me at every turn. What frustrated me was, I helped others with the formulas and experiments and yet when I turned in my assignments they always came back with a failing grade while those I'd helped received plaudits for their efforts. I spent restless nights examining avenues that might turn the situation around. All my other subjects were doing fine.

On the brighter side, our baseball team was one of the best the school had ever fielded. We finished undefeated. Our success was largely due to Johnny Whitton. He pitched in five of our games. He threw two three hitters, one two hitter and a five hit

285

game. Our last opponent was Hotchkiss, a much larger school. It was the best game in which any of us participated. For twelve innings, Johnny pitched no hit ball. The Hotchkiss pitcher had held us scoreless, even though we had five hits. At the top of the thirteenth, Jack McKinney hit a home run putting us in the lead 1 to 0. Taking the mound in the bottom of the thirteenth, Johnny threw a ball over the plate which the Hotchkiss first baseman drilled wide of our shortstop on the third base side. From nowhere, Ed. Nash dove for the ball and caught it about a foot from the ground. It was spectacular! The next batter went to a full count. Johnny threw his pitch low and away. The batter hit the ball and it slowly came towards me at second base. I ran to it, picked it up and threw to first. It went high but Ed. Frost jumped and reached for the ball, caught it and came down on the bag. The runner was out. A pinch hitter was put in, a tall muscular guy. Johnny got two quick strikes on him. His next pitch was a little wide and called a ball. Everyone was nervous and shouting at Johnny that he could strike the guy out. His next pitch was right over the plate. The batter drove it high down the left field line. It looked like a home run. As it descended it started curving and dropped about a foot out of bounds. We all whooped it up. Johnny then reared back and threw his fast ball. It sped by the batter as he swung late. STRIKE THREE! We had won the game and Johnny had pitched a no-hitter. Our joy was indescribable. It was the last sporting event I played at Salisbury. The end was better than I could have ever hoped.

The school crew team also had a great season. They were never beaten. The performance of those two sport units did wonders for the morale of the school. It was a very positive ending of our athletic activities. Only a small group of students seemed removed from the resultant high spirit. Nearly all were younger boys who clung to the trail of Bill Thompson. It was unreal and uncomfortable to witness.

The final weeks never found me free from worry of what was to be the outcome of the unhappy situation in my chemistry course. It seemed as if I was doomed to fail. In panic, I searched the archives for previous final exams. I found seven or so, studied every one, put them away and a week later brought them out to review again. The more I studied, my confidence escalated. Classmates kidded me about being paranoid over the subject. I couldn't help it, I was worried.

While all this turmoil was happening, four times a week I was receiving letters from Betty. She loved to write, was good at it, was chatty, funny and enclosed little stories she had written for her school newspaper. She also inundated me with plans of things she wished for us to enjoy together. Perhaps, I answered two or three of her epistles. I didn't know what to make of her. Instead of thinking her a nuisance, she was becoming a friend. However, no romantic thoughts entered my mind. Those were reserved for Marian.

The most memorable day of that spring had nothing to do with school, Marian or my letter writer. On May 8, 1945 Germany surrendered!! The thrill of that announcement can never be overstated. The allies had won, Hitler was dead and now perhaps Japan would soon join the Nazi on the trash heap of history. Many who were graduating were immediately going in to the service. Some had already been drafted but been deferred until their graduation. Others had or were going to enlist. A few of us were enrolled at accelerated programs at various colleges before entering the military. Now we wondered if any of us would see combat. If we did, it would be against the Japanese. Invading that island country was considered inevitable and it was believed the fighting would be terrible with hundreds of thousands killed. But now, the full force of the allies would be concentrated on the pacific theatre, which should hasten the end. Many of us were also fearful of the Russian intentions. How they behaved would determine much of our future.

Exams arrived. All were at least two and a half hours long. Answers had to be written cogently, without grammatical mistakes. I felt, I had done well on them all, even chemistry.

When the grades were posted for all to see I had passed them all. However in chemistry, no grade was posted next to my name. I couldn't believe it and immediately sought Mr. McEnery. When I knocked on his door, he opened it and said:

"Yes? What can I do for you?"

"How come no mark has been posted for me?"

He grinned and said:

"I couldn't read your paper."

"I don't believe you. Why not?"

"It was too difficult to make out."

"You've got to be kidding."

"No, I'm not. You'll have to take another exam."

I was speechless and extremely hurt. I thought of going to the Head Master and asking him to look in to it all but realized he would just relish my predicament. Looking at McEnery, I said:

"Okay. You want to give me a hard time. When can I take it?"

"Tomorrow morning, at nine o'clock."

"I'll be there."

When I told Harry and other friends of what Mr. McEnery had said, they were nearly as shocked as me. No one could understand why I was being given such a hard time. The next morning at nine I arrived in the chemistry lab to take the exam. Mr. McEnery was not there. I waited for over forty-five minutes and still he had not shown up. I went to his quarters and knocked on his door. When he opened it, he said:

"Chuck, what are you doing here?"

"I've been waiting in the Chem. Lab since eight fifty-five to retake the exam."

"Oh, that's good. I've decided to have you take it at two thirty this afternoon."

"Why didn't you advise me?"

"Because, I wanted your fat rear end to wait. I've never liked that you are such a big deal in this school. You're not to me."

I swallowed my temper, looked him straight in the eyes and said:

"I'll be there and hope you will as well."

I took the exam that afternoon as scheduled. It was totally different from the one before and more difficult. Fortunately, most questions were from the previous seven exams I had studied. I raced through it and felt confident I had done well. When I turned it in I asked when he would have my grade. The answer was typical:

"When I have corrected it and decided on the grade it warrants."

That afternoon I happened to bump in to Mr. Tappert and Coach Myers. They immediately told me they were aware of what Mr. McEnery was doing and cautioned me not to worry. The whole faculty knew he was going overboard to give me a hard time. His enjoyment over my misery was all too obvious. This knowledge infuriated me but I realized the little game would have to be played out. The day before graduation I received my grade. It was a 78. Passing was 65, so my graduation was assured.

The longed for day arrived. The ceremony was to be at two o'clock. I expected my parents to arrive around noon. To my surprise, Jack Zimmerman showed up shortly after ten thirty. He had come to see Harry and I graduate and also to tell us he would not be at Princeton when we got there because he had been drafted. We were very disappointed to hear the news because we had so looked forward to the three of us being at the same university. Just before lunch, my folks arrived.

Promptly at Two o'clock, the graduates marched in to the hall to receive their diplomas and say their farewells. The ceremony started with a prayer given by Reverend Langdon. It was quickly followed by some remarks from Coach Myers, the assistant Head Master. He dwelled on the strong historical traditions of the school and how they should better prepare us to deal with the paths our future took. Mr. Corbin was next outlining the high-lights of the year. It was then my turn to speak about our class, the school and its' influence on us and the warmth of feeling we had for the institution. This was followed by the award ceremony for athletics. That over with, the Reverend Langdon announced the three major award winners: the Carr Medal for best student of the class, the athletic medal for the best all- around athlete and the Quaile Medal for the student graduating who had contributed most to the school. Desmond Henn won the best student award, I won the Athletic Medal and Bill Thompson the Quaile Medal.

It was then time for Reverend Langdon to give the final fare-well and outline his hopes for our future and the future of the school. It was anything but a joyous speech. He talked of his vision for the school, which was nothing but a manifesto declar-ing a relaxation of regulations, the installation of greater extra curricular choices, the de-emphasis of competitive sports and a broadening of independent courses that would deal with the need for social change. It was all I could do to sit still. He ended by looking directly at me and saying how happy he was to see the last of the "Quaile Boys". As we marched out, I noted the shocked faces of the faculty members who had been there under Mr. Quaile and then I caught Dad's eye. I had never seen him look so upset.

The next hour was spent saying goodbye to all my friends, the masters and some of their wives. I went up to Rev. Langdon and put out my hand to shake his. He took it gingerly, said nothing and turned to another. My humiliation was deeply felt. Next to approach was Mr. McEnery. He looked at me and smiled. I put my hand out and he shook it saying:

"Chuck, you are one unusual boy. I know I tortured you, I've always thought you were too highly thought of but you proved to me you are one tough individual. I wish you luck." I was completely taken aback. His comment made the day a little easier.

Back at my room, I found my folks, Jack, Harry and his folks and Ed. Nash. It seemed an unhappy gathering. For the first time in memory, Dad put his arm around me and said:

""I'm very proud of you. What Reverend Langdon said was unspeakable. Let's get out of here."

We did but not before I had an emotional parting with Wim and Jane and Coach Myers and his wife.

As we left, I shouted to Harry I'd see him in Princeton on Monday.

One chapter of my life had ended and a new one was unfolding. The next ten years saw many unexpected developments. Some were extremely happy, others excruciatingly painful, one of great disappointment and then finally a lifting out of turmoil to unbelievable happiness. Perhaps another time I'll divulge it all.

Yes Margaret, I was a Lucky White Boy.

EPILOGUE

THE FOLLOWING IS a quick synopsis of what happened to some of the major players involved in my early life.

Johnny McCullough, half of McVan Photo Company, graduated from Bronxville High School and Yale. He served several years in the Army and then became part of our Intelligence Agency. He married and had eleven children and traveled to many parts of the world. I saw him again only once and that was twenty-five years after this story ended. He died in May 2007. His older brother had called me from out of the blue in April to let me know that Johnny was dying of cancer and wanted to hear from me. I called him. We had a great conversation. I followed this with a letter to him with attachments showing our first photographic efforts in 1938 along with our contract letter establishing our business. He was a good friend.

Lynn Vandevere, my kindergarten girl, had moved to Los Angeles, California with her family. She was a vague memory when one day, while at home in Scarsdale on furlough from the Army, I caught a bus on Central Avenue to White Plains. As I was taking my seat, I heard a voice:

"Charlie, is that you? Remember me? I'm Lynn Vandevere."

I saw a young lady my age, light brown hair, freckles across her nose with a warm smile parting her lips.

"Lynn, I can't believe it is you. What are you doing here? I thought you were on the West Coast. It's great to see you."

We rode together the rest of the way and spent another fifteen minutes talking at our stop. She loved California, was engaged and planned a wedding as soon as her guy got out of the Navy.

She seemed as outgoing and thoughtful as she had been as a child.

Johnny Fearing went to the Kent School, was Captain of the football team, a Prefect and then went to the University of Virginia. I've been told he was a very successful businessman

John Scardefield remained one of my closest friends until his death in 2001. He married a girl from Beacon, N.Y. and lived in New Hamburgh until he died. He was a character. A great athlete who played football in college, as well as baseball, played a short time in the major leagues as a pitcher, won the Albany to New York City motor boat race three or more years, knew the Hudson River better than anyone else I knew with the exception of Captain Dewit Robinson. John had a solid business career with Texaco and then IBM. He was brilliant and could have gone very far but preferred to be a small town person. He died in the house in which he was born. I miss him.

Louie lived by the pond until his death. He was a fixture at the fire department, liked by everyone and honored by the whole town at his funeral. He was a wonderful friend to me, as was his wife Mary Jo. They were one of the warmest and most cheerful couples I have ever known. They taught me much.

Wim and Jane Keur had a very happy marriage and two delightful children. When I sent my eldest son to Salisbury, after the Reverend Langdon had departed, they took my Chuck under their wing. I stayed in touch with my Godson until his death. Jane, I kept in touch with until her death in 2010. She was a terrific woman.

Coach Myers and his wife, Jo, stayed in touch with me until their deaths. When the new Gymnasium was built, seventeen years later, I was minimally instrumental in having it dedicated to Coach Myers. I really admired the man.

Lucy Mckewen, I've been told, seriously considered a movie career. Several studios had contacted her. She had the good sense to turn their offers down. In college she had starred in several plays and with her provocative looks gained notice. I also heard she married a very solid guy, raised three children and became very active in charitable work. She was really something.

Jack Zimmerman became a roommate at Princeton of Harry Bartley and me once the two of us had returned from the Army. He graduated Magna Cum Laude from Princeton, went on to Johns Hopkins to study medicine and graduated from there, Phi

Beta Kappa. He went on to become a very famous doctor. We stay in touch.

Harry Bartley, as mentioned, roomed with me at Princeton. He entered service after graduating as a chemical engineer. He then went to Wharton Business School. He retired as President of a major Chemical Company. We stay in touch, see one another occasionally and are good friends.

Gordon Ferguson didn't marry Sue. He met a great girl who was a nurse. She bowled him over. They married and had three boys. He was in the banking business in Denver Colorado until his mid- forties and then retired to spend time fly-fishing all over the world. Ambition was not one of his strong points. He became renowned as one of the greatest fly fishermen in the country. We remained close friends, even separated by miles. Unfortunately, He died in March 2012.

Mr. McEnery left Salisbury the year following my graduation. We ended our battles both the wiser. He was an unhappy soul. I'm told he went from one teaching job to another before succumbing to the bottle. He could have been a nice guy.

Bill Thompson went to Yale and returned to Salisbury as an assistant to the Reverend Langdon. He stayed three years. In the third year I've been told he was found in questionable activities with young boys. The Head Master tried to keep him on but the hue and cry would not allow it. Shortly after this, he married a girl. It lasted four days. He was a big blowhard on Long Island. No one really understood what he did. C'est la Vie. In 2010 he died.

The Reverend Langdon ran the school his way. It became extremely liberal. Discipline fell apart and standards dropped. He did accomplish one thing. That was to increase the school's financial stability. For this he deserves credit. After his retirement, the school under Ed. Ward, the new Head Master, started to turn around. Subsequent Heads have continued that path and today Salisbury is one of the very best all boys Private Schools in the Country.

Bill Ferris remained my friend until his death. We worked side by side, many, many hours, to build a home on the island under my Dad's supervision. The lessons he taught me were invaluable. Three men influenced me more than any others. Dad, Wim Keur and Bill Ferris.. All were totally different. Bill made work easy.

Marian Logan remained my secret love for ten years. We never got together. I tried writing to her several times. Did everything I could to trace her whereabouts to no avail. Her family had moved while I was in the service. I think it was Philadelphia or perhaps Kansas City. I never could find out. I called many of our old friends in hopes of tracking her down but never succeeded. Six years after graduating from college, I was with a business that had transferred me back to New York City. Two days after being in my new office, a young man walked in and said:

"Hi, I'm Bill Foster. Are you the Chuck Van Anden from Scarsdale?'

When I said yes, he continued:

"I'm Marian Logan's cousin. You are the guy she told us she was going to marry but she never found you again."

I was stunned!

"Where is she? What is she doing?"

"I don't have her address but I can get it for you, if you'd like."

I groped for words and finally said:

"No, what's the use? It's too late."

Bob Naylor came back in to my life in 1983. I was at the Waldorf Astoria Hotel in New York for a speech I was giving to a business convention. At the end of the speech, many men came up to ask questions, etc. and one man held back until the rest had left. He came forward and said:

"Chuck, remember me? I'm Bob Naylor."

Wow! A face and name from the past.

""Gee, Yes. How are you doing Bob? It's great to see you after all these years. Where are you now?"

"In Ohio, I'm with Johns Manville."

We talked about business and then he said:

"The last time I saw you it was in Princeton but you probably don't remember. I was with Marian Logan. She had called me from out of the blue and asked if I would take her to a football game at Princeton. Through the grapevine she had heard you were there after being in the Army. She persuaded me, so my girl and I took her to a game that October. We tried to locate you before the game but didn't have any luck. The administration offices were closed. We did ask around but without success. Going to the game, Marian kept looking all over for you. Towards the end it started to rain lightly. As we were walking away from the stadium, she was sure she saw you ahead of us. We pushed through the crowd and she called out to you three or four times. One time you turned around, seemed to wave and then took off in a hurry. She was devastated. That was the last I ever saw or heard from her. She kept saying the two of you had made some kind of promise to get back together again. It was quite a day!"

My heart seemed to shrivel. I remembered that day clearly. I had heard a girl call my name. I did look back and saw a gorgeous blond girl all wrapped in a raincoat. My date pulled at me and said she had to run to the lady's room. Reluctantly, I went along with her but instead really wanted to see the other girl more closely. When we got to Elm Club, I dropped off my date and ran back to see if I could find that girl. It had struck me who it might have been. I searched for nearly forty minutes, running all around campus but never found her. Now I knew, it was hard to take. A discovery so cruel could not have been more devastating. When that happened, she was still the girl I craved.

Bob and I became friends again. We saw each other every year at various functions but that is the last I ever heard of Marian.

Over the years New Hamburgh has changed. It has gone from a country town to a quasi-suburban community. Parking lots service commuters from the back country, farmland has almost vanished, boats by-pass the town dock and a marina has replaced Millard's Lumber Yard. In the late 1940's the beautiful view of Danskammer Point and its' light house was changed by the scars of progress made by the erection of a Central Hudson Power Plant. The new firehouse, the Episcopal Chapel and the Yacht Club are still going strong. Many old families still call it home and it is still a unique settlement.

When my time is done, I hope my spirit will have the opportunity to stand on the hill by the old cemetery so I can hear the old sounds, smell the good earth and see the view of the small village that contributed so much to my life.

Lightning Source UK Ltd.
Milton Keynes UK
UKOW02f0009220316

270629UK00001B/134/P